MENNONITE WOMEN

A Story of God's Faithfulness, 1683-1983

MENNONITE WOMEN

A Story of God's Faithfulness, 1683-1983

Elaine Sommers Rich

Foreword by
Barbara K. Bender Reber

HERALD PRESS
Scottdale, Pennsylvania
Kitchener, Ontario

Library of Congress Cataloging in Publication Data

Rich, Elaine Sommers, 1926-
  Mennonite women.

  Bibliography: p.
  Includes index.
  1. Women, Mennonite—North America. 2. Women in
church work—Mennonites. 3. Mennonites—North America—
Biography. I. Title.
BX8128.W64R5 1983   289.7'088042   82-15452
ISBN 0-8361-3311-0 (pbk.)

MENNONITE WOMEN
Copyright © 1983 by Herald Press, Scottdale, Pa. 15683
  Published simultaneously in Canada by Herald Press,
  Kitchener, Ont. N2G 4M5
Library of Congress Catalog Card Number: 82-15452
International Standard Book Number: 0-8361-3311-0
Printed in the United States of America
Design by Alice B. Shetler

83 84 85 86 87 88 10 9 8 7 6 5 4 3 2

To the memory of ten pioneer leaders of the Mennonite
Woman's Missionary Society

Naomi Blosser (1882-1937)
Mary Yoder Burkhard (1880-1957)
Mary Ann Nahrgang Cressman (1864-1948)
Mary Ann Smucker Gerig (1868-1957)
Stella Shoemaker Kreider (1893-1977)
Amelia Bergey Nahrgang (1873-1936)
Crissie Yoder Shank (1888-1929)
Clara Eby Steiner (1873-1929)
Martha Whitmer Steiner (1878-1928)
Ruth A. Yoder (1864-1948).

Contents

Foreword

This record of three hundred years of female Mennonite history in North America will be viewed as an important new beginning: a beginning in recognizing the significance of over half of the church's faithful workers.

Mennonite Women: A Story of God's Faithfulness, 1683-1983 succeeds well in charting where Mennonite women have come from and who Mennonite women are. The author gives us a wide range of examples from the lives of our "foremothers": Lydia Heatwole, the Florence Nightingale of Mennonite nursing; Sarah Gross Lapp, the horse-and-buggy doctor in Nebraska during the 1870s; Rose Lambert, a missionary to Turkey; Susannah Heatwole Brunk Cooprider, a wife and mother in the 1860s and 1870s; deaconesses in Virginia who until the 1920s visited and counseled "the flock." We now have a history of some of the women who helped shape the life of the Mennonite Church in North America.

Although Mennonite women, almost without exception, have been excluded from ordination, their ministry has been essential to the growth of the home, the church, and the communities in which they lived and worked. Many suffered untold hardships and worked from dawn until late in the night, toiling to raise their children and give their husbands support or to nurture the young and aged among whom they ministered. Some went even further and took on added church assignments, such as Clara Eby Steiner in 1899. When her husband found he could not attend the Sunday school conference in Wayne County, Ohio, he persuaded her to take his place on the program. I quote the following from her collection:

> I wrote the essay at night after a hard day's work staying up several nights to get it accomplished till eleven o'clock. I then sent it to M. S. (her hus-

9

band) to Dakota, Illinois, to have him correct it. I wrote plenty, expecting him to cancel and tear it all to pieces, but much to my surprise, he only changed the introduction with a few words here and there; and after reading it to J. S. Shoemaker, he pronounced it excellent.

Mennonite Women: A Story of God's Faithfulness, 1683-1983 is a volume about women for an audience of both women and men. The time may come when such volumes will no longer be needed, when interpretive history will show an awareness of both men and women as "essential actors on life's stage," who together have brought about those developments of life and society that we call history.

I am pleased to be a part of an organization (WMSC) that is making this important contribution to the total Mennonite Church. The author helps us understand ourselves. She increases our awareness of the gifts women have been using for a long time. May this volume enrich the current life, witness, and outreach of Mennonites and others who find its themes of timely interest.

Barbara K. Bender Reber
Executive Secretary
Women's Missionary and
Service Commission of the
Mennonite Church

May 1982

Barbara Miller Bender (1863-1935), Nebraska, holding her namesake, Barbara K. Bender (Reber), 1926.

Author's Preface

In celebration of the anniversary of the first permanent Mennonite settlement in the New World, at Germantown, Pennsylvania, in 1683, this book about Mennonite women is presented to readers with joy and a sense of accomplishment. It is also presented with a certain regret, for many women who should be on these pages are not here. Certain geographical areas and historical periods are also inadequately represented, as are women in business. Despite these and other shortcomings, it is hoped that this volume will serve as a foundation on which others may build.

The Scope of This Study. Mennonites in Canada and the United States belong historically to one of two streams. The first stream is made up of Mennonites from Swiss, South German, and Alsatian backgrounds, who immigrated to the eastern United States and Canada in various waves from 1683 to the 1850s. This stream includes both the Amish-Mennonite group and the (Old) Mennonite Church, two groups which gradually merged between 1860 and 1930. The stream also includes the Old Order Amish, who remain a separate group, and other smaller groups.

The second stream is composed of Mennonites from Dutch, Prussian, and Russian backgrounds, who immigrated to the Western prairies in 1874 and in successive waves thereafter, continuing to the present time. Today most of these are General Conference Mennonites or Mennonite Brethren, or belong to other smaller groups.

This book has been commissioned by the Women's Missionary and Service Commission (WMSC) of the Mennonite Church, and thus basically covers women in the first category of Mennonites. (For information about women in the second group, readers are directed to three excellent works listed in the bibliography: Mary Lou Cummings' *Full Circle,* Gladys Goering's *Women in Search of Mission,* and Katie Funk Wiebe's *Women Among the Brethren.)*

The year 1950 was used as an arbitrary cutoff date for inclusion of extensive biographical data. Women whose primary contributions have been made since then are either mentioned but briefly or omitted for three basic reasons: (1) there have been more women leaders since 1950 than can be included in such a volume as this; (2) it seemed a matter of priority to "harvest" earlier materials now—many written records already exist in various Mennonite archives for the contemporary period, while much of the material in this book came from hundreds of private sources; and (3) historical distance sharpens perspective.

Acknowledgments. All materials submitted for this book have become part of the WMSC Collection, deposited in the archives of the Mennonite Church on the Goshen (Indiana) College campus. I wish to thank each group and person who has submitted materials for this work. Some materials could be used directly; all materials submitted were used indirectly, helping to set the book's tone and guide its perceptions.

I am deeply grateful to many people and institutions for their help in the making of this volume; a few should be named:

—The WMSC Advisory Committee: Alice W. Lapp; Jocele Thut Meyer; Emma Sommers Richards; Leonard Gross (representing the Historical Committee); and Barbara K. Reber (executive secretary of WMSC), chairperson.
—Historians who submitted primary materials and answered my many queries, especially Hope K. Lind of Oregon, Lorraine Roth and Lorna Bergey of Ontario, Hazel Lapp of Illinois, Grace Showalter and Mary F. Suter of Virginia, and John E. Lapp and Carolyn C. Wenger of Pennsylvania.
—Women in local WMSC groups for their faithfulness in collecting documentation, for their research and writing, and for their wholehearted support.
—Bluffton College and Goshen College for the use of their Mennonite historical libraries.
—The Historical Committee of the Mennonite Church, and its archives, for counsel and documentation.
—The Schowalter Foundation of Newton, Kansas, for a grant to WMSC for this project.
—The *Mennonite Quarterly Review* for permission to quote extensively in chapter 11 from an article by Melvin Gingerich.
—Priscilla Stuckey Kauffman for research assistance.

—Sue Minton, Louise E. Showalter, and Doris S. Shenk for aid in typing the manuscript.
—And finally Ronald L. Rich, my husband, for his encouragement.

My life has been enriched through writing about these wonderful women. May their physical and spiritual descendants carry into the 21st century their kind of courage and faithfulness.

> *Elaine Sommers Rich*
> Bluffton, Ohio
> December 4, 1981

MENNONITE WOMEN

A Story of God's Faithfulness, 1683-1983

*"We all depended on God
and He did not fail us."*

—Rose Lambert, of her experience
in Hadjin, Turkey, in 1909

CHAPTER 1

In Search of Mennonite Women

Eleven women in a group from Krefeld, Germany, left England on the *Concord*, arrived in colonial America on October 6, 1683, and settled at Germantown, Pennsylvania. Francis Daniel Pastorius, a German pietist, had selected for them this site, which became the first permanent Mennonite settlement in the New World. The party also included thirteen men, one youth, and eight children.[1] One of the women, the "wife of Jacob Telner," returned to London in 1698. It is not known why. Barbara Umstat and two daughters—Anna Margaretha (d. 1696) and Eve (married Hendrick Pannebecker in 1699)—and Gertrude Streypers (wife of Paulus Kuster) remained in the colonies.[2]

Two women bore children on board the *Concord*. Did the ship's captain provide a private stateroom for childbirth? Or was it a semipublic event? Who attended those women? Was there at least one midwife among the other nine women in their company? Were the newborn babies colicky? These questions remain unanswered.

Even under the best of conditions the journey across the Atlantic by sailboat in those days took at least ten or twelve weeks. The *Concord* eventually landed in Philadelphia. En route from

Philadelphia to Germantown one woman died. Of what cause? In childbirth? Or typhoid or pneumonia? What was her name? Where was she buried? We simply do not know the answers to these and similar questions.

These Germantown women exemplify some of the problems in preparing this book. In recorded American Mennonite history the women are often nameless. Little has been written about them. "Sister C" wrote 37 articles for the Mennonite Church paper, the *Herald of Truth* (predecessor of the *Gospel Herald*), between 1883 and 1893. Yet her name is not known. One cannot even be certain that "Sister C" was not a pseudonym for the male editor.

Mennonite women have always been present—bearing children, working beside their men, singing, baking bread, being burned at the stake, arranging preaching services in the wilderness—but one catches only glimpses of them, never long looks. The purpose of this book is to make Mennonite women more visible, particularly in North America—to tell a story of God's faithfulness to them and of their faithfulness sometimes, by God's grace, to him. A story will unfold of their contributions to God's kingdom as wives, mothers, and teachers; as workers in local congregations and missionaries at home and abroad; as doctors, nurses, and founders of women's organizations. The story is set within the context of early Mennonite history going back to Reformation times.

The European Background

Already in the earliest years (1525ff.) of the Anabaptist movement (forebears of today's Mennonites) in Switzerland, South Germany, and Holland, many—both men and women—died for their faith. Lois Barrett reports that about one-third of the 930 Anabaptist martyrs mentioned in *Martyrs Mirror* are women.[3] Listing the names of all of them would be a formidable task. In the *Mennonite Encyclopedia* entries under "A" alone include Adriana Jansdochter, Adriane Naerken Vyncx, Aelken Jansdochter, Aeltgen Gielisdochter, Aechtgen Jansdochter, Aechten Joris

Adriaensdochter, Aeff Peters. Next come at least nine Anna's and twelve Anneken's. Nine Barbara's are listed under "B," plus Mary and Ursula van Beckum. In the initial stages of Mennonite history, women are named. In January 1523, Ulrich Zwingli said in Switzerland, "Matters have reached such a state that even the laymen and *women* [italics added] know more of the Scriptures than some priests and clergymen."[4]

The following two examples typify these many women martyrs, put to death for their faith by drowning, burning at the stake, or other methods.

Maeyken van Deventer[5]

This Maeyken—known by the Dutch city from which she came, Deventer—was arrested in Rotterdam in mid-1573. From the fact that she was about a hundred miles away from home in a day before automobiles and airplanes, one can conclude that she

The martyrdom of Anneken Heyndricks, from *Martyrs Mirror*.

was hardly a "homebody." Perhaps this "heroine of Jesus Christ" had gone to teach, preach, or attend meetings. Perhaps she had fled for her life. While in prison she wrote a lengthy letter to her four children—Albert, Johan, Egbert, and Truyken.

> I cannot leave you gold or silver, nor can I give you treasures of this world, as the world gives to her children; for this I did not take with me, but left it to your carnal father; and this I also did not seek, but I sought the eternal riches, which are imperishable. Do you also seek this way, and you shall live forever; and follow this testament and the instruction which I here write you. Even as Christ Jesus our forerunner left such to us for an everlasting testament and sealed it with His blood; such a testament I also leave you, and will likewise seal the same with my blood, even as the blessed Jesus did.... Therefore, my children, love your neighbor heartily, and this with a liberal heart. Let the light of the Gospel shine in you. II Cor. 4:4. Deal your bread to the hungry, clothe the naked, and do not suffer anything to remain with you double, since there are enough that lack.

The following prayer by Maeyken van Deventer survives:

> O holy Father, sanctify the children of Thy handmaiden in Thy truth, and keep them from all evil, and from all unrighteousness, for Thy holy name's sake. O Almighty Father, I commend them unto You, since they are Thy creatures; care for them, for they are Thy handiwork; so that they may walk in Thy paths. Amen.

Authorities put Maeyken van Deventer to death in Rotterdam in 1573.

Maeyken Wens[6]

Also in 1573, Maeyken Wens died at Antwerp. The seventeenth-century chronicler couches Maeyken's story in his quaint old language (translated from the Dutch, of course):

> The north wind of persecution blew now the longer the more through the garden of the Lord, so that the herbs and trees of the same (that is, the true believers) were rooted out of the earth through the violence that came against them. This appeared, among other instances, in the case of a very God-fearing and pious woman named Maeyken Wens.

Her husband, Mattheus, was a minister in the church at Antwerp
and a mason by trade.

Authorities arrested Maeyken in April with others of her
fellow believers and imprisoned them. Representatives of the state
church—probably priests—as well as secular persons—no doubt
civil officials—tried to persuade her to recant.

> But when she could by no manner of means, not even by severe tortures,
> be turned from the steadfastness of her faith, they, on the fifth day of
> October, 1573, passed sentence upon her, and pronounced it publicly in
> court at the afore-mentioned place, namely, that she should, with her
> mouth screwed shut, or with her tongue screwed up, be burnt to ashes as a
> heretic, together with several others, who were also imprisoned and stood
> in like faith with her.

Her fifteen-year-old son, Adriaen, brought his little brother
Hans (or Jan) Mattheus, about three years old, and stood near the

Adriaen Wens at the place of execution of his mother, from *Martyrs Mirror.*

place where his mother was being executed. Unable to take such a horror, he "lost consciousness, fell to the ground and remained in this condition until his mother and the rest were burnt." The *Martyrs Mirror* contains two letters which Maeyken Wens wrote from prison to her husband, two to her son Adriaen, and one to Jan De Metser, a minister.

Mothers do urge their children to do better, Maeyken included. She says to Adriaen:

> This, I, Maeyken Wens, your mother, have written, while I was in prison for the Word of the Lord; the good Father grant you His grace, my son Adriaen. Write me a letter as to what your heart says, whether you desire to fear the Lord; this I should like to know. But you must write it better than the last two letters were written; the one which Maeyken Wils brought, however, was good.

Were Maeyken Wens's admonitions "nagging" or "instruction"? However they are classified, they reveal her deep love for her son.

Wolfgang Schäufele reports that women members of the Anabaptist laity were forbidden to preach and to baptize and that they were not permitted to take part in the election of the *Vorsteher* (elder).[7] Yet in 1645 a group of Anabaptists from Switzerland wrote a letter about their troubles to their brothers and sisters in the Netherlands, asking for prayer in their behalf that they might "patiently endure." Five people signed the letter. Among them were Ruth Kunstel from the Berne jurisdiction, "at Muchem, a minister in the word of the Lord," and Ruth Hagen, "an elder," from the Zurich jurisdiction.[8] Ruth Kunstel and Ruth Hagen were themselves *Vorsteher*. Who can be certain they not only preached but perhaps even baptized?

Indeed, Schäufele also reports that Anabaptist women were sometimes chained in their homes to keep them from going about spreading their faith. He says, "The woman in Anabaptism emerges as a fully emancipated person in religious matters and as the independent bearer of Christian convictions."[9]

George Williams makes the following assessment:

> Nowhere else in the Reformation Era were women so nearly the peers and companions in the faith, and mates in missionary enterprise and readiness

for martyrdom, as among those for whom believers' baptism was an equalizing covenant.... The Anabaptist insistence on the covenantal principle of the freedom of conscience for all adult believers and thereby the extension of the priesthood of the Christophorous laity to women constituted a major breach in patriarchialism and a momentous step in the Western emancipation of women.[10]

Women in the Writings of Menno Simons

Mennonites receive their name from the Dutch reformer Menno Simons (1496-1561). What did Menno think about women? In one sense, not much. In another sense, a great deal.

In 1554, in Wismar, Menno had extensive debates with Martin de Cleyne, called Micron, a leader of Zwinglian refugees exiled from London and seeking refuge on the continent. They disputed about baptism, the incarnation of Christ, the oath, divorce, the calling of ministers, and the magistracy; their discussions continued for five years.[11] Menno insisted that a child begins from a seed contributed by the father and that the mother contributes nothing.

In 1556, Menno wrote *Reply to Micron* and *Epistle to Martin Micron*, including the following statements:

> Therefore I hope by the Lord's help and grace to explain to all unbiased and sensible readers with so forcible an argument from Scripture, and also from observable facts of God's ordinances, that men may see with one eye shut that procreative seed by which the human race exists and multiplies is to be sought *with the fathers and not with the mothers* [italics mine]. ... what sort of pollution occurs in women they themselves know best. It is mentioned in Lev. 15:19 and many other places. [He is speaking of menstruation.] ... You see, worthy readers, although our opponents collide as with blind eyes with these and similar passages of which the Bible is full, yet they have to leave this position to us unviolated namely that the origin and substance of the child comes from the father's body or loins, that women come of men, that mothers conceive seed from the fathers, that in the blood of the mother the fruit congeals with the seed of the father, and that in this manner mothers bear children unto the fathers, as is plain enough in the recited Scriptures.[12]

Menno's motive was high. He believed in the virgin birth and was attempting to prove that Jesus Christ had inherited nothing from a human father or mother.

The entire booklet is something of an embarrassment to twentieth-century Mennonite historian John C. Wenger, who comments:

> While no one can blame Menno for the primitive state of science in his day, yet one cannot but wish that he would have had more good sense than to waddle through the mire as he does in this monotonous and repetitious discussion. As a matter of plain fact, Menno was simply wrong scientifically in his central argument that human generation and inheritance rest with the father only.[13]

Despite Menno Simons's spirited denial of a female co-role in the conception of children, the only extant letter in his handwriting is addressed to a woman, a widow whose name is not known. This tender letter contains one of his rare poetic lines (italicized).

> Much grace and peace, and a kind greeting! Fervently beloved sister in the Lord, whom my soul cherishes and loves! Since the Lord has now called you to widowhood, my fatherly faithful admonition to you is, as my dear children, to walk as becomes holy women, and I hope that you may, even as the pious prophetess Anna, serve the Lord in the holy temple, that is, in His church with a new and upright conscience, with prayer and fasting, night and day serving the needy saints, which the virtuous widow of Sarepta in Sidon did for faithful Elijah in the time of drouth and scarcity when she received him in her hospitality and fed him with her tiny bit of meal and oil. *So shall the meal of the holy divine Word be not lacking in the vessel of your conscience, and the joyous oil of the Holy Spirit from your soul* ... Faithful sister, carry on bravely, fear your God from the heart, crucify your flesh and its lusts, resist the enemy and all his solicitations. In all things conduct yourself piously; do not carelessly cause anyone inconvenience. Take good care of your labor, your household and children ... M.S., your brother who loves you fondly.[14]

Menno Simons also wrote a persuasive letter to Leonard Bouwens's wife, which will be quoted in chapter 3 on wives. In another letter by Menno concerning whether and how the ban should be applied in marriage, he says:

> However, it shall always be done with this exception and provision: If there is a devout person, whether man or woman, who is able to live out

his faith without being hindered by his excommunicated mate, (let them live together).[15]

That Menno says *whether man or woman,* indicates that he does believe in a soteriological equality of the sexes.

Did Anabaptist women continue to be co-workers with their brothers in witnessing to the power of the resurrection? Harold S. Bender observes that "after the creative period of Anabaptism was past, the settled communities and congregations reverted more to the typical patriarchal attitude of European culture."[16] This book will tell the story of how Mennonite women in the New World found ways of serving God despite occasional cultural barriers to that service.

EXHIBIT 1

Elisabeth, an Anabaptist Martyr

A ballad from the *Ausbund*

Translated by John C. Wenger

In 1549, Lijsbeth or Lijsken (Elisabeth) Dircks of Friesland was put to death for her faith.[17] A ballad about her trial and death appears in the Anabaptist hymnal, the Ausbund (no. 13).[18] She may have been the first Anabaptist deaconess. In any case, she was active in witnessing and teaching the Christian faith. Her examiners accused her of being a "teacher" in the church, a common term at that time for "preacher."

1

A maid she was of slender form,
  Attractive, and of conduct good;
Her given name, Elisabeth.
  God's Word she truly recognized.

2

Leeuwarden: That's the home
  she had;
  Within that city did she dwell.
In fifteen hundred forty-nine
  This tragic story did unfold.

3

In January was she caught,
  Was bound, and then was questioned
  hard.
And in that town was asked on oath
  If she no man had ever had.

4

When questioned thus she answer gave,
  You asked of me that I should swear.
But that I have no right to do;
  My word can be but Yea or Nay.

5

Indeed, for me an oath to give—
  To tell the truth requires no oath!
For who his neighbor will deceive;
  He will but swear an oath that's false.

6

But I can say, In very truth
  That to no man am I betrothed.
And then they cried: You have misled
  A host of others from the truth!

7

For you a Teacher really are:
  So first you must to us declare
What sort of people you have taught,
  And to your error you have brought.

8

To them she said; My honored lords,
  You only should request of me
What sort of Christian Faith I hold;
  Then here and now I'd freely speak.

9

Before you I will simply tell
  What I believe, and do affirm.
They asked her then to tell them true
  Of mass and sacrament her view.

10

So she at once her answer gave:
  That she no ground for them could
  find.
The Scripture never mentions them,
  And so to them I cannot hold!

11

The "Evening Meal"—'tis thus it's
  called,
Of Christ Himself a Testament.
It is a witness and a seal—
  Inheritance that's without end.

12

God writes upon our hearts within

In letters spiritual and clear:
A sure foundation signify,
  And marked are they invisibly.

13

When she much Scripture introduced,
  She then was told immediately:
The devil speaks out through your
  mouth;
  Your witness no foundation has.

14

She answered them in words sincere;
  The servant is but as his Lord;
It will not better with me go:
  Of this no doubt can I e'er have.

15

Of infant baptism did they ask—
  The rite that yet is common still—
If it's required, and pious makes?
  She shall her answer give, and short!

16

She them shall show, and shall confess
  Just why it is, up to this hour
That baptism's given to those of faith—
  Thus causing many to be judged!

17

She answered that by Christ's own word
  She baptized was: but only once!
Upon my faith was I baptized—
  Just as it's written in God's Word.

18

They further asked her them to tell
  If by God's Word the holy priest
The sins of mankind can forgive.
  To this she proper answer gave:

19

The Christ Himself our High Priest is,
  No man this honor from Him takes.
Man but proclaims the grace of God
  To him who from his sin repents.

20

But he who will not thus repent,
    The Church proclaims no other end
Than that his sins will be retained:
    No grace will he receive on earth.

21

And further, in the world to come
    His judgment is already set!
No human can that judgment change—
    Regardless how adorned his words.

22

Elisabeth received no grace.
    Before the Court she then was led;
Was soon to torture chamber brought
    To her examine under pain.

23

To executioner she came,
    Who spoke to her with words like
        these:
Until this time we kindly dealt,
    With you in friendly manner spoke.

24

But now we'll have to be severe,
    And deal with you in pain so sharp.
The Judge has this prescribed for you,
    If you're not ready to repent.

25

So screws to fingers he applied:
    Excruciating was her pain.
The torture was so very hard
    That blood from fingernails did spurt.

26

She then with God on High did plead:
    The pain I can no longer bear!
O come to me with help and strength.
    O guard me from insult and shame!

27

They told her, Just confess you're wrong!
    And then we'll quickly you release.

To cry to God will do no good;
    Confess! And you will be set free.

28

She kept on praying, earnestly;
    And God did rescue her from pain!
Such courage did He give that hour
    That she was filled with quiet
        strength.

29

Distress and pain she then could bear,
    Could not God's goodness then
        deny!
She cried: My pain did God now take
        away,
    When I did Him entreat for aid.

30

Now, you may ask me what you will:
    My hope in God alone is set!
Then screws they to her legs applied,
    That her distress might greater be.

31

She cried, O put me not to shame,
    For that will you no honor bring;
That you my body thus make bare:
    O think upon your wife and child!

32

In order not to thus be shamed,
    To them she frankly did confess;
No man his hand on me has laid;
    My body never has been touched.

33

And then she sank upon the ground,
    She passed into unconsciousness;
They really thought that she had
        died.
    Yet God did her again restore.

34

When she once more received her
        strength

She unafraid to them did say:
I'm still alive. I am not dead!
Then added: Now to God confess

35
That you do err, and contradict—
While you might still His grace
receive.
And then she said, I ask by God
To seal my faith with earthly
death.

36
In March of designated year
Did she her execution meet.

The Court its judgment did declare,
And soon 'twas also carried out.

37
That she should quick in water die;
And she no mercy should receive.
For that's the "goodness" shown by
wolves;
They're always ready for the sheep!

38
In serious memory let's recall
Elisabeth of heart so brave;
How she in pain and great distress
To God did call in earnestness.

CHAPTER 2

Mennonites in the New World

In the first two centuries of Mennonite life in the New World, physical survival loomed as a primary goal. Women spent most of their time and energy in childbearing and child-rearing and in providing food and clothing for their families: gardening, preserving fruits and vegetables (in more recent years, canning); spinning, weaving, knitting, sewing. In retrospect it seems only natural that when women formed their own organizations in the first decade of the twentieth century, they continued these domestic activities on behalf of others less fortunate. They made clothing for famine sufferers in Russia during the early 1920s. They canned for city missions during the 1920s and 30s and for conscientious objectors in CPS (Civilian Public Service) camps in the 40s.

During the Revolutionary War a Pennsylvania court confiscated and sold the belongings of Mennonite families who, because of their Christian conviction against going to war, refused to be a part of the Continental Army. Mennonite writer John Ruth notes that the recorded lists of items sold "evokes the flavor of their lives."[1] For instance, the following belonged to the Jacob Yoder family:

> Churn, spinning wheel, walnut table, scythe, sickles, chisels, currycomb, augers, cow chains, ax, saw, shovel, rakes, leather and wool, harrow, plows, hayforks, clock, two stoves.

It had taken the Yoders over half a century of hard work to achieve this degree of material security. Later in this chapter the story will be told of Eva Yoder and Esther Bachman, two courageous women who dared to confront that Pennsylvania court.

In 1802, 33 families moved from Bucks County, Pennsylvania, to Lincoln County, Ontario. Frank Epp in describing their life says:

> The girls all learned to milk cows, to plant vegetable gardens, to weave wool, to spin flax, and to sew their own clothes. Every home had its loom, its apple cider barrels, and its vegetable cellars.[2]

This chapter will highlight a few women from the early colonial period. Chapters 3 and 4 will tell stories of nineteenth-century women.

Mother Eberly

Oral tradition has handed down reports of Veronica Ulrich, later known as Mother Eberly. Evelyn K. Mumaw, a contemporary Mennonite writer, says that after hearing about this courageous woman from three different people on three separate occasions she determined to find out what she could about her. This is what she discovered.[3]

Veronica Ulrich, born in Switzerland in 1685, and her husband, Heinrich Eberly, moved with many Mennonites from Switzerland to the Palatinate on the Rhine in Germany. In response to Hans Herr's glowing reports, they decided to go to Pennsylvania to escape the oppression they faced in the Palatinate. In 1727, 348 families numbering 1,240 persons prepared to migrate to America. Heinrich and Veronica and their six children, ages one to twelve, made their way to Rotterdam to the ship *James Goodwill*.

While Heinrich left the ship to return home for something, the ship sailed, leaving him behind. Evelyn Mumaw says:

> One can only imagine the anguish of the young mother with her family . . . as the grim reality of her situation weighed down upon her. Through all the journey and for many months and years she probably lived on the hope that he would follow in a later ship and one day they would be reunited. But the months and years passed by, and Veronica never heard of Heinrich again.

Veronica and her children went westward from Philadelphia with fellow immigrants to a little settlement called Hickory-town, an area now known as North Queen Street in Lancaster. Several years later Veronica Eberly bought a tract of land that measured about a square mile in an area now called Durlach in northern Lancaster County. The account of the move merely says that they unloaded her scanty household furniture under a big white oak tree near a spring. The nearest neighbors to the Eberlys—Indians—lived two miles to the southeast.

A story about Mother Eberly, handed down through the generations, gives us an inkling of how bleak and barren of sweetness her life must have been. When her son Jacob was grown and married to Maria Huber, he farmed his mother's land, and she lived with him and his family. He infrequently made the sixteen-mile trip to the nearest store, in the village of Lancaster. Once when Jacob needed to purchase supplies, Mother Eberly took a coin worth about twelve cents from her meager coffer and asked him to buy some molasses for her.

In the store Jacob saw a cowbell. Perhaps he thought of the many hours he had to spend hunting through the woodlands for the cows and of the frustration of not being able to find them when he wanted them. What a difference it would make to have the strong, clear sound of a cowbell coming over the hillside from the woods! His own money all gone, he spent his mother's coin on the cowbell and rang it exuberantly as he approached home. But when his mother discovered what he had done, she was so disappointed that she wept bitterly.

In 1920 a stone was erected by Veronica Eberly's descendants in the family burial ground at Durlach. It reads:

IN MEMORY OF
THE PIONEER EBERLY FAMILY IN AMERICA
The Mother Eberly and Her Six Children
Jacob - Michael - Peter - Ulrich - two Daughters
Who came from Switzerland and settled in this vicinity in about 1730.

The sons are named; the daughters are not. But perhaps their names are written in the lamb's book of life, and perhaps for their mother, heaven has a sweetness surpassing that of earthly molasses.

Sister Grube and Sister Hershey

The diary of the Lititz Moravian congregation says that in 1767

> Brother and Sister Grube, visiting in the country, lost their way not far from Manheim and came to a house where abide the only couple of Indians remaining in this Province. The man was not at home but the woman was as happy as a child when Bro. Grube began to speak to her in the Delaware tongue, which she slightly understood—although she and her husband are Conestoga Indians. At the time of the Lancaster Blood Bath, these two Indians were in some danger of being murdered, but the Mennonite with whom they were living for 15 years hid them in his cellar, where they had to stay all winter until the excitement had somewhat abated.[4]

These two Conestoga Indians lived with farmer Christian Hershey. Who was Mrs. Christian Hershey, and what part did she play in the story? A Mennonite woman fed and cared for two Indians hiding in her basement for an entire winter in order to keep them from being harmed, perhaps killed. This unfamiliar part of the heritage of Mennonite women should be known. Not *all* white people mistreated Indians.

Who was Sister Grube? Perhaps she was not a Mennonite at all but a Moravian, for the account of the Grubes's visit to the Indians was translated by C. H. Martin from a Moravian document.

Eva Yoder and Esther Bachman

The period of the American Revolution severely tried Pennsylvania Mennonites, Moravians, Dunkards, and Quakers. The earliest record of American Mennonite women attempting to influence government in the United States comes down to us from this time. On September 9, 1778, Eva Yoder and Esther Bachman made an eloquent plea "To the Honorable the Representatives of the Freeman of the Common Wealth of Pennsylvania in General Assembly met."[5]

The Continental Army forced Mennonite farmers to furnish horses and food for them and sometimes conscripted the farmers to carry provisions with their teams and wagons, a service for which the farmers received no pay. A court in Upper Saucon Township, Northampton County, Pennsylvania, summoned ten men to appear: Jacob Joder (as it was spelled in the document), George Bachman, John Deisinger, Abraham Keisinger, Henry Sell, Jasper Joder, Abraham Joder, Henry Keisinger, Christian Joung, and John Newcomer—all peaceable, conscientious citizens, "being of the Religious Society called Menonists." The court ordered them to leave the state within thirty days, confiscated and sold their property, "even their Beds, Beddings, Bibles and Books." From some of them "all their Provisions were taken and even not a Morsel of Bread left them for their Children." Even though their iron heating stoves were fastened to the floor, the sheriff took them also. "Abraham Geisinger's wife had not a bed left her although she was Near her Time of Delivery."

Eva Yoder and Esther Bachman decided something had to be done. Winter was coming. How were they to keep warm without stoves? Why should they have to sleep on the floor with their children because their beds had been unfairly taken? What right had these government men to go against God? The two women made an eloquent plea to the Pennsylvania Assembly, not only for themselves but for all the wronged families. They said in part:

> May it therefore please this Honorable House to take the Premisses into
> Consideration and to mitigate the Severity of the Sentence of the said

Court, and that some Reguard be had to the Command of God laid down in the Scriptures of Truth, to witt, "What God hath joyned together let not Men put asunder" and that our Husbands may be permitted to continue to dwell with us, and that our Children may not be taken from us.

Perhaps a certain Dr. Felix Lynn transcribed their letter for them, for each of the two signatures is "her mark." The last sentence in the letter reads, "And your Petitioners as in Duty bound will ever pray."

The assembly did respond to the plea of Eva Yoder and Esther Bachman and asked that action be taken to right the wrong done to these people. Twentieth-century Mennonite women might learn from Eva Yoder and Esther Bachman.

One Loaf of Bread and a Strange Wedding

Two other stories have come down to us from the time of the American Revolution.

Amishman Christian Zook lived several miles west of Valley Forge, where George Washington's army camped during the winter of 1777-78. Both American and British-German soldiers foraged across Mennonite and Quaker farms in those days looking for food. Just as "Christian Zook's wife" was taking her bread out of the oven, some American soldiers came by and took all the loaves except one. Mrs. Zook wrapped one loaf in her apron and said, "This one is for me!" No doubt her descendants still make tasty bread.[6]

Then there was the wedding with uninvited guests. John Ruth describes it as follows:

> By Indian Creek, in the lap of the next valley to the Skippack, deacon Henry Rosenberger's family is celebrating the wedding of his daughter Magdalena to his indentured servant, John Swartley. John has had to pay considerable fines to stay clear of the militia. This is his happy day; the harvest is in, it is wedding season, and the sumptuous meal is nearly prepared. But there are unexpected guests. The inevitable foragers have come across the rise from Towamencin, seeking supplies for the Army. The women consult in consternation; they agree on a plan; they invite the soldiers to sit down with the guests. There is friendship and respect in the

midst of the chaos of war, and the soldiers, having drunk to the health of the newlyweds, leave without taking so much as a chicken.[7]

The success of this wedding resulted from a creative, humane way of treating antagonists.

A Fourfold Heritage

From these early years of their sojourn in America, Mennonite women have received a fourfold heritage: (1) learning to work with their hands, (2) practicing hospitality toward kinfolk and strangers, (3) being frugal, and (4) contributing to the welfare of the community in a spirit of cooperation. They were copartners with their men as transmitters of these values.

In more recent times, Anna Snyder Kauffman (1888-1975) of Kalispell, Montana, who lived to be 87, recalled her childhood in Nebraska.[8] One of fifteen children, she picked up corncobs and cow-dung chips to burn as fuel. She carried wood, pumped water, and milked cows.

Mabel Snyder of Millbank, Ontario, concurs about the legacy of work:

> Our women knew the ethics of hard work and economy. They raised produce to sell at the weekly farmers' market in Waterloo, and some of their produce was peddled from door to door, such as butter, eggs, coffee cakes. Some women made "koch kase" (cheese) to sell. The traditional methods of salt curing of meat, drying apples, soap-making, sap-boiling, raising chicks were all a part of their busy days. They tell of preserving certain fruits such as elderberries by boiling them down with sugar until in their concentrated form they kept for months in a stone crock. In the winter they had bees, schnitzing bees, butchering bees, quilting bees, and even rag bees, when they got together to tear mat rags. This spirit of cooperation has been passed on to today's generation.[9]

Recent immigrants often stayed with a more established family for weeks, months, or an entire season. Margaret Kilmer and her brothers Daniel and Christian from Elkhart County, Indiana, homesteaded in southeastern McPherson County, Kansas, in 1871.[10] In 1873, Margaret married R. J. Heatwole, and together they ran a sort of prairie hotel in their home. Such a stream of guests came so constantly that when Margaret was having a difficult pregnancy their physician advised her to go back East until the baby was born. She followed his advice.[11] The story of that baby, daughter Lydia Heatwole, is told in chapter 10.

Nellie I. Kinsie says of her mother, Mary Reesor (Mrs. Oscar) Burkholder (1888-1975):

> She had an endless stream of visitors—mostly from the U.S.A. where Oscar had been on meetings. She had a large garden and would often can 300 to 400 jars of vegetables each year, as well as fruit and meat, and even little potatoes. So she could put together a meal at the drop of a hat.[12]

Thrift was necessary in colonial times, on the frontier, during the Depression of the 1930's. For many it became a way of life.

Fannie Yordy Yeackley (1863-1955), pioneer mother, with her husband,
Joseph, in their 1884 wedding picture.

Eva Yeackley Reeb speaks of her mother, Fannie Yordy Yeackley (1863-1955), of Milford, Nebraska:

> She ingrained in her children that it is sinful to waste. She didn't discard utensils with holes. Through her much reading she learned of mending rivets. They and her soldering iron lengthened the life of many a utensil. She used a strip of leather for a hinge, a piece of wood for a door latch, bits of cloth tied to the handle of a discarded fly swatter to make a number-one device for removing crumbs from a toaster, and a tin can which she heated in coals in the kitchen range to be able to remove the ends and make a good, sharp, still-being-used food chopper.[13]

Mary Eiman Swartzendruber recalls rearing children on an Iowa farm during the Depression of the 1930's:

> I sewed most of the clothing for myself and the children, using small remnants and good parts of used clothing for them. For instance, Dwight's shirts both for play and dress were made from his daddy's old pants legs. For jackets and coats I used old coats from the grownups in the family, turning the faded or threadbare material inside out so the unworn side showed.... I also took jobs sewing for the community. This fit into my work as a homemaker and added a little to our income.[14]

This heritage of knowing how to work with one's hands, practicing hospitality, living frugally, and contributing to the welfare of the community through cooperative work constitutes a heritage that should be treasured and passed on to future generations. Values which once were necessary in order to survive in the wilderness may still be necessary in order to survive on the globe.

EXHIBIT 2

Petition of Eva Yoder and Esther Bachman to the Pennsylvania Assembly, September 9, 1778[15]

Document 267
To the Honorable the Representatives of the Freeman of the Common

Wealth of Pennsylvania in General Assembly met.

The Petition of Eve Joder, Wife of Jacob Joder of Upper Saucon Township in the County of Northampton in this State, Yeoman, and Esther Bachman, Wife of George Bachman of Upper Saucon Township aforesaid, Yeoman, As well on Behalf of themselves and their said Husbands as also on Behalf of John Keisinger, Abraham Keisinger, Henry Sell, Jasper Joder, Abraham Joder, Jacob Joder, Henry Keisinger, Christian Joung, John Newcomer and George Bachman, all of them Freeholders and Men of Reputation of the sd. County, who have always behaved peaceably & quietly and never intermedled in State Affairs But paid their Taxes & Fines, furnished Horses & Teams for the continental Service when ever demanded, and some of them have gone with their Teams as Drivers to carry Provisions to the Army of the united States for which Services they have hitherto received no pay;

That the said Freeholders were summoned to appear at the Court of Quarter Sessions held at Easton in June last past, where they appeared accordingly and the Test being tendered to them, by the said Court, which said Test they conscientiously scrupled to take (being of the Religious Society called Menonists) Whereupon the sd. Court sentenced them to be banished out of this State within thirty days after the said Court and that all their personal Estate be confiscated to the State;

That afterwards all their said personal Estate even their Beds, Beddings, Linen, Bibles & Books were taken from them and sold by the Sheriff to the amount of about forty thousand Pounds;

That from some of them all their Provisions were taken and even not a Morsel of Bread left them for their Children;

That all their Iron Stoves were taken from them out of their Houses, tho' fastned to the Freehold, they are deprived of every Means of Keeping their Children warm in the approaching Winter especially at Nights being obliged to lye on the Floor without any Beds;

That some of the said Mens Wifes are pregnant and near their Time of Deliverance which makes their Case more distressing and

That by Reason of the said Proceedings ten of the most respectful and considerable Familys in the said County of Northampton are become destitute and very much reduced:

May it therefore please this Honorable House to take the Premises into Consideration and to mitigate the Severity of the Sentence of the said Court, and that some Reguard be had to the Command of God laid down in the Scriptures of Truth, to witt, "What God hath joyned together let not Men put asunder" and that our Husbands may be permitted to continue to dwell with us, and that our Children may not be taken from us,

And your Petitioners as in Duty bound will ever pray. September the 9th 1778.

her

Eve E Joder

mark

her

Esther E. Bachman

mark

CHAPTER 3

Wives

What have Mennonite marriages been like? Do Mennonite wives have anything in common? Did Idelette de Bure, John Calvin's Anabaptist wife, influence his theology? This chapter will consider some general ideas about Mennonite wives and will then present four brief biographies.

In 1553, Leonard Bouwens's wife feared for her preacher husband's life because of the severe persecution of the Mennonites at that time. She wrote to Menno Simons begging him to use his influence to have her husband released from the ministry. Menno wrote her a letter urging her to recognize that her husband belonged first to God and the church:

> Dear sister in Christ Jesus, I trust that I by the grace of God sincerely love you with divine love in God and that I am prepared to serve you and all pious people even with my blood if need be. But dear sister, who am I that I should resist the Holy Spirit? ... Since the church so urgently desires him and since he cannot conscientiously refuse, how then shall I oppose it? I can find nothing in Leonard for which I could with Scriptural warrant oppose his call.... You are called to this of the Lord and by the operation of your faith you have yielded yourself to the service, not of your own self but of Jesus Christ and of your brethren as long as you live. I hope that you have done this heartily, cost what it may of money, possessions, and even life.[1]

In this letter, service to the Lord is clearly placed above personal desires.

One reads with some curiosity the account about Mennonite historian *Anna Cremer ten Doornkaat Brons* (1810-1902) in the *Mennonite Encyclopedia:*

> In their thoroughly happy marriage of 55 years' duration she stood faithfully at [husband Isaak's] side as a companion of equal rank and reared her large family in complete harmony with her husband. She took a lively interest in all her husband's work and was his perfect complement.

Complete harmony? Perfect complement? Does one see here a halo effect? Is "complete harmony" perceived by someone else much later? Or does it really exist? One hopes that the latter is indeed the case. Anna Brons during her lifetime worked toward her ideal, a union of all German Mennonite churches.

Ideals Concerning Marriage

The idea of marriage as a partnership of equals persists as a motif in Mennonite history. In the first half of the twentieth century, it was customary for ministers in the pulpit to speak of their wives as "companions." Roland Bainton credits Anabaptists, and later the Quakers and English Puritans, with insisting that companionability be the prime ingredient in marriage.[2] Also central to the Mennonite view of marriage is that it should be "only in the Lord" and that it is a lifetime commitment. "What therefore God has joined together, let not man put asunder" (Mark 10:9). An article on marriage in the December 1877 issue of the *Herald of Truth* (p. 186) stresses partnership, not hierarchy, in marriage.

Clara Eby Steiner (see chapter 11) read an essay at the Ohio Sunday School Conference in 1899, which was later published in the *Herald of Truth.*[3] Her husband had been asked to speak on "Temptations of the Young People and How to Overcome Them." She reluctantly consented to take his place, explaining that "pressing evangelistic duties in the West have demanded my husband's attention and services." She advised both young men and young women concerning courtship and marriage:

> Boys, will you allow flirts to turn your attention from valuable hours of
> study to them and to their entertainment? . . . My dear girls . . . you may
> wish for a strong arm to lean upon, but, remember, if you have not
> enough influence over a young man to bring him to Christ *before*, you
> have not *after*, marriage, and, that an unconverted arm is not the right
> kind of arm to make a good support through the storms and uneven
> pathway of life, but "A lonely heart that leans on God is happy
> anywhere."

She urged education for girls as well as boys in order for wives to
be partners intellectually with their husbands.

Mathilda Kliewer Voth (1899-), a General Conference Mennonite missionary to China in the 1920s, expressed shock that in
the mission of another denomination "the wives were not occupied with mission work."[4] Mennonite wives, along with their
husbands, *were* "occupied with mission work." (See chapter 8.)
Minnie Swartzentruber Graber (1902-) said of missionary wives
under the Mennonite mission board at Elkhart, Indiana, "We, as
well as our husbands, were always given an assignment."[5]

J. C. Wenger in *History of the Mennonites of the Franconia
Conference* points out the custom in Franconia of using the wife's
maiden surname as the middle name of each child.[6] He himself
carefully gives the names and dates of wives as he identifies
ministers. Concerning nomenclature Lorraine Roth says, "There
was a period when women were not called by their first
names. . . . It may have been chauvinistic, but it was considered
proper protocol."[7] Perhaps the system of naming was not after all
a demeaning of women, as is thought by today's compound-
surnames generation.

Also present at times has been the idea that a wife should live
vicariously through her husband and children. A pamphlet written in 1959 for the dedication of the C. Z. Yoder dormitory at
Goshen (Indiana) College expresses this well:

> Every word of tribute to C. Z. Yoder's memory is at one and the same
> time a tribute to Mrs. C. Z. Yoder, the former Lydia Smiley [1846-1922].
> The hospitality of the Yoder home; the delight with which neighbors and
> friends came and went from this home; the tokens of kindness, gestures of
> respect, gifts of plants, flowers, and items of usefulness that were shared,

are all remembered as evidences that back of every successful husband is the powerful influence of his wife. . . . The true wife and homemaker has not only lived her own life, but she has also lived through her husband. And as a mother, she has lived through her children. . . . The completeness of the life of C. Z. Yoder was deeply rooted in the life and devotion of his mate.[8]

A less common view, but not totally absent, states that a husband should live vicariously through his wife, that this is the only way in which he can understand, for example, such experiences as pregnancy and childbirth. A third viewpoint rejects the practice of living "through" or "behind" another person, saying that each man or woman must live his or her own life fully in Christ. Living in genuine partnership can be creative and fulfilling, but living only through another person can be a secondhand way to exist.

By the 1920s the idea of separate spheres of action for men and women, husbands and wives, was clearly delineated. In 1925, Illinois leader J. S. Shoemaker wrote in his book *The Ideal Christian Home:*

A good wife is like the ivy that beautifies the building to which it clings, twining its tendrils more lovingly as time converts the ancient edifice into a ruin.

Shoemaker opposed women's participation in "women's clubs, social betterment society meetings, home bureau meetings . . . to the neglect of home and family duties."[9]

Nowhere in print or from the pulpit has it been advocated that wives be treated as inferiors by husbands. Yet the novels of Christmas Carol Kauffman (see chapter 9), read widely by Mennonite women in the 1940s and 50s, often contained as a character a husband who mistreated his wife. Why were these novels popular? Were some readers identifying with the protagonist wife? Has the teaching of "headship" sometimes been misused to justify tyranny?

The Contribution of Wives

The intimate relationship of a man and a woman in marriage

is a mysterious closed door. One wonders about the relationship of Hans Herr (1639-1725) and his wife, Elizabeth Kendig (also spelled Kintig). At age 72 Hans, along with Elizabeth and their seven children, came to Pennsylvania, settling near Willow Street in Lancaster. How old was Elizabeth? Ira D. Landis says, "This family was a real asset in establishing this colony in the backwoods of Pennsylvania."[10] What was the nature of Elizabeth's contribution to the partnership? At about the same time Benedict and Maria Breckbill settled in Lancaster County between Lampeter and Strasburg. Who was Maria? What was she like?

One wonders about other pioneer couples: John K. (1824-1906) and Elizabeth (Zook) Yoder of Wayne County, Ohio; Benjamin Eby of Ontario and his two wives—(1) Mary Brubacher (1789-1834), mother of eleven children, who died of cholera, and (2) Magdalena Erb Erb (1780-1858), the widow of Abraham Erb.[11] A feature article, "Death of a Pioneer," in the May 10, 1883, issue of the *Holmes County* (Ohio) *Farmer* contains the following statement about Henry and Barbara (Miller) Shrock: "They battled the storms of life together for a little over 50 years, accumulating sufficiently of this world's goods."[12]

J. C. Wenger penned some beautiful sentences about the death of Salome Kratz (1839-1917), wife of J. F. Funk: "His wife Salome lived with him in holy matrimony for fifty-three years, and died September 5, 1917. As she was slipping away the old patriarch patted her cheek and said, 'It's all right, Mother, you are going home.' " Harry F. Weber says, "Amanda Eby (1876-1938), who became the wife of A. H. Leaman, was a faithful worker in and about the Home (Chicago) throughout the years of his superintendency."[13]

Gerald Mumaw considers some of his female ancestors:[14]

Barbara Weber, a Mennonite girl, married George Anthony Mumma sometime before 1750. George had arrived in Philadelphia with his German Lutheran parents in 1742. By joining Barbara's church George introduced the Mumaw family name into the Mennonite church. Either the strength of Barbara's personality or her faith or both made George willing to become a Mennonite.

Catherine Brenneman from Fairfield County, Ohio, married George
Mumaw (a great-grandson of George Anthony Mumma) in 1845. It is said
that George was biblically illiterate when he married Catherine. She not
only taught George the Bible, but also mothered 7 children.

How difficult it is to select women who could be considered
representative Mennonite wives! Any such attempt is justly subject to criticism. Yet the attempt will be made and four brief "representative" biographies presented.

Veronica Livengood Peachey Schmucker (1791-1884)[15]

This woman is said to be the first Schmucker mother to cross
the Ohio River with her husband and family as they left their
home in Mifflin County, Pennsylvania, seeking a new home in
Wayne County, Ohio. Six children made this journey, the older
ones likely walking most of the way.

Veronica's children and grandchildren heard her tell of her
husband Christian Schmucker's childhood experiences during the
Revolutionary War, when his grandfather Christian Schmucker
and others were arrested and sentenced to death because they
would not take up arms in the war. They were released upon a
petition by a pastor of the German Reformed Church. While the
elder Christian was in prison in Reading, Pennsylvania, the little
grandson Christian went with his grandmother Catherine Hesster
Schmucker to carry meals and encouragement to the prisoners.
On the way, town boys threw stones at young Christian.

Veronica's descendants heard her tell stories of her own
childhood in Somerset County, Pennsylvania, and of the War of
1812. Because her father required her to work with her four
brothers in the barn and fields and with the flocks, she did not
learn to do household tasks as did her nine sisters. However, she
was happily married. When her young husband died of yellow
fever before the birth of their son, Abraham, she was grief-
stricken. She and the child made their home with her sister in
Mifflin County. Those people are fortunate who have heard Dr.
Mary Royer, an outstanding speaker, tell of the divinely led
courtship and marriage of Veronica and Christian Schmucker.

Great-great-great-granddaughter Christina also tells the story:

> One morning Veronica and her sister rose before dawn to help the men get an early start to drive cattle to the market in Philadelphia. During a lull in the morning's work, she lay down on the bench behind the stove and fell asleep.

> As she slept, she dreamed she saw a ruddy-bearded stranger come riding through the creek bed and up the hill. He was mounted on a bay horse, and the horse had a white spot on its forehead. She awoke, and falling asleep again dreamed the same dream a second time, and a third. Each time the same stranger came riding a bay horse through the creek bed and up the hill.

> And then a stranger did come riding through the creek bed and up the hill. When he came to the door, she recognized him as the man she had seen in her dream. He was welcomed into the house and invited to dinner. While he was eating, Veronica slipped out to the barn to see if the horse was the same as the one she had dreamed about. It was. There was the white spot on its forehead, and the saddlebags were the same. Who was the stranger? Where was he from and what brought him on his journey?

> His name was Christian Schmucker. His wife had died, leaving him and his ten motherless children in sorrow and need. He had traveled a hundred miles from his home in Mifflin County southwest to Somerset County, where there was a community of his own faith. There he hoped to find a good wife, and mother for his children. He had prayed that God would guide him and bless his journey. When he came to a fork in the road, he said to his horse, "In the name of God, go the way you should go." And so Christian came to the farmhouse where Veronica was living. . . .

> The next time he came, he asked Veronica if she would be willing to be married so he might take her along home for the next Sunday when the church meeting would be at his house. It was the custom to announce to the congregation three weeks before a wedding the intention of two people to marry. But the preachers said that Christian and Veronica might be married at once so she could return with him for the church meeting. . . . By Sunday the house must be shiny clean and the dinner ready for all the people. Veronica could do a man's work in the fields, but she was only learning to keep house. She went behind the house and cried. Her new family found her crying. They said, "We will help you." And they did.

Christian's ten children were John, Christian, David, Nancy, Isaac, Elizabeth, Barbara, Fannie, Abraham, and Samuel. To him and Veronica were born Catherine, Joel, Jonathan, Lydia, Jacob, Joseph, Moses, and Peter. This kind of large combined family—his children, her children, their children—was common in the nineteenth century. (One of my great-grandmothers, Caroline Shrock Kendall Troyer (1848-1926), was matriarch of such a clan.)

Susan Ressler Good Hostetler (1845-1919)

Susan, daughter of Martin Boehm and Magdalena (Andrews) Ressler, was born in Strasburg Township, Lancaster County, Pennsylvania, and married Henry H. Good, of Rockingham County, Virginia.[16] To them were born eleven children. Henry died in 1908, having served for 28 years in the ministry. After seven years of widowhood Susan married David Hostetler of Weilersville, Ohio.

From her scattered writings in the *Herald of Truth* and *Gospel Herald*, Susan emerges as a remarkable person. She must have been a combination of Mary and Martha.

She moved a great deal—from Lancaster County to Rushville, Virginia, to Allen County, Ohio, to eastern Tennessee, to Halifax County, Virginia, to Weilersville, Ohio.

The August 1, 1893, issue of *Herald of Truth* contains an article by her entitled "A Valuable Remedy." It begins:

> For the benefit of the people in West Earl township, Lancaster Co., Pa., who have recently been afflicted with annoying and destructive insects, and all others suffering from like causes, I will give my experience in destroying them.

Susan tells of visiting a sick neighbor whose son-in-law had recently been released from the county jail. He told about a prisoner who was never bothered with lice because he kept oil of cedar with him. She continues:

> On my way home as I was thinking over what the man had said, I passed

some nice cedar trees. I concluded to take some of the twigs and make a strong tea or wash for the parts of our house affected with bed bugs. I had spent much time and labor to get rid of the vermin, and all to no purpose, and was only too glad to hear of something that might possibly give me relief.

Her remedy worked, and as a practical Mennonite housewife with the highest of standards, she wished to share it with others.

The May 20, 1909, *Gospel Herald* includes the following field note:

> Sister Susan Good of Wolftrap, Virginia, writes that there is an opening for possible work at Buena Vista, Va. Ministering brethren who happen to be passing that way might do well by writing ahead to Henry Camden, Buena Vista, Va., telling him when and how long they can stop there, and directing him to make appointments for them. May God bless the work.

Behind that note is the presence of a woman eager to extend the work of the church.

The April 15, 1909, *Gospel Herald* carries an article by her entitled "The Minister's Wife."

> Christian women should be humble and submissive. In the meaning of these two words lies the secret of a wife doing her duty to her husband. Not all women are naturally humble and submissive; but disappointments, afflictions, fervent prayer and true conversion can bring them there.... Webster says, "Humility does not require us to underrate ourselves." ... To help a minister in his work consists not alone in telling him where to find passages of Scripture, or to help him with quotations, or to tell him the meaning of words, although she should be well enough acquainted with the Scriptures to do this.... She should arrange her work in a way that if he wishes her to go with him to visit a sick neighbor she can go.

Susan urges the minister's wife to serve regular meals, to avoid food that is hard to digest, to make Saturday nights times of quiet.

With her emphasis on knowing the Scriptures and the meanings of words, Susan herself might have made an excellent minister. At her death in 1919 her youngest daughter, Mary M. Good, then a missionary in Dhamtari, India, prepared a collection of her poems and meditations, which was privately printed. It includes a poem about a "flitting" (moving) written when Susan was thirteen years old, many poems on the occasion of a death, and various meditations.

(It should be noted that the privately printed book is not uncommon for Mennonite women writers. Examples include Stella Cooprider Erb's *Through Tribulation to Crown of Life, The Story of a Godly Grandmother* [quoted in chapter 4], Irene Horst's *Reflections of 704* [quoted in chapter 5], Lydia Oyer's book about Lydia Heatwole [quoted in chapter 10], a booklet about Esther Ebersole Lapp [quoted in chapter 8], Ursula Miller's poetry, *Prairie Praises*, Mennonite Press, North Newton, Kansas, 1978).

Alice Troyer Yoder (1888-1959)

Of this minister's wife her daughter said, "Her main loyalty and passion was for Dad. She encouraged him, listened to all his problems, supported him in any venture he felt best. His ministry was her ministry. There was very little they didn't discuss together."[17]

Born to Amos P. and Delilah (Yoder) Troyer in Cass County, Missouri, Alice moved to Hubbard, Oregon, with her family in 1892. Her father became the first bishop of the Zion Mennonite Church there. As a young person she was interested in and loved the church. She had a close relationship with her father. He often counseled with her about the work of the church. He learned, as did her husband later, that she would never betray a confidence.

The summer Alice was nineteen she and several other girls went to the Mennonite community near Minot, North Dakota, to cook in a "cook-car" for a threshing crew there. Edward Z. Yoder, from West Liberty, Ohio, headed the crew. At the age of 27 he was homesteading a claim and sometimes also worked in the mines. This summer his job of maintaining the machine often kept him up most of the night. Alice noticed how hard he worked and saw to it that he had warm water to wash up or an extra glass of milk. He was not a Christian at this time, having left his home community bitter about the church. Alice's Christian testimony shone clearly. He told her he had decided even before he met her that the only way to live was to come back to God. They were married in 1909, and the Zion Church near Hubbard, Oregon, ordained him to the ministry two years later.

Thus began a long team ministry. During World War I Edward went to the camps to look after the needs of conscientious objectors. Non-Mennonite community people at Hubbard threatened his life and erected a scaffold for him. "Al," as she was now called, had two babies and was expecting a third. She stayed at home, milked all the cows, and did the farm work alone. Evidently the malicious zeal of the townspeople subsided, for her husband was not harmed.

At times of death in the community, Alice Yoder helped lay out the body and arrange food for the family. At times of sickness and dying she provided nursing and comfort, even in a diphtheria epidemic. A daughter recalls, "Every winter, as a child, I remember how the telephone would ring during the night, and Dad and Mom would go to pray with some sick person in the community."

Often Alice did farm work along with her husband. She planned the music when he had a worship service, funeral, or wedding. She accompanied him in visitation and in conducting services once a month at a tuberculosis sanatorium, an old people's home (as it was called then), and a boys' training school.

She served as church and Sunday school chorister and taught the kindergarten Sunday school class, ages two to five, for over 35 years. She sewed the white net head coverings for the women of the church.

Along with other women in the community, she worked at the Woodburn Pear Cannery each fall to supplement the family income. And she canned a thousand quarts of food each summer to set the winter table for their seven children. "No matter how tired she was, she was always jolly and loved to laugh." Alice Troyer Yoder was indeed a "helpmeet" to her husband.

Elizabeth Horsch Bender (1895-   )

This brilliant, modest woman is the not as well-known half of a scholarly partnership that produced such notable works as the *Mennonite Quarterly Review* and the *Mennonite Encyclopedia.* She says of her husband Harold S. Bender's work, "You know, I suppose I read everything he wrote. I'd make suggestions or change little things here and there."[18]

Elizabeth was born in Elkhart, Indiana, to John Horsch, an emigrant from Bavaria, Germany, and Christine Funck, from Württemberg, Germany. Her father, later a well-known Mennonite historian, had studied in Europe under Ludwig Keller. The family moved from Elkhart to Berne, Indiana, then to Birmingham, Ohio, where John Horsch worked in an orphanage operated by J. A. Sprunger. There Elizabeth was baptized at age twelve by immersion. They also lived in Cleveland for a while. In 1908 they moved to Scottdale, Pennsylvania, where Aaron Loucks

Elizabeth Horsch (Bender) (1895-   ), scholar-helpmeet, 1917.

had started what later became the Mennonite Publishing House.

Elizabeth recalls that at Scottdale, as the only Mennonite in the local high school, she wore plain colors and long sleeves. She played on the girls' basketball team, but if a church meeting conflicted with a game, she went to the church meeting. As valedictorian of her class she gave a speech entitled "The Quest of an Ideal." Rather than dress like the other graduates, she wore a plain white dress with long sleeves. The mother of one of her classmates asked her daughter who the girl was that "looked like an angel." Following high school graduation Elizabeth worked at the publishing house, reading proof and operating the Linotype for German periodicals.

In 1915 she took a first year of college at Hesston, Kansas— one year being all that was offered there at that time. She spent the next two years at Goshen College, earning her bachelor's degree in three years, in 1918. Because most of the young men were still in camp, only two men—both theological students— graduated in that class: J. N. Smucker and Harold S. Bender. The January 1918 issue of the *Goshen College Record* carries an article by Elizabeth entitled "Ignorance vs. Error." It contains a carefully reasoned argument that ignorance is worse than error. The first and last sentences read as follows:

> History tells us that man has not always been an intelligent being—that the history of society has been one of development from a savage state to his present state of reason and intellectual supremacy, which has brought on the condition known as civilization. ... Therefore, we can safely conclude that the discovery of the truths of which we have been boasting for the last two or three centuries would still be unknown if we had been in ignorance up to that time, that error, though not desirable in itself, was the means of progress.

A girl who looked like an angel and had a mind like that! Is it any wonder that young scholar Bender was attracted to Elizabeth Horsch?

The next two years she taught Latin, Greek, Spanish, geometry, and psychology at the new Eastern Mennonite School (now College) in Harrisonburg, Virginia. Hubert Pellman says of

her: "At Eastern Mennonite she became registrar, librarian, preceptress, director of Ladies' Chorus, and, of course, teacher. In the
two years she served on the faculty, she taught eight subjects.
Students remember her thorough scholarship and her insistence
on higher social standards, including etiquette."[19] During the next
years she taught at Hesston, worked as a linotypist in Pittsburgh,
and taught in a high school in Johnstown, Pennsylvania. At
Johnstown, in 1923, she and Harold were married, after duly
receiving permission from the school board and agreeing to keep
the marriage secret, for married women were not allowed to be
employed full-time.

The next year the couple sailed for Germany, where Harold
eventually received his doctorate from Heidelberg University.
Elizabeth "studied right along with him." He received credit and
a degree. She received neither, but "studied whatever subjects
were being offered." She remembers lectures by Karl Barth and a
course in European historical geography.

In 1924 the couple returned to Goshen, Indiana, where she
taught in the academy and later German at the college. During
Professor D. A. Lehman's final illness, she taught his courses in
analytical geometry and calculus, for she had long been interested
in theoretical mathematics.

Of her husband's doctorate she says that although he spoke
Pennsylvania Dutch very well, his High German was not as good.
"This did not stop his preaching in Europe, however, for the
people were very considerate with him. But when it came to publishing, it had to be better than that." So she edited his entire
dissertation for grammar and German usage.

In 1943, Elizabeth received a master's degree from the
University of Minnesota, as a result of the urging of her husband
and of her professor, Dr. Maessen. She was taking courses—this
time for credit—while her husband represented Goshen College
at a seminar. She wrote her thesis on "Mennonites in German
Literature." In 1958 the older of her two daughters, Mary
Eleanor, received her doctorate from Indiana University under
the direction of the same professor.

Elizabeth Horsch Bender did extensive work in proofreading, editing, and translating for the four-volume *Mennonite Encyclopedia,* published 1955-59. She says, "I think I read every one of those articles three times, once for every proofreading stage. If I had a good memory, just think what all I'd know!" For this work she received 75 cents an hour.

Since her husband's death in 1962 she has continued to do volunteer proofreading for the *Mennonite Quarterly Review.* She also aids researchers, including Leonard Gross and Leland Harder, in translating materials from the German.

Elizabeth Horsch Bender is a scholar in her own right. Would that some heaven-oriented university would grant this humble woman a "Doctor of Humane Letters"! She has a sparkling sense of humor, plus great depth and breadth of both knowledge and spirit.

**Myra Kendig (Lehman) (1896-   ), age 18,
later the wife of Chester K. Lehman.**

The list of other Mennonite couples whose names and work are inextricably intertwined is a long one including: G. L. and Elsie (Kolb) Bender, Isaiah W. and Tina (Neuhauser) Royer, J. A. and Lina (Zook) Ressler, Christian and Rosanna (McGonegal) Yoder, A. J. and Alta (Maust) Metzler, Oscar and Mary (Reesor) Burkholder, Chester K. and Myra (Kendig) Lehman, Paul and Alta (Eby) Erb, J. D. and Minnie (Swartzendruber) Graber. May the partnership of Mennonite husbands and wives continue.

CHAPTER 4

Mothers

Mennonite women have been, above all else, mothers. They have cared for and brought up children. A common sentence in obituaries of the last century and the first half of the twentieth was "To this union was born eleven (ten, seven, you fill in the blank) children." Children called their mothers "Mem," "Ma," "Mamma," "Mother."

Deaths of Infants and Mothers

In colonial and pioneer days, dangers accompanied pregnancy and childbirth. Women died of puerperal ("milk") fever. Infant mortality was high; children died of smallpox, diphtheria, and other feared diseases. Dr. Benjamin Rush, prominent colonial physician, calculated in 1790 that of every 100 children born in Philadelphia only 64 lived to reach age 6; 46 made it to 16; only 3 lived to 66.[1] Over half the children born did not reach adulthood.

A sample obituary in the February 1, 1900, issue of the *Herald of Truth* begins as follows:

Annie M., little daughter of Bro. E. C. and Sister Ida Shank, departed this life December 27th, 1899, aged 1 year, 9 months and 4 days. She suffered

nearly two weeks of menengitis [sic] of the brain. It is very sad for the
parents to be called upon to give up another one of their jewels, this being
the fourth one.

The following tombstones in the old Mennonite cemetery near
Bluffton, Ohio, are typical:

Mary Ann	Anna
wife of	Wife of
Peter Luginbihl	Abraham B. Amstutz
Died	died
March 29, 1858	Aug 17 1858
aged	Aged 24 ys 5 mo 20 ds
22 ys., 10 mo 20 ds	

Why did they bother to count the number of months and days
lived in addition to years? Was it because life was so precarious
that every day was indeed precious?

Two college girls took a walk through a small cemetery just
south of the Goshen College campus during the late 1940's.
Returning, they met Mennonite historian John Umble (1881-
1966), many years their senior. They expressed surprise that there
were so many tombstones for young women in their twenties. He
shook his head and said with deep feeling, "You girls just don't
understand. You don't understand." Indeed, it was not uncommon for one man to have three successive wives during a lifetime.

Small tombstones of children also abound in cemeteries of
the nineteenth and early twentieth centuries. (It is appropriate to
be reminded that many countries of the world have high infant
mortality rates even today.)

Despite the diseases which took many, children did survive.
Seven representative Mennonite mothers have been selected for
inclusion in this chapter.

Barbara Schultz Oesch (c. 1803-81)[2]

In 1803, King Maximilian—ruler of Bavaria, admirer of Napoleon—seized Catholic cloisters in Bavaria and invited Amish
and Mennonites to farm these lands. Johannes Oesch responded

to Maximilian's invitation, migrated to Bavaria in order to escape Napoleon's military conscription, and there married sixteen-year-old Barbara Schultz. In 1823, Johannes and Barbara listened eagerly to the stories of adventurer Christian Nafziger. He had come back to Rothsee, Bavaria, after a year and a half of absence. What stories he had to tell! Of faraway places like Amsterdam, New Orleans, Pennsylvania, and Canada. Nafziger told, wonder of wonders, of syrup flowing out of trees. For the Oesches—living in a damp, cold Bavarian cloister in the winter—times were hard. Under Maximilian they had little hope for the future. They decided to emigrate.

Barbara packed flour, grain, dried fruits, and dried and cured meat for the long journey. With three children—Christian, Freni, and Johannes, the last barely six months old—they left Neuberg, Germany, on June 1, 1824, along with the Jacob Steinman family. When they reached the new settlement in the forests of Wilmot, Canada, they experienced warm hospitality inside the small, roughly made cabins of the settlers—Schwartzentrubers, Kropfs, Goldschmidts, and Brennemans.

Johannes and Barbara quickly settled into the life of this new and growing community. On the anniversary of their departure from Neuberg, Barbara gave birth to her fourth child, a son, Daniel. The bearing and rearing of children, the production of food and clothing for family in this primeval forest, completely absorbed her energies. It was true in a sense that syrup flowed from trees, as Christian Nafziger had said, but it was not without a great deal of work. Barbara learned that it took many hours of boiling the maple sap before it became syrup or sugar. While the work was hard in Ontario, for the first time the fruit of their labor was their own.

After they had been in Canada for five years, the lot fell on Johannes, and he became a minister in the Amish Church. Five years later the congregation chose him to be bishop. In twenty years he had acquired 200 acres of land, and Barbara had given birth to fifteen children. Oldest son Christian married Catherine Zehr from Woolwich and worked the home farm, thus relieving his father for his work in the church. Oldest daughter Veronica married John Gerber, a widower with three children, later ordained a deacon in the Wellesley congregation.

The next part of the saga is repeated again and again in the stories of other families—a restless man, eager to pioneer once more, and his home-loving wife, reluctant to leave hard-won comforts, but loyal to her husband, and moving again.

Johannes heard stories of cheap land in the bush country north of Wilmot. He heard that at Ebytown (later Berlin, now Kitchener, Ontario) several families had moved to within a few miles of Lake Huron. Only 56, still strong, father of eight sons, he decided to move again. So Johannes, Barbara (pregnant with her eighteenth child), the young children, and their earthly possessions on several wagons followed the Huron Road west and north to Bayfield, where the family would live until a house was built on the 200-acre site Johannes had selected. At Bayfield, Barbara gave birth to her last child, Elizabeth.

A year later, on March 12, 1850, suddenly, unexpectedly, Johannes died of a ruptured appendix. Now another oft repeated story takes place—a widow and her children working hard to survive in a new settlement. Barbara and her children completed the family house and tilled the land.

She would have been glad to see them satisfied with what they had, but she recognized in them the restless spirit of their father. Over the succeeding years she saw her family scatter far and wide. Christian and his family went to Iowa and eventually to Missouri. Magdalena and David Kropf also settled eventually in Missouri. Daniel and Barbara (Roth) Oesch and Catherine and Jacob Bechtel settled in Indiana, and Joel and Katherine (Erb) Oesch in Nebraska. Barbara saw some of her children die—Hans, Freni, Catherine (at 46), Rudy (in a threshing accident at age 34), daughter-in-law Barbara Gascho (Hans's wife, at age 46).

Through these times of grief Barbara nevertheless rejoiced in the development of the community and congregation in Hay. Her family's move, and perhaps even their tragedies, had spurred other settlers to join them. During the last years of her life she

lived with daughter Leah and her husband, Christian Schwart-
zentruber, on the home farm. She had lived through a difficult
but exciting era—the migration of a people to a new land where
they prospered materially and the church grew in numbers and in
vitality. She died on January 18, 1881. In her obituary is this
sentence, "The Amish Church has lost a shining light."[3]

Elizabeth Gerig Meyer (1817-1905)[4]

Elizabeth, eldest of the thirteen children of Jacob and Elizabeth (Zimmerman) Gerig, was born in Pfastatt, Alsace, France,
now part of the city of Mulhouse (Mülhausen). When she was 55
and a widow, she and her two sons—Jacob and Albert—immigrated to the United States, where two of her brothers—Sebastian
and Benjamin—had already gone. She loved books, and she loved
telling stories. Here are some of the stories she told her children
and grandchildren.

Because of the poverty of the Gerig family, Elizabeth and
her brother Christian worked in a large woolen-cloth factory
about two miles from their home when they were thirteen and
eleven respectively. One evening as they, tired and hungry, were
wending their way home through the twilight, they came to the
bridge near their home. A wolf had come out of the forest and was
sleeping on the bridge right in their pathway. He seemed to be
asleep, but they decided not to find out. Tired though they were,
they retraced their steps and went home another way. As they
neared their home, Christian declared, "I will say my prayers
before I get into the house so I can eat immediately when I get to
the table, as I am so hungry." Many years later in Wayne County,
Ohio, Elizabeth—now Grandmother Meyer—would end this
story by saying to her grandchildren, "You are very fortunate and
must always be grateful to God that you live in a land of plenty
and do not need to go hungry."

Another of her stories told about the birth of her youngest
brother, Benjamin. Elizabeth had passed her 25th birthday when
this brother was born. Her mother confided to her that she feared
older son Christian resented having another child born into the al-

ready large family. Elizabeth felt sorry for her mother and spoke
privately to Christian about the matter. When the baby came, big
brother Christian, age 23, took Benjamin into his arms and "made
a great fuss over him." The scene caused their mother to shed
tears of joy in her relief. This baby grew up to be quite influential
in Elizabeth's life, for following their mother's death he and the
next-oldest brother, Sebastian, made their home with Elizabeth
and her husband.

When Elizabeth was sixteen, she obtained a position as a
cook on the large Helman estate. What a change for her! The
Helmans lived in a mansion and employed gardeners, coachmen,
stable boys, maids, governesses. But Mrs. Helman, also a Christian, and Elizabeth soon became fast friends, and Elizabeth
served the family faithfully until she married at age 29 and established her own home. One of her later stories told about serving flaming plum pudding at huge dinner parties.

During her time in the Helman house, romance entered
Elizabeth's life in the person of John Jacob Meyer, a young
engineer in the big cotton mill of Dollfus, Meig and Company of
Mülhausen. As a wedding gift Mrs. Helman handsomely
furnished the young couple's home in order to show her appreciation for Elizabeth's faithful service. Both the Meyer parents and
the Gerig grandparents rejoiced greatly when their first child and
first grandchild, Jacob G. Meyer, arrived in 1846.

Two years later Elizabeth's mother died. Cemeteries in
France at this time were controlled by the Catholic Church, and
Protestants were not permitted to bury their dead inside the en-
closure, only outside the fence. But the church authorities voted
that Mother Gerig had been a good enough Christian to be buried
inside the fence, even though she was a Mennonite! Following
their mother's death the two youngest brothers, Sebastian and
Benjamin, came to live with their sister and her husband.
Benjamin was six years old at the time. Out of deep love for and
loyalty to her family, Elizabeth brought up these two brothers
along with her own two sons, Jacob and Albert. The Meyers's only
daughter, Alice, lived for just two years.

Both Meyer boys were studious and learned readily. In order to finance his education Jacob worked as a copyist for an attorney, typewriters not yet having been invented. Meanwhile, both Gerig brothers had immigrated to the New World. Sebastian went with a Schlatter family to Canada, then on to Iowa. Benjamin went with a Sommers family to Ohio.

In Mülhausen the older Meyer son, Jacob, was drafted. While he was away, his father died suddenly of pneumonia (on February 16, 1868). The Gerig brothers in America, now prosperous farmers, urged their widowed sister to join them in the land of opportunity. They would help her now, as she had helped them when they were orphaned.

Already 55, Elizabeth nevertheless decided to go. She and her two sons sailed from Havre on a British ship and spent seventeen seasick days crossing the Atlantic. They landed in New York on July 4, 1872, and were alarmed at the shooting noises they heard. What was happening? Elizabeth told a man who could speak German that they had come here to escape war. He explained the Fourth of July holiday and its harmless noises.

Elizabeth spent the rest of her life in Wayne County, Ohio, where she and her sons made the transition from urban to rural life, from German and French to English, from Europe to America. Jacob married Anna Stucky in 1875. After three years of marriage Anna died, leaving three children. Four years later Jacob married Mary Conrad (1857-1935) of Louisville, Ohio. Elizabeth's granddaughter Katherine Meyer Yoder said of this family:

> This was one family with no reference whatever to step-mother. . . . Elizabeth was Grandma, and Mother was mother to all of the twelve, while Father was head of the family. . . . What a happy home life we enjoyed. . . . We were taught that spiritual values are much more important than possessions. We were urged to be industrious and thrifty. Our parents instilled into us a love for God and the Church, and were pleased when their sons and daughters were useful in furthering the cause of Christ. Under this teaching, these twelve all became affiliated with the Church of their Elders early in life and all grew to maturity in this faith.

Elizabeth Gerig Meyer died on February 1, 1905, at the age

of 88, after an illness that had confined her to her bed for two days.

Catharine Holly Stoltzfus (1807-84)[5]

In 1826 a petite, energetic nineteen-year-old bride, Catharine Holly, bid farewell to the Big Valley, Mifflin County, Pennsylvania, to travel over a hundred miles by horseback with her amiable 21-year-old husband, John Stoltzfus, to their new home in Lancaster County. Their household possessions were shipped down the Juniata by riverboat. For the next 46 years they were busily involved as Christian leaders and farmers in Lancaster County—and as loving parents of fifteen children, thirteen of whom grew to adulthood.

In spite of mothering fifteen children, spinning, knitting, gardening, marketing, and helping her deacon husband visit the sick and comfort the sad, Catharine found time to add touches of beauty to her home and to have a large flower garden. Although an effective disciplinarian, she had the courtesy never to scold her children in the presence of guests.

As successful farmers, John and Catharine used their resources to bless their children by buying farms for them. In 1872, attracted by the gentle climate and inexpensive farmland, John and Catharine and five children, with their families, and other fellow believers colonized near Concord in Knox County, Tennessee. This settlement acquired the name of Dutchtown because of its Pennsylvania Dutch colonists. Moving from "the garden spot of America" to a land depleted by plantation farming and ravaged by the Civil War, the Stoltzfuses worked hard during those early years in Tennessee. They introduced bronze turkeys and Jersey cows to the Southern farmers. These quiet, peace-loving Northerners became neighbors and friends of Confederate Army veterans, sharecroppers, former planters, and slaves.

Less than a month after John and Catharine arrived in the South, Debbie Neuhauser, their three-year-old granddaughter, died and was buried in the apple orchard, which John donated as a cemetery for the Concord Church. At first, Sunday school was held in homes, until John donated land to the congregation and financed the building of a church house. After John was ordained bishop, a preacher by the name of Lantz commended John's leadership and Catharine's faithfulness. John and Catharine's compassion and concern for people was reflected in their being able to hold together a congregation of unusually diverse elements—Amish-Mennonites, Virginia Conference Mennonites, Plymouth Brethren, and local Tennesseans of various denominational backgrounds.

When Jake, the youngest of the fifteen children, was married, Catharine and John turned over their farm to the young couple and moved into the "grandpa wing." By this time the effects of a strenuous life of hard work and childbearing had left Catharine in frail health, but she remained a gracious hostess and · an indulgent grandmother. Her granddaughters took turns keeping house for their beloved grandparents. After supper each evening the aging Catharine would sew or knit, while snowy-haired John read from the family Bible and sang several favorite hymns before they bowed for evening prayer. Jake often heard his father fervently pray for all his and Catharine's descendants in future generations.

On Saturday, December 27, 1884, Catharine busily prepared for a belated Christmas dinner. She baked bread, tidied the house, scrubbed the veranda, and assembled plates of treats for the younger grandchildren and the great-grandchildren. Suddenly she developed severe chest pain and died while the bread she had baked was still warm and the porch she had scrubbed was still wet. During her painful last moments she sang from a favorite hymn:

Jesu, rufe mich von der Welt,	(Jesus, call me from the world
Dass ich zu dir eile, nicht verweile,	So that I may hasten to you.
Jesu, rufe mich.	Jesus, call me.)

This hymn stanza—in German—is inscribed on Catharine Stoltzfus's tombstone.

Susanna Heatwole Brunk Cooprider (1839-1909)[6]

Susanna (or Susan), sixth child of John S. and Nancy (Swank) Heatwole, was born on the Heatwole homestead near Harrisonburg, Virginia. She remembered her mother as an invalid, who died soon after her tenth child was born.

After the mother's death the father married a young woman who did not live happily with her new family. When the older Heatwole sisters married, they would not allow young Susanna to remain at home. She had to "work out" for other families. In later years she often told of having worked for 75 cents a week, which was considered an excellent wage for a girl. She was expected to take a hoe, go to the field, and plant corn along with the men. That was hard for her, as she was shy and reserved. She said she always managed to start ahead of them, and they never caught up with her. Even in her old age she could scarcely talk of that experience without tears in her eyes. Susanna also told of a corner cupboard with glass doors and a lot of maple sugar in plain sight. "Do you think they ever gave me a taste?" she would ask. (Echoes of Mother Eberly!)

On November 17, 1859, Susanna married Henry G. Brunk, a mason, who often plastered houses. A son, John Albert, was born in 1860. The Civil War cut short the happiness of the young couple, for Henry felt that he could not serve as a soldier and remain true to Christ. In 1861, Confederate soldiers captured him and 69 others as they were attempting to ride out of the war zone. The rebel army confiscated the seventy horses, saddles, and bridles for the cavalry. They placed the seventy men into the Richmond County jail and gave them three choices. They could (1) put on the uniform and take up arms, (2) haul supplies as noncombatants, or (3) be prisoners. They chose noncombatant service. But Henry's conscience still bothered him. He felt his work was still a part of the machinery of war. One day he simply left his team of horses and went through the orchards and woods to his home, a deserter with a price on his head.

While Henry hid in attics, sometimes making willow whip baskets, Susanna, pregnant again, cared for young John Albert.

Baby Sarah arrived on September 17, 1862. Less than two months later—Susanna alone at the deathbed—Johnny died. The father attended the funeral, but had to act like a stranger and leave during the last hymn, for scouts at the funeral were searching for him to put him into the rebel army.

Seventeen fugitive Mennonite men managed to cross into territory held by the North, then made their way to Hagerstown, Maryland. Henry got a message to Susanna that she should meet him in Maryland. She put her possessions into a one-horse spring wagon, took her baby daughter and headed for Maryland, along with her sister Mrs. Rodgers. The women drove between the two armies, moving northward as the Union Army fell back. At one point Confederate soldiers seized Susanna's horse, but she clung to the bridle, refusing to let go, even after they had the horse unhitched. Then the cry "Yanks! Yanks!" rang out. The soldiers ran and ordered her to follow. She said, "I'll do no such thing!" She hitched up her horse and continued northward. (Her granddaughter Ruth Brunk Stoltzfus calls this "sanctified spunkiness"!)

When the women reached Harper's Ferry, they found the bridge burning and crossing over it impossible. A miller showed them a place where some people drove across the river. Clasping her baby to her, Susanna plunged in and drove the spring wagon across safely. She drove into Hagerstown, Maryland, looking right and left, not knowing which way to go, praying for guidance. Her granddaughter tells the story this way:

> As she passed a store front, she glanced at the window, and there beheld the object of her search! For there was the husband and father, working at the shoe trade. Their eyes met, and soon they were together with conflicting emotions of joy and tears. Together they thanked God for the marvelous way He had led them.

The Brunks moved to a farming area near Geneseo, Illinois, where Susanna bore five more children in eight years. They then took a covered-wagon trail to the "West"—the American story.

Post-Civil War feelings in Missouri still strong, Missourians did not allow settlers going to "free" Kansas to drink from their wells, and travelers drank from streams and ponds. In October 1873 the Brunks arrived at their destination six miles west of Marion Center, Kansas, where Susanna's brother Reuben J. Heatwole awaited them with farm claims staked side by side. Sick when they arrived, Henry unharnessed his horses, turned them to graze on the prairie, went to bed under a crude board-wigwam shelter, and never got up again, succumbing to typhoid fever after eight days.

Susanna—age 34, a widow, eight months pregnant—had six young children, all sick, and no roof to cover their heads. Henry G. jr. was born on December 6, just 36 days after his father's death. Thirteen days later five-year-old Fanny died of typhoid. Just before the little girl died, she reached upward with a look of joy on her face. (Similar experiences are reported by other families

Susanna Heatwole Brunk Cooprider (1839-1909), pioneer mother.

of dying children.) Another three days and the oldest girl, Sarah, died. In the spring the baby died.

Now Susanna had four children, ages 2, 4, 6, and 8. George R. Brunk, the two-year-old, said in later years that among his first memories was a glimpse of his mother standing by the table in their one-room cottage, crying as she was cutting her husband's clothing into garments for her two little boys. A few years later her son Joseph's left arm had to be amputated just below the elbow as a result of an accident.

Yet life still had much good in store for Susanna. In 1878 she married Matthias Cooprider, whose wife had died, leaving him three motherless sons. Together Susanna and Matthias had three children and 31 years of marriage.

Susanna Heatwole Brunk Cooprider "had an aversion to foolishness." It is said that the first time she laughed after a succession of deaths in her family she had to cry for fear she had done wrong. Once she ironed a dress and left all the ruffles unironed! She was remembered for her faithful church attendance, her good cooking, her love of Bible reading, her concern for the spiritual welfare of her children. She died on March 21, 1909, at the age of seventy.

Anna Swartzendruber Yoder (1858-1949)[7]

Anna Swartzendruber, the daughter of pioneer parents, was born in Johnson County, Iowa. At age eight—in 1831—her father, Frederick, had emigrated with his family from Mengering-hausen, Germany, to Baltimore. The Amish-Mennonite family of her mother, Sarah Yoder, born in Pennsylvania in 1829, had come in a much earlier immigration. When Anna was 76, she looked back and told her life story. These are her words translated from her mother tongue, Pennsylvania German:

> My parents were married in 1848. They came to Iowa in 1851 and bought a farm two and one-half miles south of where Sharon Center now stands, for which they paid $2.50 per acre. Their land was mostly covered with timber and hazel brush. It had a small one-room log house in which they lived for about six years. With not even a door on the outside, Mother

tacked a quilt over it at night, as they could often hear the timber wolves howl around the buildings after dark. She was often alone when Father went 35 miles to town. It took him several days to make the trip in the wagon.

They had no cellar; so they made an opening in the floor and dug a hole underneath it where Mother put her milk and butter and could reach it from the opening. Then in a few years they built a good frame house, three rooms upstairs, and three rooms downstairs, with a full basement. They moved into the new house about the year 1857....

In the spring Mother and the older girls helped shear the sheep. Then we washed the wool and sent it to the factory to have it carded. After harvest the spinning time came. Mother dyed the yarn and wove it into flannel and made our winter clothes. We knit our own stockings and mittens. We never thought of buying anything like that. I learned to knit my own stockings and mittens when I was nine years old.... The corn was planted by hand.... I remember that very often we had hired men. We always had supper at five o'clock in the summer. Sometimes on Saturday evening Father said, "Now we will have 'fier ovid' " (a holiday evening); so we had supper at 4:30. There was nothing done after supper but the milking. Father and Mother would sit on the porch and talk and visit. The hired men lay around and rested and Oh, it was so nice and pleasant!...

On Sunday ... Father used to hitch up the team to the wagon and Father and Mother and some of the children went to church. We had church in the houses.... Now this was a lovely home, and it seems that my childhood days were the most pleasant days as long as my dear Mother was with us. When I was nine years old she died and left ten children. My oldest sister, Barbara, was seventeen years old and baby Helena, nine days old. But oh, the change this made—the dearest one on earth had left us and after nearly three months little Helena joined Mother in that heavenly home.

How sad a home is without a mother! There was so much work to do and very often I went to bed and cried myself to sleep as I was so homesick for Mother.... In four years my father married Betsy J. Yoder. My two older sisters were then married; so Delila, fourteen, and myself, thirteen, kept house six months till stepmother came into the home. She was a good stepmother, but in about two years and two months she passed away suddenly of heart trouble. Then the responsibility of the home again rested on my sister Delila and me.... In 1885 Father was again married to widow Barbara Yoder Mast of Davis County, Indiana.... For thirty years Father was a minister and bishop in the Old Order Amish Mennonite Church near Kalona, Iowa.

When Anna was 21, she married Christian S. Yoder and subsequently became the mother of thirteen children, including two sets of twins, one set of whom were stillborn. Chris farmed but also owned and operated a steam engine for threshing grain during the summer and for sawing wood in the winter. Because of this work he was gone for weeks at a time, and Anna had the responsibility for a large and active household. This is undoubtedly why her son Sanford Calvin Yoder connected his later memories of church, communion service, and preaching almost entirely with his mother.

Anna learned to read when her children started to school. Two issues divided Amish-Mennonite communities at this time: the use of English in church services and the establishment of Sunday schools to teach the Bible to children. Anna favored both. She also favored mission activity; it was an unheard-of opinion among many of her people. Because she and Chris were not in agreement with the Sharon Center, Iowa, community on these issues, they and like-minded people moved to Eagle Grove in Wright County in northwestern Iowa.

Here they granted permission to seventeen-year-old Sanford to attend high school. Legend says he became the first child of Amish-Mennonite parents west of the Mississippi to graduate from high school (1901). Surely Anna's interest in reading and in missions influenced the life of this son, who was president of Goshen College from 1923 to 1940 and first secretary, then president, of the Mennonite Board of Missions and Charities from 1921 to 1948.

Anna died at Chappell, Nebraska, on July 22, 1949, at the age of 91. Her granddaughter LaVerne Hostetler says of her:

> These things in her life seem of special significance to me as she worked out her faith and commitment to God: her ability to learn to live and to take on the responsibilities of her household after the death of her mother and then her step-mother; her concern for and broad understanding of the work of the church; and her ability to move and adjust from primitive frontier-pioneer conditions to a life of trains and cars, telephones and radios, air transportation and a world in which her postcards and quilt tops followed the children and grandchildren all over the world.

Barbara Bachman Heiser Eyer (1861-1926)[8]

This mother endured many hardships and remained faithful. After eight years of happy marriage she suddenly became a widow with three sons to raise in a new community. On the advice of men in her congregation, she married a man who proved to be an alcoholic and emotionally disturbed. She cared for a mentally retarded son and a senile mother. She lost a son in the great World War I flu epidemic.

Barbara Bachman was born in Tazewell County, near Morton, Illinois, on June 5, 1861. Her father, Johannes Bachman, had been born in France and spoke French more fluently than English and German. Although he was an ordained minister, he seldom preached at their Amish-Mennonite house meetings, in which the German language was used exclusively. Her mother, Barbara Sutter, had been born in Detenfield Village in Germany

Anna Swartzendruber Yoder (1858-1949), pioneer mother.　　Barbara Bachman Heiser Eyer (1861-1926), pioneer mother.

in 1827 and had come to America in 1850 with her parents, four sisters, and four brothers.

Barbara had a twin sister, Elizabeth; another sister, Lena; and two brothers, Joseph and Andrew. Her parents also raised John Grundt, a neighbor boy whose father was killed in the war. It is thought that John Grundt's father was a paid substitute in the Union Army for some young man in the Bachman family, and they were thus obligated to him, for he kept in contact with the Bachmans until his death and was considered a close relative.

Barbara, like so many other Mennonite girls, became a "hired girl" when she was quite young. Money was scarce, and the hardworking girls of German background were in great demand. Barbara helped with the cooking, cleaned the house, washed clothes, milked cows, and helped to sack wheat and oats after harvest. For all this she earned fifty cents a week, a quarter less than Susanna Heatwole had earned in Virginia.

When the strong, handsome Joseph Heiser who lived nearby asked her to marry him, twenty-year-old Barbara gladly accepted. They were married on December 11, 1881, and established their first home on a small farm south of Morton, Illinois. The new Amish-Mennonite meetinghouse had been built close-by. Andrew Ropp was the minister—a good spiritual leader and one who helped the poor. A year after her own marriage Barbara's twin sister married Joseph Heiser's brother Jacob. Sisters married to brothers! Barbara and Joseph's first son, John, was born on December 4, 1882. Two years later a second son, Amos, was born.

Fertile, inexpensive farmland always seemed to lure nineteenth-century settlers. Johannes Bachman investigated land in Champaign County, near Fisher, and the entire extended family decided to move. When Barbara's third son, Aaron, was born on August 22, 1888, Grandfather Bachman looked at the infant and said, "Du armes Kind! Dass du auch musst zu dieser verkrüppelten Welt geboren sein" ("You poor child! That you also must be born into this crippled world"). Johannes Bachman died unexpectedly two months later and never got to live in Champaign County.

Moving day came in March 1889. How exciting the train ride was for young Amos and John! At last they reached Gibson City, where Uncle Jacob met them and took them ten miles south to their new home in a heavily wooded area along the Sangamon River. Not long before, the Potawatomi Indians had lived here and hunted buffalo. They had given the river the name "Sangamon," meaning "plenty to eat." The Heiser boys later followed a well-worn buffalo trail to school. Barbara and Joseph thanked God for a safe journey and for leading them to this new land.

Even before they had set aside land for a cemetery, death came to the newly established community. A week after Joseph and Barbara's arrival, a four-month-old nephew—son of Peter and Barbara (Heiser) Zehr—died of measles. Three days after this burial some of the men were helping Joseph unload hay in the barn for his livestock when he was suddenly stricken with a fatal pulmonary hemorrhage. What a shock!

Barbara had not been in the new community for two weeks; yet she, like Susanna Brunk and many before her, was now a widow, with three sons to bring up alone, and she had a farm to manage. She took little Aaron into her arms and, from that day on, called him Joseph, after his father. She would have to hire help to get the spring planting done. Barbara found that it was not easy to find men who were dependable. Single, the hired men usually boarded at her house. Some of them rough characters, used alcohol and language that was unacceptable to her. Above all else, Barbara wished to rear her sons in a godly way, as their father would have done had he lived.

Years of hard work and loneliness ensued for Barbara. One winter she had only fifteen dollars to spend. Yet she managed. She patched clothes over and over. They ate what they grew in the garden. The children's lunches often contained two slices of bread pressed together with molasses. Barbara's mother and unmarried sister, Lena, came to live with her. Lena, a frail young woman, died at age 29, four years after Joseph's death.

The men of the church understood the hard life of this young widow. When a young man from Germany, Andrew Eyer, came into the community looking for work and a home among the Mennonites, they strongly advised Barbara to marry him. She was inclined to refuse, but saying "no" would have meant being dependent for help upon these very brothers in the church and relatives advising her to marry. On June 17, 1894, Barbara and Andrew Eyer were married.

The marriage only increased Barbara's difficulties. She soon learned that Andrew drank wine to excess. Andrew began associating more and more with a German-speaking neighbor whom Barbara considered ungodly. Eventually it was learned that this neighbor practiced witchcraft. Andrew became increasingly involved over the years to the extent that he finally lost his sanity and had to be confined to an institution.

A son, William, was born to Andrew and Barbara on February 8, 1895. When he was about two years old, he became very ill, enduring a high temperature for several days. The child recovered physical health but was permanently damaged mentally and required much care.

The church was one bright spot in Barbara's life during these difficult years. Eager to see a meetinghouse built and for her sons to have friends of the same faith, she rejoiced at the coming of the Birkys, Schrocks, Unzickers, and Griesers to their community. And she rejoiced when a church building was erected close-by, on the banks of the east bend of the Sangamon River. The congregation dedicated its meetinghouse in September 1895 and ordained Barbara's beloved son Joseph as bishop of East Bend Church in 1921, an office he held until 1952. Sons John and Amos also participated actively in this church.

Another Eyer son, Daniel, was born in 1899. As the retarded son, William, grew older, he became willful and easily angered. No one could handle him but his mother. Her kind ways and patience seemed to calm his restless, troubled mind. Barbara's mother became senile and hard to manage. Barbara had to watch her so that she would not leave home, for she longed to go back to her old home in Tazewell County. In 1918, Barbara's son John died in the great flu epidemic, leaving his wife, Mary, with six children under eleven years of age.

Barbara died on March 24, 1926. Despite her many trials she kept the faith. Her granddaughter Edna Heiser Cender says:

> She is remembered still by her grandchildren for the delicious angel food cakes and huge sugar cookies she made and had ready to give when her children came to visit her. Her garden was bordered by neat beds of chives and other herbs she used to season her otherwise plain food. Verbenas, deep red and purple, bloomed all summer in flower beds around her house.... Barbara's spirit did not fail. Because of her trust in God, she gave the church on the east bend of the Sangamon River her loyalty, her children, her offspring.

Alta Mae Hostetler Hooley Yoder (1893-1972)[9]

Alta Mae, oldest daughter of Adam and Emma Hostetler, was born near Emmatown in northern Indiana. When she was

Alta Mae Hostetler Hooley Yoder (1893-1972),
resourceful mother.

nine, her mother died at the time of the birth of a third set of twins. Her father subsequently married a widow with four children and moved his family to Tuleta, Texas, where a small group of Mennonites lived and hoped to get rich from oil wells. Alta too "worked out" as a hired girl, and at age 21 married Paul Jacob Hooley. She went with her husband as he attempted to make a living in Protection, Kansas, then Harper, Kansas, then Jet, Oklahoma.

Once in Oklahoma, when her husband was attending a church conference in Kansas and she was left to care for the three children, a terrific storm arose in the night. Sensing that this was no ordinary storm, she moved their table to her bed and moved the three children into the bed with her. No sooner did she complete this task than the house twisted and jolted, and dirty water came pouring in, reaching the level of the bedsprings and stopping. Straw appeared on the window beside the bed. Throughout the episode the kerosene lamp remained upright and continued to light the room. While the children slept, Alta kept an all-night vigil.

In the morning she crawled out through a window to assess the situation. The house had been swept away in the flood. Where were they? While she walked to the nearest neighbors, the children awoke and wondered why there were cornstalks around the house, mud on the floor, and no mother.

Eventually the little family settled into their home again. Later Alta and Paul lived in Limon, Colorado, and in Idaho, where Paul died of a stroke. She was president of the Indian Cove, Idaho, WMSA (Women's Missionary and Service Auxiliary [now Commission]) from 1936 to 1939 and from 1943 to 1946. Alta later married a childhood friend, Ammon Yoder, who took her back to Shipshewana, Indiana. She taught a Sunday school class and was active in the sewing circle. She became a widow a second time and lived to be 81, another faithful mother.

Extraordinary Ordinary

The women whose lives were chronicled in this chapter did

not aspire to achievement outside their homes. Their homes were their achievement. Their husbands, children, homes, churches constituted their world. The amount of hard physical labor that it took to sustain that world was truly phenomenal—cooking, gardening, canning, baking, sewing.

C. Henry Smith says of his mother, Magdalene Schertz Smith: [10]

> Mother died in the prime of life, at the age of fifty-four, as a sacrifice to her family and to the traditions of her people. I was told by those who long had known her that she was beautiful in her girlhood; but the bloom of youth passed early from her cheek. I remember her as prematurely wrinkled, with form bent and hands calloused from hard toil. Her work was never ended. Seven days in the week, from early morning to late at night, she was busy with her family cares and routine of household drudgery—cooking, scrubbing, sewing, and mending. Even Sunday, a day of rest to all the others, for her was often the hardest of all. Her four older children were boys, and the four younger, girls, who were able to help her only after it was already too late.
>
> Her exacting household duties left her little time or opportunity for enjoying many of the luxuries of life. She never saw much of the world. She spent her whole life within the boundaries of two adjoining townships, and seldom stepped outside. Beyond a few trips to Peoria, she had never seen a big city. She never attended a county fair, and never rode on a railway train.
>
> The greatest tragedy of all was that this life of self-denial was so unnecessary. We were not poor; Father was considered well-to-do by his neighbors. My mother's lot was not exceptional at that time, but rather the common experience of most of the Mennonite farm women of her day. Like them, she had become the slave of earlier habits of thrift and industry, now no longer necessary, a slave to the needs of her growing family and to the conventions and ideals of her people.

The women of this chapter would have been the first to consider themselves quite *ordinary*. The later perspective of history shows how *extraordinary* they really were.

Adella Brunk Kanagy wrote about her mother, Alice Yoder Brunk (1886-1977): [11]

> Today I see Mama's ninety years of *ordinary* living as a witness to her faith, as a pattern, as an unspoken statement of values.

She made Bible reading a daily habit. She trusted Jesus as Savior. She frequently quoted, "I go to prepare a place for you. . . ," and looked forward to that prepared place. Christian faith was woven through her everyday living, as Mama's heart truly followed the first and second commandments of love.

Mama's hands kept busy *doing*. The *ordinary* doing that goes with caring for a family of five children, as well as keeping boarders sometimes during depression years. The *uncomplaining* doing required to parent two small sons alone while Papa went to do relief work in Constantinople after World War I. The *extra* doing of welcoming many visitors, always having room for the children to bring home friends.

The *loving* doing of sharing with neighbors, attending sewing circle faithfully, helping quilt for relief, piecing quilts and knitting afghans for children, grandchildren, and great-grandchildren.

Evelyn King Mumaw wrote to her mother, Cora Elizabeth Shank King (1888-   ), on her ninetieth birthday:

I am so glad to see you happily, comfortably situated in your apartment in Laura's home, still braiding rugs, growing roses, loving music and the Word, helping out in household tasks, rubbing a weary grandchild's back, writing letters to your children and attending church quite regularly.[12]

All these mothers built better than they knew. We arise and call them blessed.

CHAPTER 5

"Aunts"

Every Mennonite congregation has at least one of them, fortunate congregations more than one. These women are called "aunts" (or "grandmas" or "sisters") not only by their own nieces and nephews (or grandchildren, brothers or sisters) but by entire Sunday schools or communities. Although a myth holds that they live alone, usually this is "an ill-founded belief held uncritically."

Collectively, these women have done every job in the church. They have taught Sunday school and summer Bible school. They have been janitors and church treasurers. They have given generously of their means, have visited the sick, and cared for the elderly. The Catholic Church has orders of sisters and nuns. The Mennonite Church has had a large group of women who, although not organized into religious orders, have spent their lives in loving service, not to one man or one family only, but to a much wider circle of people in need.

Of one such aunt—Lydia Neuhauser (1859-1929) of Knoxville, Tennessee—a niece wrote:

> When she lay in her last sleep, hundreds of her "children," rich and poor, black and white, illiterate and schooled, lowly and prominent, looked

upon her kind face and called her blessed. For she had given herself freely
to that larger relationship of the kingdom which transcends home and
family and includes the "least of these" for Jesus' sake.[1]

Which of these women should be chosen for inclusion in this
chapter?

Susan Johnson Dettwiler (1848-1924) acted as grandma to the
children at Brutus, Michigan, in her time.[2] Martha Yoder of Middlebury, Indiana, recalls her "Anne Hathaway cottage" and her
old pump. Children went to her home to get into their angel or
shepherd costumes at Christmastime. "Auntie" Lizzie Frey
LeFevre (1866-1963), Sterling, Illinois, went into her in-laws'
home during the flu epidemic of 1918 and took care of all of
them, seeing a sick baby through convulsions.[3] Annie Kauffman
(1876-1968) spent many years in mission work in Knoxville, Tennessee; Tampa, Florida; and at the Welsh Mountain Mission near
New Holland, Pennsylvania. Before the days of summer Bible
school as it is now known, she conducted her own "Aunt Annie's
Bible School" in a garage near Intercourse, Pennsylvania. She
willed her house to the Eastern Board of Missions and Charities at
Salunga, Pennsylvania; the house is now used for missionaries on
furlough.[4]

      Pearl Schmucker Aschliman (1893-   ) has shared her
home in Archbold, Ohio, with 32 people since moving to town
from the farm.[5] "Aunt Annie" Bixler Gerber (1870-1939) was
known and loved in the Sonnenberg congregation of Wayne
County, Ohio. Mary I. Groh of Scarborough, Ontario, recalls her
Aunt Mabel's "inspiring ministry in the Wanner congregation."
Mabel Groh (1884-1962) as a young woman volunteered to the
mission board to go to India but was rejected for health reasons.
She helped bring up younger brothers and sisters, nieces and nephews. With her sister Esther she cared for aging parents. An
outstanding Bible teacher, she taught the women's Sunday school
class for many years, wrote articles for church publications, and
helped both young and old in their spiritual development. Helen

Alderfer says of her Aunt Lena Conrad (1876-1950), Sterling, Illinois:

> Aunt Lena, 11 years older than my mother, never had a home of her own, but spent her whole life working in the homes of others, 20 years in my parents' home.... I remember that home was warmer and happier and kinder because she was there. She modeled servanthood for me as long as she lived.[6]

The more complete stories of three such women will be told in this chapter, with full awareness that many more remain to be told.

Barbara Oberholtzer (1890-   )[7]

Barbara gave up marriage at age 21 to keep a promise she had made to a dying woman. She took care of the Ulysses Delp family in Lititz, Pennsylvania, for 45 years. During this time she also reared Mr. Delp's orphaned niece, Mildred Brookmyer (Hess). Then she took care of Dr. Elizabeth Bricker for 12½ years, of Kathryn Young for 3 years, and of her sister Elizabeth and her

Barbara Oberholtzer (1890-   ), "Miss Barbara," age 22.

two children for many years. Sometimes she peddled her homemade cookies on the street to raise funds to help these people.

In an interview with Sarah Weber in 1980, Barbara recalled some of the events of her life. Daughter of Barbara Ann Stoner and Amos B. Oberholtzer, she was third in a family of ten children living on an 86-acre farm near Lancaster, Pennsylvania. Among her earliest memories is an experience of fetching the sixteen cows when she was eight years old. One day after a heavy rain and thunderstorm, her father said, "Barbara, it's your turn to bring in the cows. It's late; so hurry on, and don't come home without them. If you do, I'll have to use the strap." Her father did use the strap for disobedience but never on her, Barbara recalled.

Usually the creek was shallow, but on this day it was much deeper because of the rain. Barbara and their dog Tippy crossed the creek at one place but went a half mile farther before they found the cows. The little girl drove the cows into the water with a stick, and the dog took them home. Here is the rest of the episode in Barbara's own words:

> There I was on the other side of the deep rushing water. I knew the water was deeper by then. I was all alone, far away from everyone. Father always said, "If you ever need help, call on God. He will help you, no matter what the need." So I looked up to the sky and said, "O God, you can see me." I stretched up my hands high above my head and entered the water, which was to my shoulders, and I kept my eyes on the sky saying, "O God, don't let me drown. Please don't let me drown." I could feel the water lift my feet up and down; but I knew God would not let me drown. As I crawled over the bank I saw my father come running down through the meadow. He asked me what happened. When I told him I was afraid of the strap and took a chance, he wept and asked for forgiveness. He said he would never do such a thing again. That was my first answer to prayer.

As happened frequently in families of that time, two of the children—Ellen, 6, and John, 9—died in a diphtheria epidemic. The doctor predicted that three-year-old Sara, the youngest, would be next. Barbara was determined not to let her die. Her mother said, "Our lives are in God's hands, and there is nothing we can do." But Barbara would not give up, as she later recalled:

I sat by her crib and held her little hot hand in mine, and every once in a while I would say, "Sara, I'm here. I'll take care of you." And silently within myself I asked God not to take away all of our children. "Please, God, let Sara live with us." I would not eat. I simply held on to her hand all day. When night came, Mother asked me to go to my bed, but I told her, "No, Mother, Sara will die if I let go of her hand. She can breathe better when I hold her hand. I tried it out and I know."

Next morning the doctor stopped by and asked Mrs. Oberholtzer, "What did you do besides giving my medicine? It's a miracle, praise God." And for Barbara it was the second answer to her "childish" prayers.

As a young woman of 21, Barbara was asked by her father to take care of a good friend of the family, Mrs. Delp, in Lititz, Pennsylvania. Four months later the woman died of tuberculosis, after having elicited a solemn promise from Barbara, against her own wish, to care for the Delp son when his mother was gone. After Mrs. Delp's death Barbara realized what she had done:

I gave a solemn promise against my own wish. I gave up my beloved boy friend. I felt lonely and sorry for myself. I was unhappy and became bitter—bitter towards life, bitter against my father for asking me to care for Mrs. Delp. I even felt bitter towards God and hardly knew how to pray.... Then one day as I was pushing the sweeper in the same room in which Mrs. Delp had passed away, I was humming a tune ... "You can be a blessing if you only try." While I was humming ... a loud voice came down through the ceiling saying, "But you are not trying." That loud voice told me three times that I was not trying. Then I stopped the sweeper and asked God, "Are you speaking to me, God?" It seemed like a large heavy hand guided me over to the bed where Mrs. Delp had passed away, and I fell on my knees and repented of all my selfish bitterness, and I re-dedicated my life to the Lord, and I begged Him to show me how I could be a blessing. Then that same hand motioned to me, and the same voice said, "Look! Right across the street is a dying woman. Go help her and go now." I knelt there for a long time. My pride was crushed. My selfish spirit was shattered. While on my knees I asked God to use me and make of me a vessel through which His Spirit could work. I prayed for strength, for wisdom, for guidance. I prayed for Him to fill my heart with love and sympathy for others. I laid my body, my soul, my spirit, my all on the altar for His service. I got up from my knees and washed my face. I was a new person in Christ Jesus.

Barbara's employer, Mr. Delp, gave her permission to help

the family in the house across the street where the mother lay sick
with cancer. With the fourteen-year-old daughter of the family,
Barbara entered the sickroom.

> The patient was a very heavy lady. She lay on a cot on an enclosed bal-
> cony under a tin roof. The room was hot and ill ventilated.... She put
> out her hand and said, "I lay here all summer praying for God to send
> someone to help me. Now you are the answer to my prayer. Could you
> give me a bath and comb my tangled hair? I have had no bath all sum-
> mer. My daughter has enough to do to care for the children."

For 38 years Barbara Oberholtzer also taught Sunday school,
gathering children from non-Christian homes. We may echo the
Apostle Paul's question about himself, "Did Barbara Oberholtzer
not have the right to marry and have her own family as most other
women do?" Of course she did. But she kept a promise she had
made. And God gave her a large spiritual family. Alice Lapp says
of her, "Miss Barbara is my idea of a living saint."

Margaret Horst (1893-1970)[8]

"Sister Margaret" operated an influential home for working
girls in Reading, Pennsylvania, which numbers among its
alumnae many ministers' wives, teachers, nurses, and missionaries. She established the Mennonite Domestic Employment
Agency. And during her later years in Kansas she operated a
Christian bookstore in her home.

Margaret, daughter of Michael E. and Mary (Stauffer)
Horst, was born at Trousdale (now Zimmerdale), Kansas. Her
father and mother died of flu within a few days of one another
when Margaret was 21 (1915). She attended Hesston (Kansas)
College for four years, graduating with a BA in 1922, and did
graduate work at the University of Kansas. At her Hesston com-
mencement she gave an address entitled "Corsica or Calvary?"
She said, "I got the suggestion from one of Mr. Prescott's
Universalist papers. I attempted a comparison of Caesar's cheap
ambition with Christ's supreme sacrifice." During the years of
1924-27 and 1928-31, Margaret served as dean of women at

Hesston College, where she also taught Bible, English, and education courses.

She became matron at the Reading Home in 1936 and served there until its closing in 1948. She said, "Surely girls away from home should have a place to go where they can feel at home. We have spent much to provide homes for our student girls on a Christian campus, with a Christian faculty back of them. This is right. Does it not seem reasonable that a similar investment be made for our Christian girls in cities?"

These are the board and room rates listed for the Reading Home in the 1930's:

Board and Room for one week	$5.00
Board and Room for one day	.90
Lodging for one week	1.50
Lodging for one night	.25
Breakfast	.15
Lunch	.20
Dinner	.30

Margaret Horst (1893-1970), "Sister Margaret," friend of working girls.

But the girls received comparably low wages as domestics. Ann Jennings Brunk says, "For ten dollars per week I paid off my Eastern Mennonite School debt."

Hundreds of working girls affectionately called the Reading Home matron Sister Margaret. When the home closed, Margaret went west to the community of the Red Top Mennonite Church, at Bloomfield, Montana. She taught country school there for a number of years before returning to Harper, Kansas, to live with her sister Mary S. Kuhns. In Harper, Margaret opened a small bookstore, which she continued to operate until she moved to the retirement community of Schowalter Villa at Hesston, Kansas. With her younger brother Paul she set up the Michael E. Horst Memorial Scholarship, a revolving loan fund, to help students receive a Christian education. A niece, Edna White, who was with her when she died, reports that after they talked for a while, Margaret said, "I cannot talk more with you now, as I feel the winds of heaven blowing across my face." And she fell asleep peacefully. Margaret Horst provides an example of many Mennonite women who have remained unmarried for the sake of the Kingdom.

Martha Buckwalter Guengerich (1889-   )[9]

Martha—daughter of Benjamin F. and Mary Buckwalter, New Holland, Pennsylvania—lived on a small, rocky farm, where each spring the children picked up rocks that frost had brought to the surface. They used the rocks to build stone fences. In 1905 the family moved to a rural area near Newton, Kansas, and lived on a farm near the old Pennsylvania Church. Martha graduated from Hesston Academy in 1912.

After that, she helped the Chauncey Hartzlers at the Kansas City Children's Home. When the Hartzlers left, she remained to help the J. D. Miningers in regular mission work. She lived in the Mininger home, assisting in the care of guests and doing visitation work during the week. On Sundays she helped in the Sunday school. At age 34, on September 11, 1923, Martha married William S. Guengerich—a minister from Iowa—at Hesston, Kansas, becoming stepmother to his daughter, Clara.

The couple spent the next year at Manitou Springs, Colorado, serving in the mission church there. They lived next-door to the church. Martha did the janitor work, visitation, and taught in the Sunday school. Will and Martha often sang duets together. In 1924 they moved back to Iowa and became active in the Daytonville mission.

Two traits characterized "Aunt Martha": (1) her active concern for other people and (2) her love for and work in the church. When a family who had lost four children during a tornado continued to suffer hardship in the Colorado drought years, Uncle Will and Aunt Martha invited the family to move to Iowa, promising them a place to live and a job. The Guengerichs divided their house, and this family of four lived with them for a year.

When her youngest brother's wife died in childbirth, Martha and a sister went to the funeral by train. Will Guengerich told the story this way:

Martha and Esther left, and I did not know what they were going to do. One night when I came home from a church meeting, I saw a light in the

Martha Buckwalter (Guengerich) (1889-1982), "Aunt Martha."

house and knew she was home. I went to the barn to put the horses away, and as I was walking to the house, I heard a baby cry. Then I knew what she had done.

Martha took care of that baby for several months, until the father could move back to Iowa.

In their later years Martha's parents built a house across the road from the Guengerichs and lived there as long as they were able. Martha took into her home and cared for both her own mother and Will's mother prior to their deaths.

A list of Aunt Martha's work in the church would be a long one. She often gave talks to the children. She taught Sunday school, was Sunday school superintendent, led singing, organized Bible school. She helped organize the Daytonville Sewing Circle and served as its president for a number of years, and was president of the district sewing circle. It is said that "she handled the business graciously and efficiently." The women collected food and clothing for the Kansas City Children's Home. They regularly sent truckloads of fresh produce, home-canned fruits and vegetables, baked goods, bedding, and clothing.

From 1947 to 1964, Will and Martha participated actively in the Seventh Street Mennonite Church in Upland, California (now Mountain View Mennonite). They retired to Pleasantview Home in Kalona, Iowa, where Will died in December 1967. At this writing, Aunt Martha—in her tenth decade—can repeat whole chapters of Scripture from memory, even though her memory has slipped a bit (when asked where she got a vase filled with carnations, she answered, "I just can't remember, but I wish I could. Someone had more love than they could keep, and I wonder who it was!").

Miss Barbara, Sister Margaret, Aunt Martha, your lives have blessed many. Thank you.

CHAPTER 6

In the Home Congregation

In the traditional Mennonite church the men sat on one side of the center aisle and the women on the other. Small children sat with the women. Unlike some Protestant churches in which women and children were the majority, the numbers of men and women were usually about equal. Now, families often sit together during worship services; seating is not usually segregated by sex.

It would be a false impression to assume that because in Mennonite circles ordained ministers have traditionally been men, women have participated little in local congregations. A woman in her 80's says, "I've done everything in the church except teach the men's Sunday school class, and I've enjoyed every minute of it!" This chapter will explore briefly the work of women in local congregations, first giving attention to the office of deaconess. It will tell the story of a "lady baptizer" in the Virginia Conference, will mention women who began congregations, and will present short sketches of a few representative workers. The chapter will conclude with a brief biography of a lay minister.

The Office of Deaconess

Although Mennonites have never been a creedal people,

they have from time to time formulated summaries of their faith, such as the Schleitheim (1527) and Dordrecht (1632) Confessions. Article IX of the Dordrecht Confession specifically includes deaconesses as one of the "offices" in the church. The article states that congregations should "ordain and choose honourable old widows to be deaconesses, that they, with the deacons, should visit, comfort, and care for the poor, weak, ill, distressed and needy people, as also for widows and orphans, and help to alleviate the needs of the congregation to the best of their abilities."[1]

In the United States, the Middle District of the Virginia Conference practiced the ordination of deaconesses from sometime prior to 1880 (death date of Elizabeth Good Rhodes) until 1928. They ordained as deaconesses widows or wives of ministers, deacons, or laymen. Deaconesses counseled women, assisted women in the ceremonies of baptism and foot washing, and prepared bread and wine for the communion service. Grace Showalter, librarian at the Menno Simons Historical Library in Harrisonburg, Virginia, has prepared a chart listing Virginia deaconesses (see exhibit 3 on page 101). The chart contains a threesome—three generations—from one family: grandmother, Elizabeth Shank Showalter; mother, Mary Showalter Blosser; granddaughter, N. Pearl Blosser Suter.

Marietta Hunsberger Detweiler (1866-1929)[2]

An interesting incident concerns a Virginia deaconess who eventually moved west. Grace Showalter says of Marietta Detweiler's ordination in Virginia:

> She was an import from Pennsylvania and lived here a very short while. My guess is that she must have had an overpowering personality if she came in from the outside and was ordained so soon as a non-Virginian.[3]

Marietta and her husband, David F., moved their family from Pennsylvania to Virginia to Colorado and finally to Idaho because of his health, thus becoming the first Mennonites to settle in the

Filer area in the Snake River country of Idaho. In 1911 they rented a farm near Kimberly, part of it still in sagebrush; they built a three-room, tar-paper shack and nearby a bedroom shack. The children went to school eight miles away by covered wagon.

A few years after a Mennonite congregation was organized at Filer, Marietta (also known as Mattie), or someone at Filer, sent her deaconess certificate to the Pacific Coast Conference, assuming that it would be recognized by that body. The reply of the executive committee follows:

> Dear Sister, Having in hand your deaconess certificate which has been forwarded to us, the ministerial body of the Pacific Coast conference now in cession *[sic]* at the zion church *[sic]* we wish you God's richest blessings in your service for the Master as a Sister in the church and tenderly inform you that thus far this body has not seen fit to appoint, or authorize, regular deaconesses and kindly ask you to receive the returned certificate as personal property until the Lord may direct otherwise.[4]

Apparently the Lord never directed the Oregon brethren otherwise, or if he did, they failed to hear him. However, the congregation at Filer did confirm Marietta in the office of deaconess.

A Missouri Deaconess

When the congregation at White Hall in Jasper County, Missouri, ordained Joseph Good as deacon in 1882, they at the same time ordained his wife, Anna Brenneman Good (1851-1948), as deaconess.[5] Daughter Esther Good Horst recalls that Anna baked the communion bread and made the grape juice. She washed the towels and generally looked after the things necessary for communion and foot washing. She assisted the ministers with baptism.[6] These activities may well have been carried out by wives of ordained men in most congregations, even though the women were not specifically ordained. In 1926 the Goods moved to Hesston, Kansas. Joseph died in 1940. Three years later Anna moved back to Missouri, where she lived to be 96.

"The Lady Baptizer"

An unusual story comes out of the Virginia Conference about

a "lady baptizer." Mary Catherine Funkhouser Tusing (1869-1951), known as Kate, lived in Hardy County, West Virginia.[7] Sometime before 1919 (his death date) her father, John, became desperately ill, was converted, and wished to be baptized. Kate tried to get in touch with the ordained ministers at Broadway, Virginia, who held preaching services in their community, but she was unable to reach them. Her father begged his daughter to baptize him, and she did. John Funkhouser lived, and Broadway churchmen accepted his lay-performed baptism. Grace Showalter comments:

> I doubt if many of her contemporaries in the Valley churches of Virginia would have been as free as Kate Tusing to do this service usually reserved for ordained men. Perhaps the rigors of Kate's mountain life, where it was necessary to face things as they came, made her willing to take hold of this unusual situation without fear and trembling.

Kate Tusing's obituary says:

> She and her daughters (Ora and Lynn) were weavers of old-fashioned coverlets. This drew many visitors, who experienced a cordial welcome to the home.[8]

Service Without Ordination

The full-fledged participation of women in the life of the church has not always been accepted. When the language of Mennonites changed from German to English, some loss of status for women occurred. *Gemeinschaft*—the Christian community, the body of Christ—was translated *brotherhood*. *Geschwister*—sibling, male or female—became *brother*. Although no conscious attempt was made to omit women, the English language did, in fact, in these cases omit them, and to the extent that language shapes reality, a subtle loss of status occurred for women.

The following is from a letter, written in a flourishing hand, which is dated December 12, 1876, and is apparently addressed to John S. Coffman from a brother in Ohio:

> In the Articles of Incorporation (article VI I think) it is stated "Any mem-

ber of good standing etc. shall be eligible to election as a field member."
Should it not read "any brother" instead of "member"? I do not suppose
that it is intended that a sister might be elected as a field member. Or how
is it?[9]

Despite the fact that they may not have been ordained specifically to the offices, Mennonite women have done the work of
evangelists, ministers, and teachers. Often they have
demonstrated at the practical level "the universal priesthood of
believers." Most Mennonite congregations have been founded as
cooperative ventures of both men and women. Yet one finds
stories of congregations that might not have been established or
have survived without the work of a particular devoted woman.
(Maude Buckingham Douglass's labors in Arkansas are mentioned in exhibit 9 on page 180.)

Mary Keck Shrock

Mary Keck Shrock kept an Indiana church from dying. In
Howard and Miami Counties a church split had occurred
between 1856 and 1863, between conservatives (Amish) and
progressives (Mennonites). The conservatives flourished more for
a time than did the progressives. The Mennonites had been
without a minister and for quite a while had had no meetings. Because Mary (Mrs. J. Benj) Shrock did not like that state of affairs,
she invited the young people to her home one Sunday. They sang
and enjoyed themselves so much that they decided to meet every
two weeks. At last the older people became interested and also
came to the singings. In this way the church got started again.[10]
Oral tradition says that Mary got the group together for the singings by going to the pasture where the young men were playing
ball—that she caught the ball, halted the game, and convinced
the players that singing and Bible reading were also good Sunday
activities. She could catch a ball, and she was persuasive![11]

Fannie Rohrer Hershberger (1861-1941)[12]

Early in the twentieth century the Canton, Ohio, church was
about to be closed because of lack of attendance. Fannie Rohrer

Hershberger, one of only three members left at that time, regularly walked three miles to church to help keep the services going. She pleaded with ministers who came in to preach, not to discontinue the work. In 1904 the question of whether to close this church came before the Ohio Conference. Fannie wrote a letter with a strong appeal for the preservation of the church. The conference assented, and established the Canton mission. Gladys B. Hostetler reports that today this is an active, independent congregation with a strong community emphasis. She says of Fannie:

> She was intensely interested in the work of the church and was a regular attendant at services until the last several years of her life, when physical conditions made that impossible. Although her husband did not disapprove of her activities, he did not help in any way, as he had still not become a Christian. When no longer able to attend church services, she continued an active prayer life, with an ever growing list of names, developed from reading the *Gospel Herald*.

Ella Shoup Bauman (1892-1969)[13]

Would Rockview Church at Youngstown, Ohio, exist if it had not been for the work of Ella Shoup Bauman? Before Ella's marriage she served on the staff of the Mennonite mission on West Federal Street with T. K. Hershey as superintendent. She pioneered in harboring abused and homeless women and children. Indeed, the mission had a department called Temporary Shelter for Deserted Wives, and Widows and Children.[14] Because of a complex set of causes, including some opposition by Columbiana and Mahoning County Mennonite churches, the Youngstown mission closed in 1923. But Ella Shoup did not forget the place. Her vision came to fruition forty years later.

When Ella—daughter of Joseph and Barbara (Ziegler) Shoup of Holmes County, Ohio—was quite young, her father died. Her mother later remarried. Ella loved school and considered learning a privilege, but her stepfather thought an eighth-grade education was sufficient. She had to wait until she was "of age" and "on her own" before she could attend Goshen Academy and spend two years at Goshen College. There she met

Norman Bauman from Floradale, Ontario. They shared an interest in foreign missions and were married on June 12, 1919, intending to go to seminary and then to South America as agricultural missionaries.

Health problems kept this dream from coming true. Norman worked at a variety of jobs. They rented one farm, then another, moving a number of times but always staying in the area of the Leetonia (Ohio) Mennonite Church. Three children were born to them. At some point Ella developed asthma. In the late 1940s she went regularly to Youngstown for medical treatment. The Briar Hill area of the city had changed. German immigrants had moved out; blacks had moved in. Each time Ella made the trip for medical treatment, she filled a bag with inexpensive Christian books and spent some time at Briar Hill selling the books.

Carolyn Augsburger tells a now legendary story in this way:

> One day . . . a rain storm stopped her colportage work. When she stepped into the recessed empty store front, several children sought refuge there with her. As she waited for the streetcar to return her downtown, she used the time to tell those children a story or two. They were spellbound. The Spirit told her this was another key. When she asked if they would like her to return to tell them more stories, they eagerly begged her to come back. That summer she told stories to children on Boone's and Davies' porches off Pershing Street.

> When cold weather came, homes were too small for the large group of children attending. Ella looked around and found an empty small store by the coal tipple of the steel mills along West Federal Street. She rented that, changed the weekly Bible story hour to Sunday afternoons and begged the country churches for help.[15]

For the next five years Ella shouldered the responsibility for starting the church, although her husband, now working in an industrial plant, helped with the finances. Five women and several teenagers became members of the church. Bishop Steve Yoder baptized the people. In 1952 the Ohio and Eastern A. M. Conference sent a pastoral couple, Fred and Carolyn Augsburger, to the fledgling church. Carolyn says, "It is a miracle of God that this little asthmatic, gasping, weak woman had so much vitality and strength for the services she started." Mrs. Augsburger also remembers Ella as a highly creative teacher.

During the last years of her life Ella Bauman was bedfast and blind. She spent hours with her Braille New Testament. "Praise God for the vision of this quiet woman and for her daring to go out and start a church."

Sunday School Work

Women have been active in Sunday schools since their beginnings. In 1879 the Clinton Frame congregation in northern Indiana listed as teachers Lydia Burkey, Amanda Smiley, Amanda Smoker, and Mary Schrock. Mary Schrock was treasurer of this Sunday school in 1883 and secretary in 1884.[16]

Women spoke to the large regional Sunday school conferences. Often a topic was assigned to both a man and a woman. At a Sunday school meeting held in the Allensville (Pennsylvania) Amish-Mennonite Church on October 21 and 22, 1909, participants gave a series of presentations on "Four Elements of Strength in Sunday School." Ruth Kauffman spoke on "Preparation," Maude Yoder on "Inspiration," and both John T. Hartzler and Rachel Esh on "Reverence." Lena Yoder and Oliver H. Zook spoke on "How Shall We Grade the Sunday School to Get the Best Results?"[17]

The same year at a Sunday school conference held near Albany, Oregon, on June 11, Mollie King spoke on "Purpose of S.S. Conference," Emma Kennel on "What Are the Most Urgent Needs of Our Sunday Schools?" Lydia Maurer on "Blessedness of Obedience in Sunday School Work," Sadie King on "How Best Remedy the Lack of Interest and Study in the Sunday School Work," Lovina Hooley on "Parents' Duty in Sunday School Work," and Katie Widmer on "Qualifications of Workers."[18]

Lois Gunden Clemens reports that her mother, Agnes Albrecht (1888-1963), met her father, C. J. Gunden, at an Illinois Sunday school convention, where she had presented such a "topic." (These conference presentations were not called speeches or sermons.) Although women did not hold offices in the church conferences, they did in Sunday school conferences. For example, in the aforementioned meeting at Allensville, Pennsylvania, D. E. Plank and Maude Yoder are listed as secretaries. The Sunday school movement utilized the gifts of women.

Because farm work slackened in the winter, many congregations set up "winter Bible schools" lasting from two to six weeks during the months of January and February. Women sometimes served as instructors in these schools. Before she went to India as a missionary in 1913, Fannie Hershey (later Mrs. George Lapp) taught in such a school at Canton, Ohio, along with George M. Hostetler and J. S. Hartzler.[19]

During the first two decades of the twentieth century, women sometimes presented the Sunday morning message; it was a particularly acceptable practice for missionary women on furlough. Reporters preferred the term "talk" rather than "sermon." The March 4, 1919, issue of *Gospel Herald* carried an article entitled "The Evangelization of India"; it was an address given by Anna Stalter (1874-1933) at the LaJunta, Colorado, church prior to her departure for India. Mary Yoder Burkhard preached the sermon during a Sunday morning service at her home church— Bethel in West Liberty, Ohio—in 1908.[20]

Women often wrote essays and presented them at "young people's meetings" on Sunday evenings. The *Gospel Herald* later printed some of these as articles. Mary Graber Conrad Wade Good (1887-1982) recalls this activity from her Iowa girlhood:

> My sister wrote essays in German. I wrote a whole bunch of them too, read them on Sunday nights for Young People's meeting.[21]

Mary Good also recalls her years in the congregation at Sterling, Illinois:

> I worked in the Home Department. Four of us worked with people who weren't in church at all. We visited people in their homes and talked to them and invited them to church. Mrs. Apple, a member of West Sterling, told my daughter Doris, "Dearie, Mary is the reason I found Jesus. She came and visited me for thirty years, never gave up on me."[22]

The activities of local congregations have provided the channels through which Mennonite women could witness to their faith and serve others. Additional representative Mennonite women are presented in exhibit 4 (p. 104) at the end of this chapter, which now concludes with the story of a remarkable lay minister from southeastern Pennsylvania.

Mary Mensch Lederach (1898-1980)

Mary Lederach taught Sunday school from 1917 until 1978, a period of 61 years. John L. Ruth said in a memorial tribute to her:

> I think it's obvious that Mary had more leadership ability than most men, but she lived in a time when women were asked to keep silent in church. A few opportunities did emerge, like speaking to girls' and women's groups, teaching Sunday school, or speaking in "Young People's Meetings," but there was no openness, as there would be today, to her using her speaking talents among her own Mennonite fellowship.
>
> If you could have seen her standing before the Salford congregation, leading in a pastoral prayer for some special occasion or project and spreading her hands before God as she stated, "These are my people," you would have carried with you the image of a shepherd-hearted mother and leader.[23]

Virginia Glass Schlabach says:

> I remember going to hear Mrs. Lederach speak to a group of women and girls when I was about ten years old; she was well-known in southeastern Pennsylvania for speaking to mothers and daughters about sexuality, a subject still rather "hush-hush" at that time.[24]

Emma Richards says:

> I recall few women who spoke in chapel at Goshen College when I was a student there. But I remember Mrs. Lederach. She spoke on "The Best Is Yet to Be" and began with "Grow old along with me." I was much impressed.[25]

Mary Mensch, the only child of Jennie and Abraham Mensch, grew up in Skippack, Pennsylvania, dearly loved by her

Christian parents and grandparents.[26] In 1914 she graduated from Skippack Elementary School and in 1918 from Millersville State Normal School. At about age sixteen she was baptized and became a member of the Mennonite Church. She wore the cape dress and prayer veiling required by her church, and this special mode of dress came to mean much to her.

Her first teaching position, in 1918-19, at the small Iron Bridge Public School in Rahns, Pennsylvania, became available because the students had scared the former teachers away. Mary wrote:

> When I first approached the school on a Monday morning, I saw all the boys perched on the porch rail like a row of crows awaiting their next victim. I kept them busy, tending the stove, getting water from the well, and cleaning, and I kept my eye opened to spot the leader. When I was sure who it was, I gave him a note for his parents and told him not to come back to school unless accompanied by his father. That settled the troublemakers. I was asked to return the next year.

Mary Mensch Lederach (1898-1980), a shepherd-hearted mother and leader, with her husband Willis.

Mary taught at Hesston College in Kansas for one year, 1919-20. Then she returned to Skippack and married Willis K. Lederach, a young banker from Lederach, Pennsylvania. The couple served at the Norristown mission from 1921 to 1928. Later they moved to Trooper, Pennsylvania, where Mary gave many family-life talks to civic and church groups, including the Jewish Women's League. At Trooper both the Democrats and the Republicans once asked her to run for the school board. They assured her she need not make any preelection appearances, because the community knew and respected her convictions. But she declined to run.

During Mary's last illness one of her daughters said to her, "Mother, if you were in your prime today, you might possibly be a minister." Mary answered without hesitation, "I was a minister. I filled many pulpits." She once wrote:

> Since coming to Lederach, I have spoken to various groups on various topics, making more than 200 appearances.

In addition to this public ministry Mary had a secret ministry that few knew about until after her death. She worked part-time at the Lederach post office, and she had a real estate license in order to help her husband in his office. She used all the money she earned, and later all of her social security money, to buy food, clothing, and medical treatment for the needy people she sought out. Mary Mensch Lederach may not have been an ordained-by-men minister, but she was an ordained-by-God minister.

For Mennonite women the local congregation has often been an area of freedom through which they have found much joy in service for Christ.

EXHIBIT 3
Virginia Deaconesses
Prepared by Grace Showalter, Harrisonburg, Virginia

Name and Dates	Husband	Parents	District	Date Ordained
Elizabeth (Good) Rhodes 1789 - 1880	Henry Rhodes —layman	Jacob and Frances (Gro) Good	Middle	
Magdalena (Hildebrand) Rhodes 1810 - 98	David Rhodes —minister	Jacob and Anna (Brenneman) Hildebrand	Middle	
Rebecca (Rhodes) Burkholder 1821 - 1900	Martin Burkholder —bishop	Bishop Samuel and Eliz (Funk) Rhodes	Middle	
Elizabeth (Burkholder) Hartman 1815-88	David Hartman —layman	Bishop Peter and Eliz (Coffman) Burkholder	Middle	
Elizabeth (Shank) Showalter 183? - 1913	Michael Showalter —layman	Bishop Samuel and Eliz (Funk) Shank	Middle	
Annie (Weaver) Brunk 1823 - 89	John Brunk —layman	Samuel and Eliz (Rhodes) Weaver	Middle	
Sarah (Weaver) Sharpes 1839 - 1918	James Sharpes —layman	Samuel and Eliz (Rhodes) Weaver	Middle	
Magdalene (Heatwole) Rhodes 1820 - 84	Frederick A. Rhodes —deacon	Gabriel and Polly (Swank) Heatwole	Middle	

Name and Dates	Husband	Parents	District	Date Ordained
Susanna (Hartman) Brunk 1843 - 1913	Samuel Brunk —layman	David and Eliz (Burkholder) Hartman	Middle	
Fanny (Rhodes) Driver 1846 - 1928	Joseph N. Driver —bishop	Deacon Frederick and Magdalene (Heatwole) Rhodes	Southern	
Fanny (Rhodes) Heatwole 1850 - 1921	Joseph F. Heatwole —minister	Peter and Annie (Beery) Rhodes	Middle	
Sarah (Heatwole) Coffman 1859 - 1958	Joseph W. Coffman	Joseph and Lydia (Rhodes) Heatwole	Middle	
Marietta (Hunsberger) Detweiler 1866 - 1929	D. F. Detweiler —layman		Middle	
Elizabeth (Heatwole) Brunk 1857 - 1928	Elias Brunk —deacon	Joseph and Lydia (Rhodes) Heatwole	Middle	
Annie (Wenger) Brenneman 1858 - 1934	Benjamin Brenneman —deacon	Jacob and Hannah (Brenneman) Wenger	Warwick	before 1919
Mattie (Martin) Shank 1856 - 1934 Born Hagerstown, Maryland	Lewis Shank —bishop	Jacob and Eliz Martin	Northern	before 1910
Emma (Bixler) Showalter 1886 - 1940. Born Columbiana, Ohio; died California	Frank B. Showalter —layman	Joseph and Mary Bixler	Middle	1914

Mary (Showalter) Blosser 1862 - 1927	Daniel Blosser —layman	Michael and Deaconess Eliz (Shank) Showalter	Middle	1914
Rebecca (Coffman) Hartman 1868 - 1926	Perry D. Hartman —layman	Bishop Samuel and Frances (Weaver) Coffman	Middle	1914
N. Pearl (Blosser) Suter 1888 - 1958	J. Early Suter —minister	Daniel and Deaconess Mary (Showalter) Blosser	Middle	1928
Betty (Brunk) Keener 1878 - 1967	H. B. Keener —minister	David and Elizabeth (Hartman) Brunk	Middle	1928
Mollie (Coffman) Heatwole 1883 - 1956	Melvin Heatwole —minister	Joseph W. and Sarah (Heatwole) Coffman	Middle	
Lydia F. (Lahman) Shank 1875 - 1959	James H. Shank —minister	Martin and Catherine (Shank) Lahman	Middle	
Elizabeth (Hershey) Weaver 1855 - 1931 Born Pennsylvania	S. H. Weaver —deacon	Joseph and Fannie (Hartman) Hershey	Southern	
Lydia A. (Heatwole) Grove 1841 - 1931	Henry Grove —layman	Joseph and Maria (Rhodes) Heatwole	Southern	
Maude (Shank) Driver 1892 - 1973	Daniel Driver —layman	John F. and Eliz (Zigler, Shank, Myers) Shank	Southern	

EXHIBIT 4
A Partial Listing of Women Active in the Local Church

Dora Shantz (Mrs. Will) Gehman (1897-   ), retired nurse, became an
elder at Prairie Street congregation in Elkhart, Indiana, when she
was 75 (September 1972). She carries on a "tape ministry," taking
church services recorded on tape to shut-ins.[27]

Clara Hooley (Mrs. Guy F.) Hershberger (1896-   ) spent nearly forty
years in the Christian education program of the College Mennonite
Church in Goshen, Indiana, where she was something of a pioneer
in early childhood education.[28] *The Mennonite Encyclopedia* says:

> The first strictly Mennonite summer Bible school was started by Dean
> Noah Oyer of Hesston College, Hesston, Kansas, although Edwin Weaver
> had conducted a community vacation Bible school in 1922 at Wakarusa,
> Indiana.[29]

Clara remembers these beginnings well. Dean Oyer had the vision,
but Clara directed the school and turned the vision into reality.
Another of Clara's accomplishments occurred many years later.
During 1949-50, when her husband represented the Mennonite
Central Committee (MCC) Peace Section in Europe, she was
hostess at the MCC headquarters in Basel, Switzerland. She
initiated a "knitting circle" which brought together women of the
Holee congregation—member of the French Conference—and the
Schenzli congregation—member of the Swiss Conference. Previous
to "Tante Clara's" coming, these two groups of women had been
strangers to one another.

Lizzie Wenger Hershberger of Des Allemands, Louisiana, is described as
"a devoted woman," who "had a burden for the work there," who
"lived up the bayou, helping mothers with large families to patch
and sew."[30] She spent time trying to keep services going. In the
summer of 1925, J. B. Brunk of Gulfport, Mississippi, got William
Jennings to help in a series of evangelistic meetings at Des Allemands. Since no suitable meeting place existed, Lizzie contributed
money for the building of a tabernacle. Brunk and Jennings put it
up in five days. Many of the people who came into this congregation were of French background.[31]

Trella Risch (Mrs. Paul) Jacobs (1889-   )—born in Johnstown, Pennsylvania, daughter of Joseph and Almira (Blough) Risch—brought up eleven children. She taught Sunday school for many years at Carpenter Park and Kaufman Mennonite Churches and was active in the women's work at Kaufman (Hollsopple, Pennsylvania). She often led devotions and presented talks at annual district meetings of the Southwest Pennsylvania Mennonite Woman's Missionary Society in the 1930s and early 40s.

Barbara Matthews Kauffman (1826-98) of northern Indiana took her children to revival meetings at the old log-structure Clinton Brick meetinghouse three miles from her home, walking the six-mile round trip by lantern light, so eager was she that her children should hear the gospel.[32]

Pearl Headings (Mrs. Ivan S.) Kropf (1907-   ) of Hubbard, Oregon, drew up the original plan for the Zion church building, first used on Thanksgiving Day, 1957.[33]

Ruth Smucker (Mrs. Carl) Magnuson (1898-   ) served as lay worker in the churches of Pleasant Hill and Highway Village, East Peoria, Illinois, for over forty years. She taught Sunday school, vacation Bi-

Christian educator, Clara Hooley (Hershberger) 1896-   ), Indiana.   Amelia Bergey Nahrgang (1873-1936), Ontario, servant of her congregation.

ble school, and helped with the women's organizations. She says, "I taught Sunday school for nearly 50 years."[34]

Lydia Bauman (Mrs. Simon) Martin (1900-76) began service in 1924 at Sherkston, Ontario, under the Ontario Mennonite Board of Rural Missions. Earlier she had attended Eastern Mennonite College, where she took her young daughter Elsie along with her to classes. She brought up eight children, including an orphaned niece and nephew. The family moved to Strasburg near Kitchener, where they earned their living by farming and marketing. Lydia baked between 100 and 200 dozen cookies and 70 to 80 loaves of bread weekly to sell at the Kitchener Farmers Market. (She made 100 pounds of noodles for the 1935 General Conference held in Kitchener.) After the children were grown, she and her husband served at a rural mission church at Monetville in northern Ontario, for the first time receiving financial support. It is said that "she knew how to live a godly life and through it blessed many."[35]

Amelia Bergey (Mrs. Menno) Nahrgang (1873-1936)—oldest child of David and Louisa (Bowman) Bergey, Waterloo, Ontario—longed to be a schoolteacher like her father.[36] (Her father also did some legal work and was secretary for the Ontario Mennonite Church organization.) Millie, as she was called, was told that she must stay home to care for six younger children. And of what use was a high school education to a girl? Millie refused to relinquish her dream. She completed work at Berlin High School, took a teacher-training "short course," and began to teach at Conestoga Public School in 1898. She enrolled in the seminary course at the Elkhart Institute in 1901 and received a junior college certificate from Goshen College in 1907, following an interruption during which she taught near Breslau, Ontario.[37]

In April 1909 she married Menno Nahrgang. A surprise snowstorm piled snowdrifts as high as the axles of the buggy wheels on that day. Her friends said, "Poor Millie! She waited so long to get married, and her husband is only a farmer!" But Menno's aunt, who helped "keep house" for her nephew, held a different opinion. She said, "Poor Menno! He waited all these years to get married, and now he just got a schoolteacher!" The new household included Menno's mother and two bachelor brothers.

The Lord blessed this marriage, and Millie spent the remainder of her life in service to her congregation. In 1919 she became the first superintendent of the primary Sunday school. Also that year she, Curtis Cressman, and his wife, Amanda, became the first church librarians in the Biehn congregation. With the coming of the Russian Mennonite refugees in the early 1920s, Millie's home became a depot for collecting clothing and household articles for them. She became president of the local sewing circle and also of the Ontario district organization of circles. She served in both offices from 1917 to 1936, often traveling away from home to attend executive meetings. She attended the by now well-known meeting with D. D. Miller, S. C. Yoder, and S. E. Allgyer in 1927 at which the Mennonite Woman's Missionary Society was turned over to the General Mission Board. (See chapter 11.)

In addition to her church work Millie belonged to the Haysville branch of the Federated Women's Institute from 1914 until her death in 1936. And with Menno she attended the Stratford Farmers Market for many years, selling cheese she had made from milk produced on their farm; homemade mustard pickles, doughnuts, and bread; and fresh vegetables from a large garden. In 1917 the Nahrgangs took into their home a foster son, Philip Richardson,

Ruth Smucker Magnuson (1898-   )
Sunday school worker, 1924.

Lizzie Wenger Hershberger (c. 1860-c. 1945), "lived up the bayou."

whose parents had died of typhoid shortly after immigrating to the Doon area from England. At first he could not speak with their own daughter Alice, for she spoke only German. Later Philip's older brother joined the family.

Nora King Stauffer (1897-   ) of Tofield, Alberta, served as janitor of her congregation for many years.[38] She not only cleaned the church weekly but also hauled the coal for heating it. She opened her home, lodging and boarding both summer and winter Bible school students who had to come from some distance to attend. Florence Voegtlin says:

> My son and I did a rough estimation of how long a table it would take to seat her guests on both sides. We decided it would be a bit difficult to see the hostess at the far end. And just think of washing all those plates without a dishwasher, and for many years, without running water.

Bertha Reedy (Mrs. Bert) Zehr (1898-   ), a member of the East Bend Church in Illinois (see chapter 3), is known for the hundreds of international students entertained in their home over a period of forty years.[39] With her husband she has been a youth-fellowship sponsor. She has been active in the regional Mennonite Historical Society and has participated in a great many activities of the church.

Catherine Ropp (Mrs. Andrew Y.) Zehr (1872-1957) lived near the East Zorra Amish-Mennonite Church, Tavistock, Ontario, and served as custodian from 1921 to 1929. "Katie's" wages ranged from $40 in 1921 to $115 in 1929.[40]

CHAPTER 7

In Education

When, in 1862, Magdalena Miller, Barbara Burkhalter, and Elizabeth Yoder sold some property to the congregation later known as Oak Grove near Smithville, Ohio, the women made their marks on the deed, for they were apparently unable to write their names.[1] Many women (and men) were functionally illiterate during the eighteenth and nineteenth centuries. Others read and wrote German but never mastered English. And still others were well educated for their time.

This chapter will profile three early women college graduates and tell the stories of several educators. Compiling a roster of Mennonite women educators proved to be a too formidable task for this work, but two quite incomplete lists are offered in exhibits 5 and 6 on pages 120 and 124: "Teachers at the College Level" and "Teachers in Primary and Secondary Schools." Perhaps one day some scholar or group of scholars will compile a definitive Who's Who of Mennonite schoolteachers, both women and men.

Three Early College Graduates

How many Mennonite women graduated from college before 1900? Bertha Kinsinger Petter (1872-1967)—from the

Butler County, Ohio, Amish—graduated from Wittenberg College in 1896. She became the wife of the Swiss missionary and linguist Rodolph Petter and served as a missionary to the Cheyenne Indians under the General Conference Mennonites for more than 61 years. A booklet entitled *Cheyenne Mission Souvenir* was copyrighted in her name in 1911.[2]

Emma D. Lefevre Byers (1875-1946), daughter of Adam and Emma (Sigman) Lefevre, was the first woman graduate (1898) of the Elkhart Institute, which later became Goshen College. She became the wife of N. E. Byers, president of Goshen College from 1903 to 1913, dean of Bluffton (Ohio) College from 1913 to 1933, and professor of philosophy there until his retirement in 1938. Byers said of his Harvard education (1903ff.), "This financing was made possible by the sympathetic cooperation of my loyal wife."[3] Mrs. Byers was considered a capable partner of her husband. She is remembered as "quiet," "very refined," "a gracious hostess."[4]

Emma Lefevre Byers (1875-1946), first woman graduate of Elkhart Institute, with husband Noah, 1898.

A remarkable woman, Emily Strunk Kauffman (1873-1960) deserves to be more widely known.[5] She graduated from Juniata College in 1899. Born on a farm near Mount Union, Pennsylvania, the second daughter of George and Elmira (Fry) Strunk, she was severely burned at the age of 3½ while trying to put wood into a range. She was left with crippled hands, which in later life became cancerous. Both her hands were amputated when she was forty and the mother of five children.

Once as a child, Emily overheard the conversation of women cutting and sewing carpet rags in her home when her mother was out of the room. "Poor child! It would be better if she had died! She will never be able to do anything."

The little girl appeared and said, "Well, if I am willing and try real hard, I'm sure I can do as much as someone who isn't willing and has two hands."

One of the startled women responded, "Dear child! Of course you can!"

At age fourteen, after the death of her mother, Emily lived with Rachel, Phoebe, and Israel Zook, whose father was a well-known Amishman, Shem Zook. At sixteen she joined the Spring Run Church of the Brethren. Who encouraged her to attend college? That piece of the story is still missing. At any rate, Emily graduated from Juniata and became a teacher. At age 27 she married Israel M. Kauffman of Belleville, Pennsylvania, and joined the Maple Grove Mennonite Church. Nineteen years later they moved to a milder climate, to Westover, Maryland, for the sake of her husband's health, and were among the founders of the Holly Grove Church.

In 1924, Emily Kauffman, along with Ruth Hostetler, helped organize the first WMSC, then called sewing circle, at Holly Grove. Emily served as president for about 25 years. She also taught Sunday school for about thirty years and organized the Sunday evening services for the church.

Emily Strunk Kauffman painted, sewed, crocheted, wrote, typed, and served her family and her local congregation well. She died at age 87 in a son's home in New Holland, Pennsylvania. A daughter once said of her, "Mother can do more for herself with a handicap than many a younger woman with no handicap."

These early college graduates were exceptions. It should be pointed out, however, that achievement in high school and academy classes of the time perhaps equaled that in today's college liberal-arts courses. Also, intelligent young women customarily became schoolteachers by taking a "normal course." Or communities simply recognized a woman's ability to teach and invited her to do so.

A Music Educator, Maryann Amstutz Sommer (1858-1930)[6]

The Amstutz family of La Chaux d'Abel, Switzerland, engaged in dairy farming and cheesemaking. One can imagine the rejoicing when after five sons the first daughter, Maryann, arrived. Two later daughters died of scarlet fever. The Amstutz children were taught to sing and greatly enjoyed music.

In 1871 two major events happened to twelve-year-old Maryann. She was baptized in April and became a member of the Mennonite Church in Switzerland, and her family immigrated to America. This meant changing from the school which she had attended at Bendorf, France, to a rural school in Wayne County, Ohio.

Young Maryann's community recognized her as a gifted teacher of music. They invited her to begin singing schools. The first met in the shop at her home, then at the Sonnenberg District No. 10 Schoolhouse. When the ministers of the church came to realize what a blessing the singing school was to congregational singing, they invited her to conduct the school in the church building itself.

She taught the children to read notes, using the Italian syllables *do-re-mi*, etc. She struck her tuning fork on the edge of her book, held it briefly to her ear, and sounded the pitch clearly. One amusing mannerism she had at times was to bite the tuning fork sharply to get her pitch. To her dismay, one of her students was a monotone. After repeated futile attempts to teach him to sing the scales as they should be sung, she tried a new method of

Maryann Amstutz (Sommer) (1858-1930), music educator, with her brothers: (top row) Benjamin and Jacob, (bottom row) John, Abraham, and Daniel.

teaching. She grabbed a shock of his hair and pulled as she said, "Now sing higher." Another tug. "Higher!" And a final pull with "Higher yet!" It worked! Her usual methods were more gentle.

Maryann, obviously gifted and much respected, often led singing in Sunday school. The Sonnenberg Mennonite Church honored her at the dedication of their building in 1907, when she shared an hour of leading singing with her brother Dan in the afternoon service.

At age 27, Maryann married Christian Sommer, "a farmer with a rare sense of humor." People remember her for many activities. She taught a Sunday school class of ten-year-old girls. She was the first president of the Sonnenberg Sewing Circle, an office she held for many years. She was the first woman in her congregation to change from the customary heavy black silk head covering to lighter net. She had a formal flower garden with "a round raised bed in the center and four small raised beds around the circle, forming a rectangle with paths in between." She kept the cemetery neat and clean. She skillfully played her reed organ.

Two of her nieces say of her:

> Maryann was a devoted Christian. She was compassionate, kind and generous, tireless in service, and a woman of conviction. If she felt something was right, she was not deterred by criticism, custom nor convention. If it was Christian and proper, you did it.

An Oregon Singing Teacher[7]

In 1900, J. D. Mishler—bishop of the Hopewell congregation, Hubbard, Oregon—wrote to the *Herald of Truth* of the need for a singing teacher, asking for "some good young brother in the East that is willing and that understands music. . . ." a year later the congregation was practicing singing twice a week on the same nights as the Bible readings were held, and not a "good young brother" but Sister Lizzie Detweiler of West Liberty, Ohio, was going to teach vocal music as soon as her books arrived.

Christina Neuhauser Royer (1875-1967)[8]

While Isaiah W. Royer served as general Sunday school secretary for the Mennonite Church and Ohio Conference for 25 years (1915-41), his wife, Christina, was children's superintendent of the Orrville Ohio Mennonite Church Sunday school. There she taught her own three daughters and many other children to love and memorize songs and Scriptures. Her daughter Katherine says of her: "She was demonstrating in their own Sunday school effective methods of teaching the Bible to children which her husband was advocating for the church at large."

Two of her daughters, Katherine and Mary, and her namesake granddaughter, Christina Neff, also became teachers. Mary received her PhD from Ohio State University in 1950 and was a professor at Goshen College from 1933 to 1979. Katherine wrote *Happy Times with Nursery Children at Home and Church.*

Katherine wrote the following account of her mother's life:

> Christina Neuhauser, next youngest of Catharine and Christian Neuhauser's nine children, grew up near Concord, Tennessee, where her parents and grandparents pioneered an Anabaptist Community in 1872.
>
> Her childhood was gladdened by brothers, sisters, cousins, school friends, and playmates Julia and Mary Alice (daughters of freed-slave Black Aunt

Mary who worked for her mother), and by farm-hand Black Billy who told the famous Brer Rabbit folk tales still unwritten.

Her life was filled with music. Her mother's cradle lullaby "The Great Physician" and her singing-school-teacher father's beloved gospel hymn "I Saw a Wayworn Trav'ler" were among her favorite songs. Christina learned yet-unrecorded negro spirituals from Black Aunt Mary. From highland neighbors Christina and her brothers Abner, Joe, and John, learned old Scotch and English ballads which they sang and played on banjo, guitar, and mandolin. Christina's love for music was encouraged by her father's purchase of an organ and a phonograph for which he made his own recordings. At her high school graduation program in 1893 she sang in a quartet, played a piano solo, and was also organist. Later she gave piano lessons.

Christina attended Girls' High School in Knoxville before completing high school at Friendsville Academy, a school sponsored by Philadelphia Quakers. In the girls' dormitory at Friendsville, Christina and the other girls had "practical instruction in domestic duties" during the earliest days of the home-economics movement. At Friendsville at the age of sixteen she confessed Christ as her Savior under the ministry of a Quaker woman preacher and was baptized into the Concord Mennonite Church.

Following the example of her beloved oldest sister Lydia [see chapter 5], who had been her teacher, she prepared for teaching at Holbrook Normal School and at the University of Tennessee, where she enrolled in the first summer school of the south. Educators like G. Stanley Hall, P. P. Claxton (later U.S. Secretary of Education), and the Hofer sisters (renowned for work in early childhood education) taught without pay in order to establish this first southern summer school for teachers as part of the post-Civil War reconstruction program.

Christina was a farm girl as well as a school ma'am, adept at milking cows and doing other farm chores. She was an expert equestrian, a hobby which came in handy when as a teacher she rode horseback to school over the Tennessee hills with a niece in front of her, a nephew behind, and lunches and books tied to the saddle. She continued teaching primary school for ten years near her home in Tennessee, then taught in the first public school in St. Tammany's Parish near Salt Bayou, Louisiana, near her brother's home in Slidell.

In 1906 she became the wife of a young minister, I. W. Royer, whose ministries she faithfully shared in the College Church at Goshen, Indiana; the 26th Street Mennonite Mission in Chicago; and for forty years in the Orrville Mennonite Church in Ohio. While serving as Mennonite inner-city missionaries in Chicago in the early 1900's near Jane Addams' Hull

Christina Neuhauser (Royer) (1875-1967), Christian educator, with her mother, Catharine Stoltzfus Neuhauser (1833-1913).

House, both Christina and her husband Isaiah studied at Bethany Biblical Seminary.

Because Sunday school work, Bible conferences, evangelistic meetings, and Bible schools frequently took her husband away from home, Christina had additional responsibility not only for the family, but also for visiting the sick and dying, and arranging for funerals and weddings. Like her mother Catharine Neuhauser and her grandmother Catharine Stoltzfus, she had a courageous pioneer spirit. Like them, she was a loving mother, a fond grandmother, and a gracious hostess to the many guests in their parsonage. Her loving compassion and hospitality included her daughters' friends and teachers, her husband's coworkers and congregation, the bread-man's handicapped daughter, neighbors in need of body or soul, hungry transients, the friendless and lonely. She died at the home of her youngest daughter, Elizabeth (Mrs. Charles) Neff, in California "as gently and serenely as she had lived."

Martha Whitmer Steiner (1878-1928)[9]

Martha Whitmer, daughter of David L. and Anna (Otto) Whitmer, taught in three different country schools in Mahoning County, Ohio, beginning in 1895: Pine Hill, Webster Hall, and East Lewistown, all located near North Lima, Ohio.

At a Sunday school conference she met Albert Steiner, whom she married in 1903. They established a Christian home, which has been described as follows:

> . . . family worship was a vital, regular practice each morning and often in the evening also. At times they first spent time memorizing scripture as part of their worship. It was a home where the boys were expected to work, and to be obedient to their parents.

All three Steiner sons became schoolteachers and Mennonite ministers.

Son John tells the following story about Martha's teaching:

> My brother James was just starting his first year of teaching several days before Mother died. The night before she died she called James into her room and asked him how school was going.
>
> "Not too well."

She said, "It was hard for me when I started. . . . I took pieces of paper and wrote on them, 'Lord, help me to be a good teacher.' I placed them in the closet and in the desk drawer where my eyes would read them often during the difficult first days. The Lord was faithful."

When I started to teach, some of her former students would say, "John, you will be a wonderful teacher if you become as good as your mother was."

Throughout her adult life Martha Steiner served as primary Sunday school superintendent. She provided leadership for the women's organization of the North Lima, Midway, and Leetonia churches, then considered one congregation. In 1926 she succeeded her sister-in-law Clara Eby Steiner as secretary of the Mennonite Woman's Missionary Society, a position she held until her death two years later.

Martha Whitmer Steiner (1878-1928),
Christian teacher.

Amanda Frey (1890-1975)[10]

Amanda—first a schoolteacher, then a businesswoman—was the daughter of Jacob C. and Mary (Burkholder) Frey of Fulton County, Ohio. Amanda began teaching country school in 1908, taking examinations and attending institutions to qualify. After teaching for eight years she attended Hesston College and Goshen College. She taught home economics and other subjects in the Goshen-Elkhart area.

In 1933 as a result of a car accident, she retired from teaching and returned to her home community, where she opened the Archbold Dry Goods Store in 1939. She operated this business until 1972. Mary Smucker says of her:

> While keeping her books for her business, she served as treasurer for the national WMSA. She was successful and frugal and able to contribute financially to the church. She loved her church, was faithful in attendance, and taught Sunday school for many years.

"The Only Regret . . . That She Is Not a Man"

During the spring and summer of 1914 the committee setting up a new school in Virginia (later Eastern Mennonite College) searched diligently for a "capable, conservative principal."[11] The committee felt encouraged to discover a young lady who met all their expectations. Marion Charlton (Mrs. Jonas) Eshelman (1890-1973) of Williamsport, Maryland—a schoolteacher recently come into the Mennonite Church—was highly praised by all members of the faculty committee when they solicited her to teach. Daniel Kauffman said that her letter in reply was "one bright ray of promise for the success of the school." L. J. Heatwole spoke for the committee when he said, "I was so favorably impressed with all her answers that the only regret I feel about it is that she is not a man instead of a woman." If she had been a man, they would have looked no further for a principal! Marion taught at Eastern Mennonite in the year 1918-19.

Generations of children are indebted to Mennonite women schoolteachers, inheritors of the mantle of Christopher Dock. The following appendices list only a few more of them.

EXHIBIT 5
A Partial Listing of Teachers at the College Level

Bender, Bertha Burkholder (1896-1978). Graduated from Hesston in 1925. Earned MA degree. Instructor in French at Goshen College, 1926-29; dean of women, 1927-29.

Bender, Elizabeth Horsch (1895-   ). See chapter 3.

Bender, Florence (1899-   ). Received AB from Goshen College in 1922, MS from Purdue University in 1934 with two home economics majors. Held job as state supervisor of nursery education in Indiana. As a day-care consultant, helped set up national standards for nursery schools and day-care centers. Principal of a pioneer school for retarded children in Toledo, Ohio. Retired in 1967 from many years as a teacher of home economics at Bowling Green University (Ohio).[12]

Brackbill, Ruth Mininger (1906-62). Taught education and literature at Eastern Mennonite College, 1934-62. Called "Queen of Starrywood" by her astronomer husband, M. T. Brackbill.

Brenneman, Naomi (1891-   ), MA in literature from University of Chicago, 1921. Teacher at Bluffton College, 1918-61 and Goshen, 1945-46, and again in the 60's.

Brunk, Ada Zimmerman (1908-54). Dean of women at Eastern Mennonite College, 1939-49. Coauthor of *The Christian Nurture of Youth* (Scottdale, Pa.: Herald Press, 1960).

Clemens, Lois Gunden (1915-   ). See chapter 13.

Eby, Mary Emma Showalter (1913-   ). PhD, 1957. Headed home economics department at Eastern Mennonite College, 1947-67. Editor of best-selling *Mennonite Community Cookbook* (Scottdale, Pa.: Herald Press, 1950). Columnist for *Mennonite Weekly Review* "Homemaker's Corner," 1973-81.

Eigsti, Dorothea Abrahams (1900-   ). Graduated from Knox College, 1918. Taught mathematics and English at Hesston Academy, 1953-58. Registrar at Hesston College, 1958-66. Later active in WMSC work at Pekin and Morton, Illinois.

Enss, Amy Evelyn Greaves Sudermann (1878-1975). Grew up in Sheffield, England. Met and married Jacob Sudermann while visiting her uncle, the British consul in Berdiansk, Russia. Taught at the first Mennonite Russian college at Halbstadt. Husband died during her fourth pregnancy. Married Gustav Enss in 1912. Immigrated to the United States. Taught French at Bethel College (Kansas), and Hesston and Goshen Colleges. Autobiography written at age 91 is in the archives of the Mennonite Church, Goshen, Indiana.

Erb, Alta Eby (1891-   ). Daughter of Abraham and Salome (Denlinger) Eby, Lancaster, Pennsylvania. Graduated from Goshen in 1912. Taught at Hesston, 1912-40. Mary Miller says of her: "Mrs. Erb continued giving her pointed study talks in which she convinced students that blaming unprepared lessons on teachers, on long or difficult assignments, on a confusion of circumstances, or on a lack of native ability was merely transparent rationalizing. In graphic, step-by-step instruction she showed students how to prevent mind-wandering, how to master assignments, how to plan and to use study schedules, and how to develop and sustain study habits."[13] Editor and writer at Mennonite Publishing House, Scottdale, Pennsylvania, 1945 to 1970's.[14]

Alta Eby Erb (1891-   ),   Home economist, Mary Emma
Christian educator.   Showalter Eby (1913-   ).

Good, Viola M. (1907-   ). BA from Goshen, 1939. MA from Northwestern University, 1942. On staff at Goshen College, 1939-77. Originally from St. Jacobs, Ontario.

Hartzler, Sadie A. (1896-1972). Taught at Eastern Mennonite College and was librarian from 1926 to 1962. "Two requirements that her English classes never forgot were the book report on *Friendship* by Black and drawing on adding machine tape the journeys of Christian in *Pilgrim's Progress.*" She "wisely guided the library in its growth from a few hundred volumes to some thirty thousand."[15]

Horst, Emma Zimmerman (1894-   ). On staff at Eastern Mennonite College, 1923-35. Affectionately called Sister Emma by generations of students. "Dean of women, nurse, dietitian, housekeeper, counselor, and housemother."[16]

Hostetter, Ruth Stoltzfus Stauffer (1908-   ). On faculty at Eastern Mennonite College, 1928-40, 1942-   . First taught home economics, then business education.

Housour, Alta. On staff at Hesston College, 1932-40.

Kauffman, Edna Ramseyer (1910-   ). Received MA from Ohio State University, 1938; EdD, 1956. Professor of home economics at Bluffton College, 1936-65. From the Oak Grove congregation, Smithville, Ohio. Early participated in Quaker work camps and pioneered in organizing voluntary service for Mennonite women.

Kemrer, Dorothy (1898-   ). Daughter of Phares D. and Elizabeth (Kramer) Kemrer, Vintage, Pennsylvania. AB from Goshen, 1925. MA from Penn State University, 1931. Teacher of Greek and Latin at Eastern Mennonite College 1920-64. Assisted J. B. Smith on his *Greek-English Concordance to the New Testament*, published in 1955. "In 1964 . . . terminated a period of forty-four years of teaching and thorough scholarship in Greek and Latin that enhanced the academic tone of the college."[17]

Leaman, Bertha R. (1893-1975). Graduated from Goshen, 1921. MA in history from University of Chicago, 1924. Studied at University of Paris, 1927-28. PhD from University of Chicago, 1935. Dissertation topic: "French Foreign and Colonial Policy under Radical-Socialist Party Control, 1898-1905." Taught at West Liberty State College in West Virginia, 1949-63. Died at Haverford, Pennsylvania.[18] Said to be first woman graduate of Goshen College to earn PhD.

Martin, Elsie (1908-   ). On faculty at Eastern Mennonite College, 1935-42, 1947-54. Principal and supervisor of Park School. Director of teacher training.

Miller, Mary M. (1897-1963). Teacher of English at Hesston College. Library at Hesston is named in her honor. Served in France with MCC during World War II. Author of *A Pillar of Cloud* (North Newton, Kan.: Mennonite Press, 1959) [See *Hesston College Bulletin*, Oct. 1963];

Nitzsche, Bertha (1901-   ) Daughter of Julius and Barbara (Oswald) Nitzsche. B.A. from Goshen College, 1936, M.S. State University of Iowa. Librarian at Hesston College, 1936-45. Dietitian at Mennonite Hospital, LaJunta, Colorado, 1950-3.

Royer, Mary Neuhauser (1907-   ). Daughter of Isaiah W. and Tina (Neuhauser) Royer. BA from Goshen, 1930. MA from George Peabody College for Teachers, 1931. PhD from Ohio State University, 1950. Taught in education department at Goshen College, 1933-79. Writer of Christian education materials for Mennonite Publishing House. First woman to address Mennonite World Conference. See page 229.

Schrock, Alta E. (1911-   ). AB from Waynesburg College, 1937. MA from Kent State University, 1939. PhD from University of Pittsburgh, 1944. Taught biology at Goshen College, 1946-58. Founder of Penn Alps at Grantsville, Maryland, Council of the Alleghenies, and Casselwood Corporation (a furniture factory).

Smith, Verna Graber (1902-   ). BA from Goshen, 1928. MA from University of Wisconsin, 1950. Taught Latin, Spanish, and English at Goshen College, 1930-1972.

Wenger, A. Grace (1919-   ). MA from University of Pennsylvania. Teacher of literature and language, first in Earl Township country schools, Pennsylvania, Eastern Mennonite College (1943-56), Lancaster Mennonite School, and Millersville State College (1966-79). Has served as vice-president of Menno Housing—a church-related organization providing low-income housing in Lancaster, Pennsylvania—and on the Mennonite Board of Education,[19]

Winey, Lois (1910-   ). BA from Goshen, 1936. MA from New York University, 1950. Assistant business manager, teacher of business at Goshen College, 1936-1977.

Witmer, Edith (1902-1982). BS from Penn State University, 1923. MA from Columbia University, 1926. Taught home economics at Goshen College, 1926-29. Author of hymn 438 in *The Mennonite Hymnal*—"Teach Me Thy Truth, O Mighty One."

Wyse, Olive G. (1906-   ). BA from Goshen, 1926. MA from State University of Iowa, 1933. EdD from Teachers College of Columbia University, 1946. Taught home economics at Goshen College, 1926-1976. An annual lectureship has been established in her honor.

EXHIBIT 6

A Partial Listing of Teachers in Primary and Secondary Schools

Bauman, Salome (1909-   ). Made a significant contribution to Rockway Mennonite School in Ontario for 25 years. Served as principal for several years.[20]

Carper, Eva Weber (1898-   ). First child of Henry S. and Mary (Burkholder) Weber, Lancaster County, Pennsylvania. Taught in public schools of Virginia until her marriage to Reuben Carper in 1923. Helped establish Warwick River School in Newport News, Virginia, in 1942; taught there for many years; helped plan new building in 1948. Wrote a column entitled "Notes from the Garden Spot" from 1932 to 1940 for *The Rural New Yorker*. Writer of curriculum materials for Mennonite Publishing House. After retirement taught Choctaw Indian children at Macon, Mississippi. Now lives at Reba Place Fellowship, Evanston, Illinois.[21]

Coffman, Barbara F. (1907-   ). BA from Goshen, 1931. Journalist and music teacher in Vineland, Ontario. Author of *His Name Was John* (Scottdale, Pa.: Herald Press, 1964).

Cooprider, Eva (1907-   ). Teacher in public schools of Hesston and Newton, Kansas. Daughter of Thomas Jefferson and Viola Barbara (Yoder) Cooprider. Received teaching certificate from Hesston Academy, 1925. BS in education from Emporia State Teachers College, 1948. ME from Colorado State College of Education, Greeley, Colorado, 1959. Active in many kinds of church and community service.

Denlinger, Anna Ressler (Mrs. Lawrence) (1902-   ). Teacher in Amish school at Ronks, Pennsylvania, for many years.

Gehman, Vera Longacre (1899-   ). Taught in Pennsylvania, 1917-25 and 1942-62.

Getz, Mary Jane Turner (1894-1962). Teacher in Franklin, West Virginia, and Brocks Creek School in Virginia. Known for her knowledge of nature.[22]

Good, Wilma Smucker (1899-1978). BA from Goshen, 1921. Taught English in high school at Orrville, Ohio. Co-donor with her husband, Harold, of Good Library at Goshen College.

Kurtz, Ida (-   ). In 1914 opened a school for black children in an old shirt factory, Salisbury Township, Lancaster, Pennsylvania.[23]

Lark, Rowena Winters (? -1970). Teacher in public schools of Washington, D.C., Chicago, St. Louis. An active church worker.[24]

Miller, Pearl Klopfenstein (1901-   ). MA from University of Nebraska, 1925. Teacher of English in high school at Wakarusa, Indiana.

Moyer, Bessie Clymer (1901-70). BA from Goshen, 1930. Teacher at Durham, Pennsylvania.

Osborne, Eva Troyer (Mrs. Chester) (1913-   ). Graduate of Ball State Teachers College. Teacher in public school at Hesston, Kansas.

Roth, Mabel (1905-   ). Teacher at Waterford School, Goshen, Indiana.

Thut, Ada Ellen (1905-58). Teacher at Doylestown, Pennsylvania.

Troyer, Esther Freed (Mrs. Samuel) (1913-61). A pioneer teacher in the Franconia Mennonite Elementary School (now Penn View) beginning in 1945. Also served as a missionary in Tanzania.

Weaver, Florence Troyer (Mrs. Norman) (1909-　　). Teacher in Howard County, Indiana.

Wenger, Edna K. (1914-　　), Bareville, Pennsylvania. Teacher at Lancaster Mennonite High School.

Yoder, Anna E. (1884-1975). Born in Champaign, Illinois. Received BA from Goshen College in 1912. Taught at Parkside School, Goshen, Indiana.

Yoder, Rhea (1898-　　). Teacher in elementary schools of northern Indiana and at Landour, India, from 1948 to 1959.

CHAPTER 8

In Overseas Missions

Mission work overseas has been widely accepted for so long that it is difficult to realize how much people once opposed it. The first Mennonite women missionaries had to go under other boards because Mennonite boards did not yet exist. The stories of two of these women, Alice Yoder and Rose Lambert, will be told in this chapter. Other women faced various barriers. Lina Zook Ressler said philosophically about opposition to missions, "Someone must bear the unpopularity of pioneer work."[1] Phebe Yoder prayed for years before she could enter Africa. Dr. Florence Cooprider Friesen's story will be told in chapter 10, "In Health-Care Ministries."

John A. Lapp says that during the 63 year period covered in his study of the Mennonite mission to India, the 102 separate missionaries serving in India included 41 missionary couples and 18 single women.[2] These women taught, supervised their own households—sometimes under great difficulties—provided health care, and set up an effective women's organization.

A missionary woman, *Lydia Liechty (Mrs. M. C.) Lehman,* on December 15, 1915, wrote an interesting letter from India to her friend Clara Eby Steiner in Ohio. Clara founded the women's organization during those years and had informed Lydia about the opposition she was facing from church leaders. (See chapter 11.) Note that these women addressed one another as "sisters" in the faith many years before the term became popular in the women's movement later in the twentieth century.

Dear Sister Steiner:

Greetings of love. Your letter was indeed a welcome guest in our home and was circulated among the missionaries. So glad to hear from you and to learn of your marked success and progress in the work to which you have laid your hands. You certainly deserve much credit for the way you handled the situation at the conference.

The brethren will have to confess ere long that there is a work for the sisters of our church and they should be given an opportunity to prove themselves. It has been our experience here on the field that the women's work is better organized than the men's. The reasons are evident and not to the discredit of the men; but facts are facts. The men have each so many irons in the fire that they can not stop long enough to think and plan and organize. The result was, our women got together and organized themselves into a Women's Christian Work Committee and began to carry on their work with Bible Women and school mistresses through that committee. It was so satisfactory that the men wanted something like it and, in short, copied after our work. I am really surprised at the attitude some have taken and the assistance they have given and offered.[3]

A recent researcher says of the missionary women:

They had full confidence in the Christian gospel to equalize the roles of the men and women, and one woman went so far as to assert that Christianizing the women of India was the key to India's modernization! . . . Because the Society [in the United States and Canada] supported the missionary *women*, who in turn were working with the native women, there existed an amazing network connecting the North American women through the missionaries to the native women.[4]

An example of the kind of ties maintained by overseas workers with the people at home is provided by correspondence and articles by Alice Yoder.

Alice Yoder, Orphanage Worker in India

Alice Yoder of Lititz, Pennsylvania, one of the first American

Mennonite women to become an overseas missionary, went to India with the Christian and Missionary Alliance in 1897. Carolyn Wenger, director of the Lancaster Mennonite Historical Society, wrote in 1981:

> No one locally of the Mennonites seems to remember this Alice Yoder of Lititz. Of course, 1897 is about the beginning of the Christian and Missionary Alliance movement. In fact, in 1892 or 1893 about one-third of the Landis Valley Mennonite congregation's membership, half of the Sunday school, and more than sixty scholars left, although a few later returned. The issues at stake included missions, baptism by immersion, faith healing, and a greater degree of emotionalism than the more traditional Mennonites of this time desired.[5]

Five of those who withdrew, including Minnie Landis, became missionaries to China. Was Minnie perhaps the first Mennonite woman to go overseas as a missionary? Or was it Sara Alice Troyer of Milford, Nebraska, who went to China in the 1890s under the China Inland Mission?[6] Which were truer to Mennonite ideals—those who had to leave in order to become missionaries or those who remained at home unperturbed by needs overseas?

Alice Yoder worked at an orphanage in Khamgaon.[7] She spoke the sentiment of later missionaries as well when she said:

> Love must be the missionary's supreme motive. Not a narrow selfish love, but a great, wide, deep love that embraces the whole world.[8]

The first issue of the *Herald of Truth* in the twentieth century (January 1, 1900) carried a letter that Alice wrote from Khamgaon in Berar, India, on November 3, 1899. The letter is addressed to "My dear Sister." First, Alice describes the famine and resulting suffering. She describes her own troubles in trying to provide water for the 79 children in her care. Then she thanks the sister for "the offering of [her] dear people."

> I started a new well and as I moved on the money came in and when the last week's mail came I did not receive the letter with the draft at the same time I got my other mail, so one of the lady missionaries came to me and

said, "Did you receive any money this mail?" No, not yet, but I know the
Lord will not let me stick. I began the well in His name and He sent the
money thus far. And what do you think! Three days later your letter came
with the draft enclosed $38.25 just at the time needed. I was at the time
with my language teacher, a heathen, and I praised the Lord before him,
I could not help [it]. It was a God-send. We have water, praise God. We
struck a nice stream and the people are surprised, O so much. I asked the
Lord when I measured off the well to not let my hands and feet go one
inch out of the way and the stream was struck right in the middle of the
well. Pray that it may be a permanent flow, that the fountain may not fail;
as it will mean the taking in of many more famine children and that the
Lord may provide and care for them. Thank all the dear ones for me.
Much Christian love to all.[9]

Whether or not Alice Yoder's name was on a Mennonite church
roll in 1897, her writings indicate that she thought of herself as a
Mennonite.

Lina Zook Ressler (1869-1948)

The story of missions in the Mennonite church could hardly
be told without including this remarkable woman. Theron Schlabach calls her papers "especially helpful" for his study of the
Mennonite church from 1863 to 1944, because they supply "the
perspective of a very able young woman deep in the hard work of
missions and of a person struggling to keep her Mennonite church
identity and to accept church leaders' advice and discipline."[10]
Persons nurtured on the now defunct children's paper *Words of
Cheer* remember her as the "Aunt Lina" who wrote a per-
sonalized answer to every child's letter. Her answers treated each
child as important and worthy of attention. But her service to the
church had begun much earlier, in the Oak Grove congregation in
Smithville, Ohio, during the 1880s.

Lina was the firstborn of the seven children of David and
Magdalena (Blough) Zook. During her youth—along with the
Christian young people of the neighborhood—she enjoyed spell-
ing bees, Bible study classes, Christian Endeavor societies, singing
schools, and maple sugar parties. These young people came from
several denominations and shared their good times.[11]

From 1889 to 1891, when she was in her early twenties, the

Herald of Truth published at least eleven articles by Lina Zook. One of them, "The Relation of the Sunday School to the Church," had been presented to a Sunday school conference.[12] A recent researcher comments, "Usually only men tackled issues such as this. This goes beyond merely the pious and jaded verse which women usually wrote."[13]

Lina caught the missionary vision early. In "Memories of Early Missionary Experiences in Chicago," she says:

> It would be difficult to tell when I first became interested in missions. As a little girl I listened to stories about missionaries and their work.... At the time of our first Sunday School Conference, near Goshen, Indiana, my heart was thrilled as I saw the interest.... At last our church seemed awake to the needs of those who knew not the Gospel. Up to that time I had heard little about missions from public speakers in our church.[14]

Lina tells of the stirring addresses she heard at that conference, one of them by Phoebe (Mumaw) Kolb. Young Lina Zook eagerly longed to go overseas to carry out the Great Commission, but since this opportunity did not yet exist for her under Mennonite auspices, she did what many talented young Mennonite women of her time did. She volunteered for service at the Gospel Mission in Chicago.

Notebooks which she kept during these years are in the archives of the Mennonite Church at Goshen, Indiana. Schlabach reports that her manuscripts numbered 1 through 117 in the archives make up four linear feet.[15] On her first day in Chicago, September 3, 1896, Lina wrote:

> Here I am at last in the place where I have often longed to be.... I believe God intends for me to work for Him here, for the time being at least.... One of the first things that attracted my attention as we enter the city is the vast number of wicked hopeless looking faces that we see.

Lina's co-workers during her years in Chicago included Melinda Ebersole (see chapter 9), Mary Denlinger, Amanda Musselman, Hershey Leaman, Isaiah and Tina Royer (see chapter 7). These intrepid workers found hungry children and fed them, families without coal for heating during the winter and provided coal, people who died without anyone to care for the bodies, and they provided that care. The workers joked about the sporadic support for the mission. They said, "We eat dried apples for breakfast, drink water for dinner, and let it swell up for supper."[16] Lina recorded incidents from this part of her life in letters she wrote for the *Herald of Truth*. The November 1, 1897, issue carried this report: "Last Sunday there were one hundred and twenty-two pupils in Sunday school and the order was fairly good."

Dr. F. B. Whitmore, a Baptist missionary, operated a medical dispensary at the Chicago mission. Letters back home to Ohio mentioned "Dr. W" more and more frequently. The home folks became somewhat alarmed. James Lehman tells the story in his book.[17] On June 2, 1898, Lina wrote quite a letter to A. B. Kolb, president of the Mennonite Evangelizing Board. She told him that workers often felt the board was not as deeply interested in the Chicago work as it should be. She asked about India: "Shall the foothold our churches have gained in India be lost through delay?" She told Kolb that her call to mission work had come long before she met "Dr. W." "However," she went on, "Dr. Whitmore and I think that we could work successfully together, and I believe that the decision has been made with a view, not selfish, for God's glory and the advancement of the mission cause."

Lina requested a frank answer concerning whether they could be sent to the foreign field and whether she should leave Chicago to go to the newly established Elkhart Institute. Then as now, the whole church was interested in a particular young woman's love affair. Lina's mother wrote to her that ministers J. S. Hartzler and David Garber had visited Oak Grove; she said, "The Brethren are so interested in you and your circumstances out there." Hartzler told Lina's parents that Whitmore was not worthy of their daughter. Mother Zook wrote, "Pa says that she should come home for awhile."

Lina followed the parental advice and returned to Ohio for five or six months. During that time she heard newly-appointed missionaries J. A. Ressler and W. P. Page speak at her home

church. (Ressler's wife, Lizzie Bachman (1871-98), had contracted
typhoid and died in Westmoreland County, Pennsylvania, prior
to his volunteering for service in India.) Lina herself presented
some stirring missionary challenges. Lehman says of one presentation: "Few ministers could match the eloquence with which Lina
challenged that Sunday evening meeting group!" She also
traveled to Mifflin County, Pennsylvania, to make the presentation. The *Herald of Truth* correspondent reported, "Never have
we had so good an opportunity to hear of the conditions and
needs of the perishing in our cities and among heathen peoples."
He proudly proclaimed that Mifflin County was the home of
"Sister Zook's ancestors" and that her visit opened many hearts
and homes and did much to awaken an interest in city mission
work."

In November 1898, five months after Lina had made her
request of the mission board, she received an answer:

> If your love affair with Dr. Whitmore is settled in favor of the Mennonite
> Church you will have a right to expect great things from the Lord. You no
> doubt have been told what the general sentiment of our people is, that it
> would be impossible to send the Dr. as a Mennonite missionary now.

Lina returned to Chicago, but not for long. When the
Elkhart Institute opened, she became a preceptress there. She
taught Bible at the institute from 1901 to 1903.[18] In February
1902 she received a persuasive letter from Dhamtari, India—from
the widower and pioneer missionary to India, J. A. Ressler. "He
presented powerful arguments that it was neither good for a single
woman to do mission work in India nor any better for a man to
stay single in India!" Two months later Lina decided that she
would indeed accept the proposal and go to India.

Ressler returned to the States for a furlough in 1903, and on
June 18 of that year Lina Zook and Bishop Jacob A. Ressler,
superintendent of the American Mennonite Mission in India,
were united "in the holy bonds of wedlock" by Benjamin Gerig in
a German ceremony. What went on in this young woman's mind?
Outwardly confident, she was inwardly less so. Once shortly

before the marriage someone found her in tears. The engaged woman explained, "Now I won't be Liny Zook anymore, just 'Jake Ressler's frau.' "[19]

In India, Lina plunged immediately into work. After she had been there for a year, her husband wrote to his friend A. K. Kurtz:

> I wish you would tell me what to do with her—I mean Lina. She is having her old trouble of going at her work as if it had to be done right off or not get done. Of course we all like to see people work with energy but I am afraid Lina is going to overwork if she does not "watch out." I had hoped that the lack of language would give her a chance to catch up with her resting. But she was not here very long before she saw that she could help the blind and the mutes and so she got to work and now she is in it so hard that there is fear that she will not take proper care of herself.[20]

Lina spent only five years in India. During that time she bore two children in a thatch-roofed mud hut and had an ovarian cyst removed. Her only son, Luke, was stillborn on June 12, 1904. It is a profound experience for a woman to carry a child in her body for nine months, to go through the intense experience of giving birth, then to have to relinquish that child to death. Lina's second child, Ruth, survived.

Ill for a long time in India, Mrs. Ressler had no access to a foreign-trained doctor. The local Indian doctors thought she was pregnant again. At last a famous British missionary doctor, Dr. Wanless, who operated a hospital and dispensary in western India, discovered and removed a large ovarian cyst. During this crisis Esther Ebersole (Mrs. George) Lapp stayed with Lina and nursed her in a mud hut in the rainy season. In later years Mrs. Ressler often recalled how Esther sang, "Be not dismayed what e'er betide. God will take care of you." Lina believed that song brought her back to life. Because of her health problems the Resslers returned to the United States in 1908 and lived in the Oak Grove, Ohio, community, where their second daughter, Rhoda, was born. There the couple wrote a book entitled *Lights and Shades from Hindu Land* (Smithville, Ohio, 1910).

In 1911 the Mennonite Publishing House invited J. A. Ressler to Scottdale, Pennsylvania, to do editorial work. In her latter years Lina worked more and more with her husband in his office, and after his death in 1936 continued for several years as editor of the children's paper *Words of Cheer*. How she respected the dignity and personhood of each child letter-writer! "A very good letter, Wilbur. You will soon be busy on that farm. God bless you. Lovingly, Aunt Lina."[21] On January 28, 1934, a typical letter from a child said:

> I am a boy 8 years old.... We live on a farm of 17 acres. We have 48 chickens, 1 horse, 4 pigs, and 6 steers. From your loving friend, Paul N. Kraybill.

Lina replied:

> Come, again, Paul, only then it will not be a "first letter" any more.

He did come again, and again, and is at this writing executive secretary of the Mennonite World Conference.

Lina Zook Ressler edited *Beams of Light* (succeeded by *Story Friends*) from 1937 to 1946. She compiled four volumes of

Lina Zook (Ressler) (1869-1948), missionary and editor.

Rose Lambert Musselman (1878-1974), missionary to Turkey.

poems and stories for children and young people: *Poems for Our Boys and Girls* (ca. 1916-28, 2 vols.), *Helpful Stories Retold for Our Boys and Girls* (ca. 1923-36, 4 vols.), *Recitations for Young Folks, Suitable for Christmas, Easter, and Other Special Occasions* (ca. 1927). Her article "The Sewing Circles of the Mennonite Church" appeared in a 1939 issue of *Gospel Herald*.

Lina's daughter Ruth says, "For thirty-five years Mother knew that some day she would be blind. The way she prepared for it was heroic." The two Ressler daughters, Ruth and Rhoda, adopted their parents' values and served as missionaries in Japan from 1953 to 1973. A whole generation owes a debt of gratitude to Lina Zook Ressler for "settling her love affair in favor of the Mennonite Church."

Rose Lambert Musselman (1878-1974)

Rose Lambert spent twelve years as a pioneer Mennonite missionary in Turkey during a turbulent time of starvation and massacre. On May 8, 1909, she wrote from Hadjin, Turkey:

> Thousands have been massacred, and thousands of the living are threatened with starvation.
>
> There is scarcely a family in Hadjin who is not in mourning, Bro. Maurer and our two chief native workers have been killed. We need your prayers.[22]

Daughter of George and Amanda (Gehman) Lambert, Rose was born in Vera Cruz, Pennsylvania, but spent her childhood years in the Elkhart-Mishawaka area of northern Indiana except for a brief period at Peabody, Kansas. Her father, an influential promoter of missions in the Mennonite Church, made two trips to India, distributing relief grain in the famine of 1898. He was also instrumental in opening the Mennonite mission program among the Armenians of Turkey.

Rose studied nursing and orphan-school management in Cleveland before going to Turkey in 1899. She became matron of an Armenian orphan school. The church papers of the period carried various letters from her about her work. One such letter said:

The city is full of typhoid fever and although the Governor has forbidden
the tolling of bells, we are told, the processions keep marching to the
graveyard.[23]

Due to ill health Rose returned to the United States in 1910.
She married D. G. Musselman, a Chicago inventor-businessman.
The following year she wrote a book entitled *Hadjin and the Armenian Massacres* (New York: Fleming H. Revell, 1911). She
dedicated it "To the memory of the Christian martyrs and to the
suffering mothers, sisters, widows and orphans." The newly married couple bought a ranch at Salem, sixteen miles from Victoria,
in southern Texas, where they established both a post office and a
church.

When her husband died in 1933, Rose continued to live in
the Texas community, and with her children managed their
ranch. They raised rice and cattle and had oil wells. Rose practiced midwifery and was considered "the organizing center of the
community."[24]

At the age of 91, Rose Lambert Musselman recalled some of
the events of her earlier years in a letter to C. L. Graber:

> I did my utmost for them [the Armenians] and at the time felt it would be
> much easier to be with the martyrs than to live with the memories of the
> atrocities. We all depended on God and He did not fail us. . . .
>
> After peace was restored and I was ill with typhoid a mounted Turkish of-
> ficer met one of our boys on the street. He stopped his horse and asked
> him if he was one of our boys and then asked, "How is Miss Lambert?"
> The reply, "She is very ill." He said, "Allah willing she cannot die! The
> Gregorians in their churches are praying for her recovery and we in our
> Mosque are praying for her recovery. Allah *must* hear some of us."
>
> Later when I was forced to go to a lower altitude to recover, the judge sent
> a message to me to please look to the right as I rode past his home; he
> would be in the vacant lot in front of it and wished to bid me farewell as I
> was leaving the city. Another message from the other officials: "Please
> look to the left as you pass the government building. We will all be stand-
> ing on the second floor gallery and wish to bid you farewell." I complied
> with their wish. Not a word was spoken but each was in their respective
> position and gave me a solemn salute. They too accepted us as their
> friends.[25]

Crissie Yoder Shank (1888-1929)

The influence of this extraordinary woman, her thinking global in scope and ecumenical in outlook, continues to this day. She was born near Holden, Missouri, the daughter of John A. and Sadie Yoder. As a young woman she taught school in Ohio, possibly in 1910. Years later (on May 25, 1938) her principal, Jessie G. Kendig, recalled that year:

> I look back with pride and pleasure to years spent at old No. I in Wayne Township, especially the year Miss Crissie Yoder was my assistant. Well do I remember how the little boys and girls would hover about her . . . one, if not *the* most successful and pleasant year of my [37 years of] teaching experiences.[26]

Crissie Yoder received a BA from Goshen College in 1913 and the next year was dean of women and a teacher of English at Bethel College in North Newton, Kansas. In 1914 she married Charles L. Shank. In 1915 they went to India, where they spent the next four years at Dhamtari. Because of their oldest daughter Ruth's rheumatic fever, they returned to the Oak Grove community near Smithville, Ohio.

When Crissie died only a decade later, she had borne eight children, written a book, helped organize what is now the WMSC, edited its *Monthly Letter*, edited a mission column in the *Christian Exponent* for two years, and become much appreciated as a public speaker.

Her son David, only five at the time of her death, says:

> Over the years as I have spoken at various places, people have come up to me and said (not once, but tens of times!), "As you were speaking, I was made to think of your mother Crissie. She used to speak at church conferences, and she was such a good speaker. When she talked, everyone listened, because they knew it was important to hear."[27]

Mary Royer recalls:

> She was a powerful, vivid speaker. I can see her now as she spoke from my father's pulpit in our old Orrville [Ohio] Church in the 20's about her experiences in India.[28]

Crissie's book, *Letters from Mary* (Scottdale, Pa.: Mennonite Publishing House, 1924), reads well even today. She creates a fictional character, Mary, who writes to her cousin in the United States about India.

In 1924 and 1925, Crissie Shank—as departmental editor of missions for a short-lived but outstanding inter-Mennonite journal, *The Christian Exponent*—covered mission news of the Mennonite Church, telling, e.g., about the G. D. Troyer family in India, Salena Gamber and the Hallmans in South America. But she also covered mission news of the General Conference Mennonites and reported on the Tokyo earthquake of 1923, on various translations of the Bible, and on mission work among American Indians. She promoted the World Day of Prayer on the first Friday in Lent.

At the Sixth General Meeting of the Mennonite Woman's Missionary Society, held at Waterloo, Ontario, in 1923, Crissie Shank was elected secretary of literature and became editor of the *Monthly Letter,* forerunner of the *Voice*.[29] (See chapter 11.) Through this medium she promoted the reading of books about missions among the sewing circles. Mary Royer recalls:

> I remember when she was General Secretary of Literature for the WMSA—how she read and reviewed missionary books to recommend to girls and women while she rocked her little children.

Crissie Yoder (Shank) (1888-1929),
missionary, mother, speaker, writer.

Crissie Yoder Shank died of childbirth complications on October 12, 1929, aged—according to her *Gospel Herald* obituary—"41 yr., 9 m., 5 d." Her husband later married Lydia Frances Shenk, an instructor in French at Goshen College, also a devoted and capable woman.[30] The Shank children have served the Mennonite Church in the United States, Europe, Africa, South America, and the Middle East. Crissie's is a priceless legacy, not only to her own children, but to all Mennonite women who follow her in the work of the Kingdom.

Phebe Yoder (1903-81)

Phebe Yoder—daughter of C. D. and Susanna (Kilmer) Yoder of the West Liberty congregation in McPherson County, Kansas—served under the Eastern Mission Board in Tanganyika (now Tanzania) for more than thirty years.[31] At age twelve Phebe read a book entitled *Uganda's White Man of Work*. One particularly moving chapter told about the martyrdom of several African young men, burned at the stake for their faith. Tears streaming down her face, Phebe heard God calling her to go to Africa. She promised that she would one day do so.

Years of preparation and puzzlement followed. She went to Hesston College, Goshen College and Seminary. Twice she was asked to marry. Both times she said, "God has called me to the mission field in Africa. Would you be willing to go with me?" Because neither man could answer "yes," the courtships were terminated.

Still the Mennonite mission board had no mission work in Africa. Phebe began sending her tithes to the board earmarked "Africa Mission." One summer following college graduation, she worked in a millionaire's home in New York City as a baby-sitter/tutor. While sitting with the children at the beach that summer, she heard God asking her daily to take nurse's training. "I battled it, because I didn't think I could be as successful in nursing as I was as a teacher," she later recalled. But she listened to the "still, small voice" and entered the LaJunta Mennonite School of Nursing, receiving her RN in 1937.

Halfway through nurse's training Phebe learned that the Eastern Board, not the General Board, would enter Africa. The General Board transferred its Africa funds to the Eastern Board. Heartbroken, she cried, "Lord, no one in the East knows me. I'll never, never get to Africa." It was a terrific test of faith. In those days one never volunteered. "And in those days," as David Shenk puts it, "the Eastern Board was quite exclusive."

As she neared graduation, Phebe received another jolt. The LaJunta administration asked her to become a nursing instructor. Again she fled to her room and wept before the Lord. What should she do? The answer came: "Wait three weeks before responding."

About a week later a letter arrived from Orie O. Miller, Eastern Board secretary. He wrote, "I don't know you, but for nine months we have been searching for a nurse, mature in years and Christian experience, to go to Tanganyika as a missionary."

Of course Phebe went. She set up her nursing station in a garage. Her "dispensary was on the fenders of an old truck." And she started schools. She supervised the construction of ten school buildings, wrote or helped to write seven primary reading books, and spent several years traveling from school to school in a self-

Phebe Yoder (1903-1981), missionary to Africa.

designed van, selling Christian books. That was only a beginning. She taught in the schools, including a theological college; served as nurse-doctor for her area; and assisted in the translation of the New Testament into Jita and Swahili.

Including furloughs, Phebe served in Africa for 34 years. She retired to Schowalter Villa in 1971 and died there a decade later. Her body was donated to the University of Kansas Medical School at her request. Phebe Yoder's faith helped open a far-reaching Mennonite work in Africa.

It took courage for early missionary women to launch out into foreign cultures with the gospel. We can feel assured that their names and service are known to God.

EXHIBIT 7

A Partial Listing of Overseas Missionaries

Brunk, Eva Harder (Mrs. A. C.) (? -1949). Spent 38 years in India.

Eshleman, Sarah Zook (Mrs. Merle) (1907-   ). Served in Tanganyika, 1939-47 and 1949-54.

Friesen, Florence Cooprider (Mrs. P. A.). Medical doctor in India. (See chapter 10.)

Good, Mary (1890-1982). Daughter of Henry H. and Susan (Ressler) Good. (See chapter 3.) Spent 32 years in India. Principal of the Gargan Memorial School in Balodgahan, which under her creative leadership developed into one of the top-ranking schools in the district. "Miss Good planned the program of study as her master's thesis at George Peabody College for Teachers.... [It] placed much emphasis on individual growth, social relationships, and the Hindi language."[32]

Graber, Minnie Swartzendruber (Mrs. J. D.) (1902-   ). Born in Eagle Grove, Iowa. Served in India from 1925 to 1942. Also active in WMSC work. In a taped interview with Arlene Mark, Elkhart, Indiana, on September 2, 1980, Minnie reminisced about her life, reflecting on changes that have occurred. She is grateful that "legalism is no longer such an issue." She recalls having spoken to entire congregations in the Midwest in the early 1930's about mission work in India. "In the first century women worked naturally in the church. Then the church turned against women. They had to have their own organizations, but eventually that will not be necessary." Minnie expresses deep appreciation for the work of the Mennonite mission board.

Hershey, Mae Elizabeth Hertzler (Mrs. T. K.) (1877-1974). Born near Concord, Tennessee. Lived with her husband in Lancaster, Pennsylvania; Goshen, Indiana; LaJunta, Colorado; and Bluffton, Ohio, before going to Argentina with her husband and children in 1917. After language study in Buenos Aires they moved to Pehuajo, about 300 miles inland. Mae Hershey made at least three major contributions to the mission work there: (1) With Emma Shank she set up kindergartens and primary schools for children. (2) With the aid of Albano Luayza and his wife, Dona Querubina, she established The Evangelical Chain of Mennonite Women of Argentina. (3) She

Ada Ramseyer Litwiller (1900-   ) and Nelson, missionaries to South America for 42 years.

helped set up a training program for Sunday school teachers and encouraged a Bible reading program in the homes.[33]

Kanagy, Minnie (1891-1976). Daughter of Joseph and Emma (Zook) Kanagy. Member of Maple Grove Church, New Castle, Pennsylvania. BA from Goshen College, 1922. Served fourteen years in India. Assisted in the mission at Wooster, Ohio.[34]

Keener, Martha Gish (Mrs. Clayton) (1901-81). Daughter of Daniel N. and Barbara (Hoffman) Gish. She and her husband were missionaries in Ethiopia and Somalia.[35]

Lapp, Esther Ebersole (Mrs. George) (1882-1917). In 1901 she took nurse's training at Passavant Memorial Hospital in Chicago, where she met her husband and covenanted to go with him to India. Spent her first term (1905-12) in orphanage work, the medical dispensary, and village visitation. Helped open work at Ghatula during second term (1913). Contracted "blackwater fever" and died in 1917. Buried in a European cemetery in the Himalayas.[36]

Lapp, Fannie Hershey (Mrs. George) (1882-1963). Served for 32 years in India. A gracious woman with a fine sense of humor. She once said to me, "While my husband took care of the big things, I took care of the little things."

Lapp, Sarah Hahn (Mrs. Mahlon) (1869-1943). Daughter of Jacob and Anna (Eyman) Hahn, Clarence Center, New York. Studied nursing in Chicago and Elkhart. Married Mahlon Lapp in 1900. "Auntie" served longer in India than any other Mennonite missionary, from 1901 to 1942. John Lapp calls her "one of the most extraordinary of all the missionaries. Rarely ill during her long career, she stayed in India nineteen years after her husband's death. Her greatest achievement was with the Bible women, with whom she virtually lived during her fifth term in India."[37]

Leatherman, Catherine Garber (Mrs. John E.) (1914-   ). Daughter of Henry F. and Ada B. (Nissley) Garber. Attended Eastern Mennonite School; graduated from Elizabethtown (Pennsylvania) College in 1935. Married John E. Leatherman, a minister, in 1935. Served in Tanzania from 1936 to 1965. With her husband began Bukiroba Bible School, now a theological seminary. At this writing she is an elder in the Mount Joy, Pennsylvania, congregation.[38]

Lehman, Lydia Liechty (Mrs. M. C.) (1884-1969). From Wayne
County, Ohio. Served in India for 24 years. Wrote many articles for
Gospel Herald about missions in India during those years. Did
outstanding work for MCC following World War II.

Litwiller, Ada Ramseyer (Mrs. Nelson) (1900-   ). From western
Ontario. Influenced toward missions by her older sister Nancy
(1872-1924). Served in Argentina and Uruguay for 42 years.[39]

Miller, Ruth Blosser (Mrs. Ernest E.) (1893-1977). From New Stark,
Ohio. Daughter of Noah O. and Ellen (Beery) Blosser. Served in
India, 1921-37 and 1956-63. President of the Women's Missionary
and Sewing Circle Organization (WMSO) from 1944 to 1950 (see
chapter 11).

Shank, Emma Hershey (Mrs. J. W.) (1881-1939). Born in Byerstown,
Pennsylvania. Grew up at Palmyra, Missouri. Taught for eleven
years. Married Josephus Wenger Shank in 1910. Lived in Hastings,
Nebraska, and LaJunta, Colorado, prior to going to Argentina in
1917. Contributed to the church in Argentina through (1) prayer
ministry, (2) home visitation, (3) Sunday school work with girls in
Trenque Lauquen, and (4) cooperating with her husband in establishing a kindergarten and primary school in Trenque Lauquen.
Buried at Pehuajo Cemetery at the site of the first Mennonite congregation established in Argentina.[40]

Edna Litwiller Swartzentruber (1901-1976),   Esther Ebersole Lapp (1882-
        missionary to Argentina.   1917), buried in the Himalayas.

Shenk, Alta Barge (Mrs. Clyde) (1912-69). Daughter of Witmer and Elnora (Esbenshade) Barge. Moved from Illinois to Lancaster County, Pennsylvania, at age thirteen. Attended Eastern Mennonite College and Elizabethtown College. Spent 33 years in Tanganyika in a pioneering evangelistic ministry. With her husband opened three stations: in 1937 the Bumangi mission among the Zanaki people; in 1954 the Kisaka station among the Ngoreme; in 1968 Mennonite congregations in southwestern Kenya.[41] After her death her children said:

> As adults it was clear to us that Mother was on a journey.... We were astonished at the joyousness and contemporaneity of her faith. Although our parents had buried themselves in the backwoods of Africa, as it were, she was modern, understanding, sympathetic, and perceptive of the issues that we confronted in our university experiences, or in the city ghettos, or in modern suburban culture. ... She was walking with God in response to the call of Jesus Christ.[42]

Smoker, Dorothy Waterhouse (Mrs. George) (1916-   ). Grew up in Japan, the daughter of Congregational missionaries. Served in Tanzania, 1941-70. Now lives in Pasadena, California.

Stalter, Anna (1874-1933). Daughter of C. N. and Mary (Stemen) Stalter. Born near Lima, Ohio. In India for 22 years. In a report to the Chhattisgarh Missionary Association in 1907, she noted that there were 1¾ million women and girls in Chhattisgarh, of whom only two thousand could read and write. She urged that the teaching of women in *purdah* (in seclusion) include such skills as writing and sewing. She devoted much of her time to working among the girls in the orphanage.[43]

Stauffer, Elizabeth (Mrs. Elam) (1900-47). Served in Tanganyika, 1934-47. Buried on Katuru Hill.

Swartzentruber, Edna Litwiller (Mrs. Amos) (1901-   ). From western Ontario. Served in Argentina for 44 years. "It is said that Amos and Edna were harvesting hay one day. Amos pitching and Edna on the wagon loading it, when they discussed the matter and decided to offer themselves for missionary service."[44]

Troyer, Kathryn Sommers (Mrs. George) (1893-1973). Born in Miami County, Indiana, the daughter of Daniel and Elizabeth (Zook) Sommers. Served in India for thirteen years and in Puerto Rico as assistant to her doctor husband.

CHAPTER 9

In Home Missions, Service
Institutions, Publishing

Women served in missions at home as well as abroad. This chapter will tell the story of one city missionary, Melinda Ebersole, and one rural missionary, Clara Brubaker Shank. It will mention the work of women in children's homes and the Mennonite Publishing House.

The cities to which Mennonite women went from their rural communities in the 1890s and the early twentieth century often confronted them with a culture quite as foreign as an overseas culture. The first such venture, in Chicago in 1893, later developed into the Mennonite Home Mission, a training school for an entire generation of Mennonite leaders.

Melinda Ebersole (1860-1933)[1]

In 1894, Melinda Ebersole went to Chicago from Sterling, Illinois, intending to take nurse's training in order to help her cousin Dr. S. D. Ebersole at his office on Twenty-Second Street near State Street.[2] She began working with the mission and became the first "permanent" worker, remaining for the next twenty years. When the mission was officially closed because of lack of support, "Sister Melinda" did practical nursing to earn

147

money to keep the work going.[3] In his 1931 history of the Mennonites of Illinois, Harry F. Weber lists her among the ministers.[4]

Born in Lancaster County, Pennsylvania, to David D. and Anna (Martin) Ebersole, Melinda and her family became part of the "westward movement," trekking to Whiteside County, Illinois, in 1889. She was baptized by Bishop E. M. Hartman in 1890, three years before going to Chicago. The work of "three sisters" is often mentioned in the story of the early years of the Chicago mission. In addition to Melinda, they were Lina Zook (Ressler) [see chapter 8] and Mary Denlinger (see exhibit 8, p.163) from Lancaster, Pennsylvania, who continued at the Chicago mission until 1899 and then worked in the Philadelphia mission until 1924. These women did visitation work, helped with cottage prayer meetings, taught Sunday school classes, and worked in the medical dispensary.

One day Melinda accompanied Dr. W. B. Page on a call to a sick mother. The family lived on the second floor, above a saloon. No mention is made of where Melinda was standing when a dramatic incident occurred, but it is reported that she was present.

> While Dr. Page was sitting at the bedside of his patient, the saloon below was the scene of a drunken brawl, which became louder and rougher until finally a shot came up through the floor and passed right between the doctor's knees. Had he been leaning forward, he would have received the full brunt of the shot; as it was, it went through the ceiling.[5]

Many years later Bishop A. C. Good looked back on his term of service in Chicago and remembered how Melinda Ebersole had encouraged him when he delivered his first sermon.[6] The regular speaker did not show up for a Wednesday evening prayer meeting, and young A. C. substituted by doing an impromptu exposition of a text of Scripture. Afterward Melinda, whom he called "the mother of the mission," said to him, "It was a good speech." He cherished the memory of her words over half a century later.

In July 1914, Melinda Ebersole returned to Sterling, Illinois, to care for her aged mother. She remained active in the Science Ridge Church to the end of her life. Her *Gospel Herald* obituary speaks of her "quiet, unassuming life, and her ever-readiness to be of service to those about her."[7]

Other Chicago Workers

During the first years at Chicago no mission board existed to direct the work. An Evangelizing Committee shared the responsibility for finding workers. In 1896 the Mennonite Evangelizing and Benevolent Board (later Mennonite Board of Missions and Charities) was established and directed the Chicago mission.

Many women served in this mission during the next years, many for short periods of time. Elizabeth Hershberger from Springs, Pennsylvania, arrived in 1893 and became the wife of the aforementioned Dr. Ebersole. Those serving extended periods of time, in addition to Melinda Ebersole, were Anna Yordy (1885-1975), Eureka, Illinois (as a chiropractor she treated approximately a hundred patients a year as part of the mission work);[8] Amanda Eby (Mrs. A. Hershey) Leaman (1876-1938), Columbus Grove, Ohio, for 22 years, from 1898 to 1920; Emma Oyer (1886-1951), for 39 years, 1907-46. Born near Metamora, Illinois, the daughter of John P. and Mary (Smith) Oyer, Emma is known for her book, *What God Hath Wrought: In a Half Century*

Emma Oyer (1886-1951), worker at Chicago Home Mission.

at the Mennonite Home Mission (Elkhart, Ind.: Mennonite Board of Missions and Charities, 1949).

Lancaster, Philadelphia, Reading, Fort Wayne, Kansas City, Toronto

In 1896 a mission opened on North Street in Lancaster, Pennsylvania. When "an aged brother, Singerly, died in 1905, Sister Elizabeth G. Musser and her daughter were stationed at the Mission. In 1907, Sister Elizabeth Myers joined them." Alta Mae Erb says, "These sisters did faithful work for many years."[9] Other workers there included Katie Buckwalter, Nellie Becker, Ella Shank, Amanda Forrey, Anna Winters, and Mabel Brubaker. Anna Lehman did visitation work in a separate mission started in the black community in 1933.

Among workers at the Philadelphia mission on North Howard Street, begun in 1899, were the aforementioned Mary Denlinger, Amanda Musselman (1869-1940), Barbara Herr, Emma Rudy (1890-   ) [see exhibit 8, p. 164], and Alma Ruth. Mary Mellinger (1865-1927) began a sewing school at Columbia, Pennsylvania, in 1920. Workers at Reading, Pennsylvania, included Mrs. J. B. Gehman, Sallye Rhodes (Mrs. Luke) Hurst, Mary and Mabel Landis, Lizzie Musser, and Myra Stoltzfus. Nellie Burkholder Weber and her husband, Newton, were at the Fort Wayne, Indiana, mission from 1934 to 1940.

Women workers at the Kansas City mission included Mina Brubaker (Mrs. C. D.) Esch, later a missionary to India; Lena Horst; Maggie Snyder (Mrs. Allan) Good; Ella Zook; Vera Hallman; Mrs. E. C. Bowman; Anna Diller (Mrs. William H.) Smith; Susie E. (Mrs. R. P.) Horst; Ruth Mininger (Mrs. M. T.) Brackbill (see exhibit 5, p. 120); Martha Buckwalter (Mrs. William S.) Guengerich (see chapter 5); Hettie Kulp (Mrs. J. D.) Mininger, known in her later years for her work of intercessory prayer; Esther Buckwalter Gingerich; Mary E. Stalter; Blanche Roppe; and Ella May Weaver (Mrs. Samuel) Miller, later a missionary to South America and speaker on the "Heart to Heart" radio program (see chapter 12).

Women workers at the Mennonite Gospel Mission in Toronto, Ontario, founded in 1907, included Olivia Good (Mrs. Samuel) Honderich (1880-1946, later of Filer, Idaho; Bernice Devitt (Mrs. Henry J.) Harder (see chapter 11); Lena (Mrs. Irvin) Weber; and Elizabeth Brown (Mrs. S. M.) Kanagy. Elizabeth Kanagy later helped girls employed as domestics in Preston homes to begin the Fidelia Club.[10]

City Mission Work: What Was It Like?

For 22 years the writer Christmas Carol Kauffman (1901-69) and her husband, Nelson, worked at the Hannibal, Missouri, mission. For December 1935, Mrs. Kauffman kept a diary of "charity work" done at their mission, perhaps the best extant account of the type of work these institutions carried on. Beginning with December 15, the diary records:

Dec. 15. Gave one dozen eggs, five lbs. sugar, and one dozen cookies to poor family.

Dec. 16. Gave out one covering[11] and fed two tramps.

Dec. 17. Called out in the night to pray for sick child. Gave medicine.

Dec. 18. Gave one covering. Bro. Kauffman sat up with sick boy until morning.

Dec. 19. Called out to pray for sick child. Gave three tea towels and dress to member.

Dec. 20. Gave $1.25 worth of coal to member with very sick child. Gave bread to poor family.

Dec. 21. Called to the hospital to pray for little girl badly burned. Gave out twenty-five Gospels of John.

Dec. 22. Gave wood to poor family. Fed three people. Bro. Kauffman preached funeral of little girl and furnished his car. Handed out seventy-five sacks candy to Sunday school pupils.

Dec. 23. Drove twenty-two miles to give bedding to poor member quarantined with diphtheria. Gave a brother two suits underwear. Mailed box of food and clothing to a family, members who moved to New Cambria, Mo.

Dec. 24. Next door neighbor dies. Bro. Kauffman calls. Handed out two bushels apples, eight yards outing, thirty-five mottoes, seven Bibles, twelve pictures, ten pencils, fourteen purses, sixteen handkerchiefs, three coverings, three pair shoes, twelve girls' dresses, skirts, and underwear, seventeen ladies' aprons, seventeen tea towels, seventeen hot pads, seventeen doilies, five boys' shirts, fifteen baby suits, eight dolls, twelve toy elephants, fifteen boxes candy, three ladies' dresses, one coat, six pair boys' pants.

Dec. 25. Gave one dozen eggs for sick.

Dec. 26. Called out in the night to take sick woman to the hospital.

Dec. 28. Called out in the night to pray for child with spasms.

Dec. 29. Child dies. Bro. Kauffman loaned his car to the family. Fed nine poor. Gave three coverings. Gave comforter.

Dec. 30. Gave out fifteen Gospels of John. Held prayer at neighbors.

Dec. 31. Loaned out twelve books to members. Bro. Kauffman preached funeral of little boy, and furnished car. Served a midnight lunch to all members of the mission.[12]

This mission diary conveys a vivid picture of what city mission work was like in the 30s. It also reveals a woman sensitively aware of the life about her. Mrs. Kauffman's parents, Abraham R. and Selena Bell (Wade) Miller, named her Christmas Carol because she was born on Christmas day. She utilized her mission experiences to write books, which were widely read, particularly by Mennonite women. *Contemporary American Authors* and *Index to Literary Biography* both list Christmas Carol Kauffman. Some of her books were translated into German, Norwegian, Finnish, and French. Her books include *Lucy Winchester* (1945), *Light from Heaven* (1948), *Dannie of Cedar Cliffs* (1950), *Not Regina* (1954), *Life with Life* (1952), *Hidden Rainbow* (1957), and *For One Moment* (1960).

Much remains to be written about the women who worked in Mennonite missions during the first half of the twentieth century. Unselfish and self-effacing, they remain for the most part unsung heroines. Anna Yordy's statement is characteristic of their spirit:

> There is not one moment of regret in the long years spent in His service. The only regret is that not more has been accomplished for Him.[13]

A Rural Missionary: Clara Brubaker Shank (1869-1958)[14]

Because of the thorough research of a young scholar, extensive material about the life of at least one rural mission worker is available. Beginning in 1886, approximately eighty articles written by Clara Brubaker appeared in the *Herald of Truth* and later in the *Gospel Herald*. They carried such titles as "Bearing One Another's Burdens" (Aug. 18, 1886, p. 245), "The Love of God" (Oct. 15, 1886, p. 368), "Peacemakers" (Dec. 15, 1888, p. 373), "Looking to God for Strength in His Service" (Feb. 1, 1889, p. 37), "Boldness for Christ" (Mar. 15, 1894, p. 93), "Paul as a Teacher" (Nov. 1, 1899, p. 330), "A Strong Will and How to Use It" (Oct. 4, 1906, p. 373), "Our Attitude Toward the Aged" (Dec. 23, 1920, p. 766).

Whether Clara was born in Snyder County, Pennsylvania, or Shelby County, Missouri, is not clear. But her parents, John Lauver and Sarah Margaret (Horn) Brubaker, were charter members of the Mt. Pisgah congregation in Shelby County, Missouri, formed by at least 1868. At the earliest possible age, sixteen, Clara became a schoolteacher, her vocation for the next 39 years.

Clara was strongly influenced by J. S. Coffman's preaching. However, Priscilla Stuckey Kauffman points out that while her "writings and ministry in Missouri represented a revivalistic style, [they] did not lose sight of the solidly Anabaptist emphases on simplicity and consistency in lifestyle, loving service to others, and a nonresistant witness." At the first meeting of the Missouri-Iowa Sunday School Conference in 1893, Clara Brubaker was one of twelve speakers. (Four other women also spoke.) During the school year of 1896-97, Clara studied at the Elkhart Institute, probably enrolled in the teachers' curriculum.

Subsequently she joined her family, who had moved to a settlement called Birch Tree in Shannon County, Missouri. Much hard work was required to clear this hilly countryside of rocks before the land could be cultivated.[15] Clara sank her energies into the development of the new community. She bought land and donated it for the building of a school. She then became the first teacher in that school.

During this period of her life she carried on an interesting correspondence with churchman J. S. Coffman. For example, in 1898 she asked him to have the *Herald of Truth* sent to a brother who could not afford it. She wrote, "We hardly ever get to pay anything into the funds, and I have [so] many times asked them to send the paper to poor persons free that I do not like to ask them again until I can contribute something. I thought you might have it sent to them."

At about this time Clara became acquainted with John R. Shank, who became her husband thirty years later, when she was 55 and he 47. In the writing of her middle years Clara increasingly emphasized the Mennonite doctrines of nonresistance and nonconformity. In 1912 she moved with her family to the Hesston, Kansas, area and taught for ten years in a country school near Canton.

Following her marriage in 1925 her articles in the *Herald* disappeared. Perhaps her writing energy went into helping her husband write adult Sunday school quarterlies. She did accompany him on most of his pastoral journeys in the Ozarks, walking many miles to visit in the homes of the hill people. Paul Erb says, "She understood well the ways of the hill people, and her coming was a blessing both to her bachelor husband and to the church."[16] Theron Schlabach does not include Clara in the following statement about J. R. Shank's contributions, although she was clearly half the team:

In many ways J. R. Shank was the Mennonite Church's foremost rural missionary, and a model one—helpful to, kind to, and apparently loved by people in the Ozark communities where he made his circuits, self-giving and tireless on behalf of the poor. Yet he seems to have made virtually no adjustments because of cultural background when it came to enforcing the distinctives, lest he sully the purity of the church. Very probably in part because of that (although in part also due to circumstances such as displacement of people when a dam was built) the ongoing, visible results of his work were somewhat meager.[17]

During the Christmas season of 1953, church people contributed enough money to buy a new car for the Shanks, for their old one had taken quite a beating. The Shanks celebrated their 33rd wedding anniversary before J. R. died in April 1958. Clara followed him in September of that year at the age of 89. Both are buried in the cemetery of the Mt. Zion Church of Versailles, Missouri.

Workers in Children's Homes

A children's home opened in West Liberty, Ohio, in 1896, one in Millersville, Pennsylvania, in 1911, and another in Kansas City, Kansas, in 1917. Wives of the directors had an important part in the children's-home work. Among them at West Liberty were Mrs. Abram Metzler; Catherine Blosser (Mrs. John) Hilty

Mary Eiman Swartzendruber (1904-1980),
"Mama" at age 18.

(1878-1946); Mrs. Frank B. Showalter; Martha Eby (Mrs. C. F.) Yake (1894-   ), later an active hostess at Scottdale, Pennsylvania; Mrs. L. L. Swartzendruber; Maggie (Mrs. Allan) Good; Mrs. Alpheus Allebach; and Mrs. John Landis. At West Liberty, Tena Hilty Burkhart (1868-1942) and Mayme King (1876-1951) served twelve and sixteen years respectively in the early years of the institution. Katie Kyle, "a tiny woman from Lancaster, Pennsylvania," cooked or cared for the babies from 1912 to 1930.[18]

An example of the influence of these women for good in the lives of young people is provided by a woman who grew up in the home at Kansas City. Mary Berkshire says of Mary Eiman (Mrs. A. Lloyd) Swartzendruber (1904-80), whom the orphaned children called Mama Swartzendruber:

> At an age when we most desperately needed a mother, she was there—calmly, quietly upholding her Christian principles, ready to listen, accepting us as worthwhile human beings and gently seeking us out individually when she saw a need to counsel.[19]

The Swartzendrubers met while both were teaching in the rural schools of Iowa. After their marriage in 1926 they settled down on a farm to a contented though sometimes difficult life through the Depression years. In 1937 they became superintendent and matron at the Mennonite Children's Home in Kansas City, where in addition to their own two young children, they took on a family of almost sixty youngsters, ages 2 to 16. After nine demanding years they moved back to Iowa and later to Virginia. In her later years Mary Swartzendruber wrote a collection of personal stories entitled *Mountains and Prairies and a Girl Named Mary* (Harrisonburg, Va.: privately published, 1978).

A Giver to Mission Causes

One does not find many philanthropists among Mennonite women, possibly because few of them have had independent access to wealth. Those who remained single were generally underpaid. Those who married deferred to their husbands concerning dispersal of funds. An exception is Louisa Kunkleman Wohlford

Snavely (1828-1907), a member of the Zion Mennonite Church near Bluffton, Ohio. She died in the home of her pastor, M. S. Steiner. At her death the *Bluffton News* reported on the front page that during the last fifteen years of her life she had given over $50,000.[20] She gave $10,000 to the sanatorium at LaJunta, Colorado; $5,000 for the erection of a girls' home at the orphanage at West Liberty, Ohio;[21] $3,000 to the Fort Wayne mission building; $1,000 each to the Kansas City mission, the Zion cemetery, the education of missionaries; and $28,000 to the Mennonite Board of Missions and Charities. Whether this money was entirely farm income is not clear. Louisa's first husband, Amos Wohlford, died in 1849; her second, Joseph Snavely, in 1853.

Some of the children in the community thought Louisa Snavely possessed exceptional knowledge. "She knew things other people didn't know!"[22] The *News* article, no doubt written by Steiner himself, says, "She is possibly the largest Mennonite contributor to the Lord's cause in America and possibly in the world.... Hers was not a widow's mite, but a widow's opportunity well improved."

The Scottdale Women

One of the most influential of all Mennonite institutions has been the Mennonite Publishing House located in Scottdale, Pennsylvania, since 1908. Women have played a vital role in this institution in two ways: (1) as workers and (2) as community hostesses to many people from the church at large who came to Scottdale on business. An 1886 photograph of the employees at John F. Funk's forerunner Mennonite Publishing Company at Elkhart, Indiana, shows 7 women out of the total 24.[23]

Who were some of the Scottdale women? Christine Funck (1870-1966)—born in Heilbronn, Germany, the daughter of Henry and Barbara Funck—married Mennonite historian John Horsch in 1893. (For the story of her daughter Elizabeth, see chapter 3.) Christine aided her husband, and after his death, read proof for the German periodical *Herold der Wahrheit*.[24] Lina Zook Ressler's story is told in chapter 8. Daisy Cutrell (Mrs.

Henry) Hernley (1889-1960) grew up in the Congregational Christian Church at Davenport, Nebraska, moved with her family to Springs, Pennsylvania, and went to Scottdale in 1908 as secretary to A. D. Martin. Estie Miller (Mrs. Edward) Yoder (1891-   ) arrived from Springs, Pennsylvania, the same year. Together Daisy and Estie served as bookstore clerks and filled the mail orders.[25] Following Daisy's marriage she became one of Scottdale's hostesses and mother of an influential "publishing house family." Estie met her professor husband as a high school student at Hesston. After her husband's death she read proof for many years. She was known for her extensive knowledge of the Bible. Other hostesses included Amelia Metzger (Mrs. Aaron) Loucks (1861-1931), also known for her high-spirited temperament; Cora Miller (Mrs. C. B.) Shoemaker (1886-1975); Alta Maust (Mrs. A. J.) Metzler (1904-   ), especially appreciated for her counseling of young women workers; and Martha Eby (Mrs. C. F.) Yake (1894-   ).

One is curious about the wife of so influential a man as Daniel Kauffman. Daughter Alice K. Gingerich says little about her mother, Mary C. Shank Kauffman (1879-1968) in the biography of her father. Yet she dedicates the book to her mother and acknowledges her mother's assistance in the writing of the book.[26] "Aunt Mollie" was fourteen years younger than her husband. Born in Morgan County, Missouri, the daughter of Lewis Henry and Mary (Wenger) Shank, Mary was a pupil in the Prairie Valley school when Daniel Kauffman taught there. Since her father respected the young minister so highly, she consulted him concerning whether she should volunteer for service at the Chicago Home Mission. How he questioned her! Greatly embarrassed, she wondered what he would think of so unstable a person as herself. Indeed, he thought a great deal of her, and they were married in 1902. Mary must have been something of an artist, for people at Scottdale remember the lovely patterns which she created and stenciled on the walls of her home, as well as a Psalm 91 quilt which she created. Like so many wives of church leaders she had the responsibility for the children while her husband traveled out into the churches. She also practiced hospitality. "One winter the Barclays, both aged and bedfast, with no near relatives, found a haven at the Kauffman home."[27]

In the days before motels the Scottdale women were expected on short notice to entertain visitors in their homes, either overnight or for meals. Mrs. Yake once recalled that in the Depression years she sometimes stood in her pantry and asked God to help her plan a menu from the food she had, enough to feed her family of six children plus the visitors who had come. A gracious hostess, she also kept well-informed concerning affairs of the church. At this writing she lives at Landis Homes in Lititz, Pennsylvania.

Louisa Wisseman (Mrs. Michael K.) Smoker (1880-1943) became a widow in 1919, when her 43-year-old printer husband died of cancer.[28] Left alone, she brought up three children. She acquired a machine to grind peanuts and sold peanut butter to support her family. When her son George went to Africa as a mis-

Martha Eby Yake (1894-   ), as a bride, with "C.F." in 1918.

sionary in the 1940s, he sent the peanut-grinding machine and other baggage on ahead. Because it was wartime, the cargo ship was torpedoed, and the peanut-grinder—symbol of a widow's dependence on God and her own ingenuity—sank to the bottom of the ocean. Her daughter Naomi served capably as secretary to the publishing house manager, A. J. Metzler, for many years and did mission work in Africa.

Martha Mumaw, an exceptionally accurate and speedy Linotype operator, worked from 1918 to 1946 and again in 1953. Vivian Baer (1903-   ) worked in the book bindery, beginning in 1929. She recalls with gratitude that during the Depression years, when Scottdale was one of the hardest-hit cities in the entire United States and the publishing house also felt the pressure, Minnie and Anna Stull and several other local girls voluntarily worked one day less per week in order that Vivian could continue her job. Mary Schload—a capable businesswoman, now of Ephrata, Pennsylvania—worked as a bookkeeper for 32 years, beginning in 1920.

Beulah Loucks (1904-   ) retired in 1969 from 42 years of proofreading and copy editing. She graduated from Goshen College in 1927 with a BA in languages, including Latin and Greek. In the fall of 1927, Beulah began working alongside Daniel Kauffman, editor of the *Gospel Herald,* and continued on into the editorship of Paul Erb. That periodical under her meticulous work remained remarkably free of typographical errors.[29] Laura Showalter (Mrs. Dewey) Stahl (1903-   ) came from Conway, Kansas, to the publishing house in 1944 and did proofreading and copy editing for 24 years.[30] Laura became known for her practice of simple living. Over the years she lent money without interest, enabling people to buy homes for themselves. L. Virginia Kreider Weaver, a capable businesswoman and staff leader, managed the Weaver Bookstore (now Provident) in Lancaster, Pennsylvania, for the publishing house from 1948 to 1959.

Writers and Editors

Another group of women vital to the work of the publishing

house have been the writers, many of whom have not lived at Scottdale. Anna Loucks (1895-   ) wrote primary curriculum materials from 1925 to 1936. Ida Boyer (Mrs. Ernest J.) Bontrager (1907-   ), Canby, Oregon, wrote curriculum materials for juniors.

Katherine Royer (1910-   ), Orrville, Ohio, and Goshen, Indiana, produced nursery and primary materials. Mary Royer (see exhibit 5, p. 123) wrote primary Sunday school and Bible school materials. Paul Erb says of the work of the Royer sisters:

> They had high standards. They believed everything should be done just right. They taught the people here [at Scottdale] a lot.[31]

Marnetta Brilhart says:

> Many children have been taught their early values through the writings of Mary and Katherine Royer. They are very influential women in the total church.

Other writers of children's curriculum and periodical materials include Alta Mae Erb (see exhibit 5, p. 121), Betty Weber (Mrs. Nelson) Springer (1917-   ), Elizabeth A. Showalter (1907-   ), and Helen Wade (Mrs. Edwin) Alderfer (1919-   ). Elizabeth Showalter edited *Words of Cheer* and helped develop writers for the Mennonite Church. For the past twenty years she has directed Books Abroad, sending tons of books overseas.

The Youth's Christian Companion, begun in 1920 under the editorship of C. F. Yake, developed a whole generation of writers. Christmas Carol Kauffman has already been mentioned. Others include Cora M. Baer, Meadville, Pennsylvania; Priscilla Delp (1910-   ), Pennsylvania; Ruth King (Mrs. John) Duerksen; Clara Lehman (Mrs. Lowell) Hershberger (1919-52), Orrville, Ohio, and Scottdale; M. Lena Kreider, Palmyra, Missouri; Miriam Sieber (Mrs. Millard) Lind (1920-   ), Scottdale and Goshen, Indiana, author of poetry anthology entitled *Such Thoughts of Thee* (Scottdale, Pa.: Herald Press, 1952), and *No Crying He Makes* (Scottdale, Pa.: Herald Press, 1972); Cora E.

Miller (Mrs. Joseph) Stutzman, Harrisonburg, Virginia; Ursula Miller (Mrs. Enos) Miller (1882-1972), Protection, Kansas;[32] and Ida Plank (Mrs. Eli) Yoder (1897-1973), Walton, Kansas. One such writer is selected for presentation here.

Esther Eby Glass (1911-72)[33]

Esther—daughter of Amos F. and Elizabeth (Metz) Eby, and a native of Denbigh, Virginia—moved as a teenager with her family to Lancaster County. Already as a child she began to write, filling a fertilizer memo book when she was nine. She married Forrest Glass in 1934 and became the mother of two children. Despite her busy life as a farmer's wife, she wrote. Most Mennonite Publishing House periodicals carried her by-line. Sometimes she wrote on assignment, but more often out of a conviction that needed to be passed on, an urge to help and inspire her readers. C. F. Yake said of her:

> She could write fiction with a spiritual impact that made the reader unwittingly a better person. And she seemed never to spare the time and energy to create her very best. She possessed no academic degrees to give her prestige; the inspiring messages from her creative mind and understanding heart brought her appreciation from readers of all kinds.

Following her husband's sudden death in 1968, Esther continued such activities as teaching Sunday school, speaking at retreats or directing them, and working in the book department at Provident Bookstore in Lancaster. Earlier she had found time to help at the Mennonite Information Center, "where she was a beautiful interpretation for the tourists' unanswered questions." The author index of the *Mennonite Bibliography* lists 26 entries under her name.

Perhaps one day someone will study thoroughly how Mennonite women have served the Lord through church institutions, including homes for the elderly. Until then, this chapter has afforded at least a glimpse.

EXHIBIT 8

Additional Workers in Home Missions and Institutions

Bauman, Louida (1904-77). Taught Sunday school, did visitation and tract distribution for fifteen years at Toronto city mission. During the latter years of her life she was recognized as a deaconess at First Mennonite Church in Kitchener, Ontario.[34]

Brenneman, Alvina Engel (Mrs. Christian) (1884-1919). Daughter of Christian and Elizabeth Engel, Washington, Illinois. Worker at Youngstown, Ohio, mission, 1912-14, and Canton, Ohio, mission from 1914 until her death in the great flu epidemic, 1919.[35]

Byer, Anna Hiestand (Mrs. Charles) (1880-1971). Began mission work in Columbia, Pennsylvania. In 1917 moved with husband and children to Knoxville, Tennessee, where they began a mission. They started the first Mennonite congregation in Florida in Tampa in 1927, and an outpost there in 1930. "She walked two miles every Sunday morning gathering a flock of children as she went." Worked as a domestic or practical nurse during the week.[36]

Coffman, Nellie (1896-   ), Dayton, Virginia. Daughter of Joseph W. and Sarah Coffman. Appointed in 1926 by the Middle District of Virginia Conference as a field worker to West Virginia. "Miss Nellie," along with her niece Lora Heatwole, began Bible schools

Nellie Coffman (1896-   ), worker in the mountains of West Virginia with Lora Heatwole, (left) and Esther Mosemann, (right).

in the mountains of West Virginia and taught there in the 1920s
and 30s. "They visited in the mountain homes, walking miles on
the mountain trails, crossing streams on foot logs, and where there
were none, took off their shoes and waded through the streams.
They were often out three or four days, eating meals and spending
nights in the homes of the people who warmly welcomed them.
They brought encouragement and hope to the sick and elderly,
taught in the Sunday schools, and often planned and conducted
evening services." When Miss Nellie left the mission field in 1933
to care for her widowed mother, she became editor of *Missionary
Light*, a small paper giving mission news. [37]

Denlinger, Mary (1867-1958). Twin daughter of John B. and Elizabeth
(Shaub) Denlinger, Black Horse, Pennsylvania. Converted at
Mendon, Missouri, under the preaching of John S. Coffman.
Worked at the Chicago mission from 1894 to 1899 and at Norris
Square, Philadelphia, from 1899 to 1924. "On the last day of
Mary's life, even with failing eyesight, she was still sewing for the
Paradise Sewing Circle." [38]

Landis, Lizzie Moyer (Mrs. Jacob) (1882-   ). Made a significant
contribution as matron at Eastern Mennonite Home, a residence

Viola Wenger Lenhart (1890-1962), Pacific
Coast Worker.

for the elderly in Souderton, Pennsylvania, from 1927 to 1952. At this writing she has almost reached the century mark in age.[39]

Leaman, Amanda Eby (Mrs. A. H.) (1876-1938). Attended Normal School at Ada, Ohio (now Ohio Northern University). Taught in Richland Township, Allen County, for several years. Appointed missionary to Chicago Home Mission in 1890. There met and married A. H. Leaman in 1902. Served at Chicago Home Mission until 1920.

Musselman, Amanda (1869-1940). Started Norris Square mission in Philadelphia with Mary Denlinger and worked there for forty years.

Musser, Lizzie (1875-1950). Worker at Reading, Pennsylvania, mission, beginning in 1922.[40]

Musser, Lizzie (1903-78), Lancaster, Pennsylvania. "After forty years of service to others she wished she had given more."[41]

Oyer, Siddie King (Mrs. Noah) (1884-1963), West Liberty, Ohio, and Goshen, Indiana. Following her husband's death she worked as matron of a men's dormitory at Goshen College for many years at an annual salary of $750.

Rudy, Emma (1890-   ). Pioneer mission worker at Welsh Mountain Mission near Lancaster, Pennsylvania. Living at Landis Homes in Lititz, Pennsylvania.

Ruth, Alma (1900-   ), Bucks County, Pennsylvania. Pioneer mission worker at Welsh Mountain Mission near Lancaster, Pennsylvania. Now living at Landis Homes in Lititz, Pennsylvania.

Wenger Lenhart, Viola (1890-1962). Born at Canton, Kansas, the daughter of Samuel and Elizabeth Ann (Landes) Wenger. Taught pedagogy, English, and missions at the first winter Bible school held by the Pacific Coast Conference (1925-26). Taught at Hesston College in Kansas and Beulah College in Upland, California. Served for thirteen years at Portland, Oregon, mission and for many years with MCC. Began a children's home in her residence at Nampa, Idaho, sometimes caring for as many as nineteen children. Married at age 71. Died of leukemia slightly over a year later.[42]

CHAPTER 10

In Health-Care Ministries

Mennonite women have been physicians, healers, midwives, and nurses. This chapter will begin with the stories of two "horse-and-buggy doctors," who practiced medicine in Nebraska and Oregon in the 1800s and early 1900s respectively. Next will come accounts of several midwives and a practical nurse. Mennonites have operated schools of nursing at Newton, Kansas; Bloomington, Illinois; Goshen, Indiana; Hesston, Kansas; Freeman, South Dakota; and now at Bluffton, Ohio. But the story of Mennonite women in nursing within the scope of this study seems most inextricably bound to the story of the school of nursing at LaJunta, Colorado, in existence from 1914 to 1957. That story will be told briefly with special attention to the contributions of Lydia Heatwole, Malinda Liechty Erb, and Maude Swartzendruber. The chapter will close with the stories of two recent physicians.

Horse-and-Buggy Doctors
Sarah Gross Lapp (1837-1902)[1]

The state of Nebraska granted Sarah Lapp a medical practitioner's license in 1879. She practiced in the Roseland community for many years. She grew up in Bucks County, Pennsylvania, and studied obstetrics under Dr. Keller of Harleysville. In 1879 she and her husband, Samuel, a deacon in the Line Lexington congregation, moved to Nebraska. There they helped establish the Roseland Church at Ayr, organized in 1880.

When Sarah's son George was born prematurely, she made an incubator for him, without which he would likely not have survived. She used a dresser drawer kept warm with hot water in fruit jars. This same George, later a missionary to India, once told John E. Lapp that his mother had delivered over 1,200 babies, and that only a dozen or so had not survived.

Sarah Lapp bore seven sons and four daughters, five of whom reached adulthood. All four sons became ministers and, eventually, bishops. Her son Mahlon apparently inherited his mother's aptitude for medicine. On the way to India as a missionary he took a crash course in tropical medicine in London, enabling him to treat many Indians who were otherwise without medical services. He was the husband of "Auntie" Sarah, mentioned in exhibit 7 (p. 144).

Sarah Gross Lapp (1837-1902), horse-and-buggy doctor, with her husband Samuel. She delivered over 1,200 babies.

Delilah Yoder Troyer (1857-1934)

Sarah Lapp had a license and some formal training. Delilah Yoder Troyer had neither, but she did have a kind of apprenticeship under a Dr. Shoore, who recognized her ability. Concerned about her husband Amos's health, Delilah (later called Lyle) made a reconnaissance trip from Cass County, Missouri, to Oregon in the early 1890s. "Delighted with the fertility of the land and the mild weather, she went back to Missouri carrying proof of her 'Canaan'—potatoes, huge apples with no worms, and jars of canned fruit which Mennonite ladies in Oregon gave her."[2]

The Troyer family moved by train to Hubbard, Oregon, in the autumn of 1892. While Amos rode in a boxcar to take care of their animals, Lyle took care of the seven children in a passenger car. She had packed enough food for the entire trip. In the baggage were also a medicine chest, medicines, medical books, and a pair of forceps for extracting teeth.

During the next years Lyle Troyer grew herbs for medicinal purposes and bought drugs from a homeopathic drugstore in Portland. For children she soaked little white sugar pills in medicine to make it more palatable. She dispensed quinine in clear gelatin capsules and often used rue, sassafras, and wormword—the latter two especially as spring tonics. In the spring she required each of her own children to drink a small glassful of "bitter tea" every morning. Daughter Emma Kenagy, remembering the taste with a grimace, recalls, "We were glad spring wasn't all year." Lyle also made a highly regarded inflammation salve. "It worked." Although she did not do surgery or repair work, Lyle "doctored" until alcohol, one of her staples, became unavailable either because of World War I or prohibition.

Midwives

In the eighteenth, nineteenth, and early twentieth centuries, most Mennonite communities had midwives, who assisted at births in the honorable tradition of those noble Hebrew midwives Shiphrah and Puah (see Exodus 1). Mary Liechty (Mrs. Peter) Graber (1700s)—whose granddaughter Mary Graber (Mrs. Christian) Miller (1819-1907) managed a brickyard in Canton, Ohio, from the 1870s on—is said to have been the first woman granted permission by the medical society of Besancon, France, to use instruments in delivery. She was a self-trained midwife, whose ability was recognized among both nobility and commoners in the 1780s.[3]

Bessie Hailey of Stuarts Draft, Virginia, at age eighty reminisced about the three women who served her community in this way: Betty Treavy Brydge (1848-1937), Isabelle Henderson Brydge (1871-1961), and Osa Henderson (1871-1953).

> We had little contact with other churches, as transportation was walking or driving horse and buggy. We lived about ten miles from another Mennonite Church. There were about 17 families in a radius of two miles. . When children were born, these three women acted as mid-wives. They took care of the delivery, washing, dressing, feeding and looked after the mother for several days. In fact, the mother stayed in bed for ten days. The nearest doctor was twelve miles away and could only be reached when someone rode horseback to his office. He in turn, had to drive a horse and cart to see the patient. This changed somewhat about 1915 when my father had a telephone put in our home, and the neighbor folks used this to call a doctor. Medicine used was camphor, wormseed oil, calomel, soda, catnip tea, epsom salts, liniments, sassafras tea, etc. Mothers nursed their babies. These three women would see about giving the medicine to the children in the neighborhood. Also sat up at nights and made clothes for the needy children, as they had no time in the daytimes, as they were busy doing things for their own families.[4]

Most communities had women who performed such services. Someone should compile a list of who they were.

Mattie R. King (1877-1958)[5]

"Aunt Mattie"—daughter of Levi and Nancy (Yoder) King of West Liberty, Ohio, youngest of seven children—kept house for her father following her mother's death until his death in 1916, then spent the rest of her life in home nursing. By 1927 she had helped deliver more than 400 babies. She kept a careful record of each baby's name, the parents, and the birth date. Unfortunately, when her house burned to the ground in 1929, her records burned too.

People who engaged Mattie's services at the time of a birth often expected her to do all the housework and laundry as well as to care for the mother and baby. She was often expected to milk cows, and a niece reported that sometimes when another baby was due, people would have a room ready for Mattie to paper "in her spare time."

On one occasion when complications could have set in following a birth, Mattie made herself a bed on the floor to be near the mother in case of need. Although some of her "clients" did not pay promptly, if at all, she nevertheless decided to tithe. She reported that following that basic decision she always had money "for the Lord's work and to pay bills." Mattie King was highly regarded by many.

Pioneers at LaJunta Mennonite School of Nursing
Lydia Heatwole (1887-1932)

The school of nursing at LaJunta, Colorado, became quite influential in the training of Mennonite nurses, although many did attend other schools. A book entitled *The Lamp in the West* tells the story of this institution. Author Maude Swartzendruber says:

> . . . as Florence Nightingale is the founder of modern nursing, so Sister Lydia Heatwole is the founder of Mennonite nursing. Her life on this earth was but a brief 45 years. . . . It seems unbelievable that in her 14 short years of professional life she and her co-workers could have established so solid a foundation for Christian nursing.[6]

Lydia Heatwole was the youngest daughter of Reuben J. and Margaret (Kilmer) Heatwole. Chapter 2 tells how the rigors of pioneer life threatened the health of Lydia's mother. On the advice of their physician the family set out across the prairies in a covered wagon in September 1886, and drove to Elkhart, Indiana, whence they took a train to Rockingham County, Virginia, Reuben Heatwole's childhood home. There Lydia was born on March 2, 1887. After fifteen months the family retraced their route to Kansas.

At age fourteen Lydia publicly confessed Christ as her Savior and Lord and became a member of the West Liberty Mennonite Church near Windom, Kansas. As a young woman she worked at the Mennonite Old People's Home in Rittman, Ohio, and in a rescue home for unwed mothers in Kansas City.[7]

After completing the year of residence required of homesteaders in Colorado, near Brandon, she went to LaJunta and enrolled in the first class of student nurses, along with Emma Rohrer and Stella Sharp Lehman (see exhibit 9, p. 183). They spent eighteen months of their training affiliating in Denver. Lydia remained an additional six months to study tuberculosis nursing at the Phipps Sanitarium (now known as Fitzsimmons Army Hospital). Upon her return to LaJunta she became director of the nursing school, a post she held until 1932. During those years she worked carefully with the State Board of Nurse Examiners, setting high standards for nursing procedures in the succeeding years.

Lydia Heatwole (1887-1932), founder of
Mennonite nursing.

At that time the nurses and students lived in the hospital. Sleepy young trainees did not always share Miss Heatwole's enthusiasm, especially at 2:00 a.m. In her biography of the nursing school director, Lydia Oyer says:

> Due to crowded conditions it was frequently necessary for nurses to give up their beds for emergency cases during the night. On such occasions Sister Heatwole was usually first to vacate her room. One night she gave up her room for an obstetric patient, and bunked in the "scrub room." A second obstetric patient was admitted. Sister Heatwole again gave up her bed and finished the night elsewhere.

> If any of us ventured to express unfavorable opinions about doctors overcrowding the already filled rooms, she exclaimed, "Why girls! That is what we need. It's up to us to make room." Her joy seemed to be full because the hospital was growing, and each year we could graduate a few more nurses.[8]

Lydia Oyer remembered her teacher as a woman of prayer:

> She often resorted to a small supply closet just off the operating room.... On another floor some other closet or cubbyhole served just as well for her prayer room.... Visiting LaJunta one time [when the old hospital was being torn down], I accompanied several nurses on a tour of the deserted building, as workmen were busily employed with crowbars and other house-wrecking tools. Finding our way to the once busy operating room, [we found] the little closet!... With hushed tones one said, "Here Sister Heatwole was often found upon her knees."[9]

A reader of the Oyer biography can only marvel at the incredible schedule maintained by Heatwole. Malinda Liechty (Erb) said of her: "Sister Heatwole was not only director of nurses, but also supervisor of floors, of surgery, of obstetrics, and was on night call. She served as dietitian and as nursing arts and science instructor."[10] Did that inhumane schedule contribute to her premature death?

When Lydia Heatwole died in 1932, Correspondence Secretary Loma Kauffman wrote to her fellow alumnae:

> We all keenly feel our loss in the passing of Sister Heatwole. She took to her bed March 17 and suffered much throughout her illness. She felt that

her work was not finished and was much burdened for the spiritual welfare of the church and training school. However, she was resigned to the will of the Lord and peacefully fell asleep at 4:00 a.m., April 21.[11]

Malinda Liechty Erb (1887-____)[12]

Malinda Liechty, a graduate of the second class (1921), filled the position of acting superintendent of nurses during Lydia Heatwole's final illness and until the summer of 1933. She then returned to her home in Archbold, Ohio.

Malinda was the oldest of ten children, born at Leo, Indiana, to Christian S. and Mary (Witmer) Liechty. At age twenty she gave up a young man whom she loved, because of differences in faith. Following family moves to Davenport, North Dakota, and back to Archbold, Ohio, the oldest Liechty son, Noah, contracted tuberculosis. Malinda knew about the Mennonite Sanitarium at LaJunta, took her brother there for treatment, and herself began nursing. When Noah's illness worsened, he begged to go back to Ohio to see his family. Malinda took him home by train. She settled him in bed, and the family—parents and nine other children—gathered around. Deacon Jacob C. Frey led in Bible reading and prayer. Noah went to sleep and never awoke.

Malinda's niece Mary Liechty Smucker says of her:

> She studied to get her high school diploma to register in Ohio. She attended Moody Bible Institute. She worked at the hospital at Wauseon, Ohio, doing private duty nursing. She supported missions, helped her sister and husband and family, missionaries in rural Michigan. She taught S.S. and cared for the sick in the family and community and managed the housework and child care as well. Talk about the new wholistic health care! She practiced it, but they called it private duty nursing in the home.

Mrs. Smucker says further:

> Malinda Liechty (Erb) and Amanda Frey, my two unmarried aunts, were well established in their careers, respected and educated women before education became an issue in the Mennonite Church. . . . They were spared the insignificant social position of many unmarried women in their day. Malinda was a registered nurse, and Amanda was a public school teacher. As a child, I decided I'd become one of these, and thus I'd never need be concerned whether or not I married.

At age 75, Malinda married widower Allen Erb, longtime administrator of LaJunta Mennonite Hospital (1916-52). What a delightful couple they were! They were married for eleven years prior to his death. At this writing she is an alert nonagenarian, living in Schowalter Villa at Hesston, Kansas.

Maude Egli Swartzendruber (1905-____)[13]

In the story of Mennonite nursing education, the name of Maude Swartzendruber appears more often than any other. Born in Tazewell County, Illinois, to C. B. and Emma Egli, the fifth of thirteen children, she moved at age seven with her family to a farm in Manson, Iowa. In March 1927 she married John Swartzendruber, whose death in December 1928 changed the course of her life, for the next month she enrolled in the winter Bible term at Hesston College. She continued there, earning her high school diploma in the spring of 1931. She received her RN in 1934, following three years of work and study at LaJunta Mennonite School of Nursing. A scholarship enabled her to attend Colorado State College of Education at Greeley the following year. In 1937 she received a BS from Goshen College.

Back at LaJunta, Maude taught the nursing sciences for a year. Then from 1938 to 1943 she taught and supervised in the surgical nursing division of the hospital. In 1943 she was appointed director of the school and nursing service at the Mennonite hospital. After a summer of study in nursing administration, she assumed this position for the next thirteen years, resigning in the summer of 1956, when the nursing program at LaJunta was discontinued. She served a five-year term as a member of the Colorado State Board of Nursing (1948 to 1953).

After the LaJunta years Maude went to Bloomington, Illinois, where she spent the next six years as director of education at the Mennonite Hospital School of Nursing there. In the fall of 1963 she accepted the challenge of setting up a department of nursing in the new Huerfano Memorial Hospital at Walsenburg, Colorado (administered by the Mennonite mission board), a post she held until 1966. Next came a much deserved year of travel; it included attending the Mennonite World Conference in Amsterdam and a stint of voluntary service at the International Guest House in Washington, D.C. From 1967 to 1972, Maude served as the college nurse at Hesston College. In 1972 she retired to an apartment at Schowalter Villa in Hesston, Kansas, where she edits the LaJunta *Alumnae News,* writes, travels, and visits.

At least 89 alumnae of LaJunta Mennonite School of Nursing have served one or more terms under a mission board, MCC, CPS, or voluntary service.[14] The mottoes which various classes chose reveal something of the philosophy of these women: "For God and Humanity," "Service Above Self," "Serving Christ Through Serving Others," "As unto Him."

This chapter opened with the stories of two "horse-and-buggy doctors." It will close with the stories of two more recent physicians, Florence Cooprider Friesen and Esther Smucker Hodel. Dr. Friesen's story has been told in *Full Circle* by Lois Barrett.[15] It is retold here because Mrs. Friesen's daughter Grace Slatter supplied WMSC with additional details of her mother's life.

M.D.: Florence Cooprider Friesen (1887-_____)

Florence—daughter of John Albert and Henrietta (Brunk) Cooprider, of rural McPherson, Kansas—had much experience with illness as a child. Her three brothers died in infancy. When she and her three sisters were quite young, the family was quarantined for diphtheria. A small room was built near the house for those who needed to be isolated. When the quarantine was lifted, the family permitted Florence to go to a cousin's house to visit. A neighbor girl lay sick on the couch all that day with scarlet fever. Florence succumbed, and once again the Coopriders were quarantined. Later, as an eighth-grader, she contracted tuberculosis but recovered.

As a girl, Florence heard missionary-on-furlough J. A. Ressler speak on the effect of famine in India. In 1906 she and her sister Stella (who became the first Mrs. Allen Erb) attended Goshen College Academy. There they heard Mary Burkhard—whose husband, Jacob, had died in India, leaving her with three children. Mrs. Burkhard emphasized the need for medical work among the women of India; she said that Indian men would often prefer to have their wives die rather than see a male doctor. Hearing this, Florence remembered a youthful promise to God to serve him wherever he wished. Later the college pastor, probably I. W. Royer, asked whether she would consider studying medicine to go to India as a doctor. Florence was so shy that the thought overwhelmed her. But she cherished verses like 2 Corinthians 12:9—"My grace is sufficient for thee: for my strength is made perfect in weakness"—and Philippians 4:13—"I can do all things through Christ which strengtheneth me."

Florence told her parents about her call to India. They were sympathetic, but her mother said, "I don't see how you can do it. You are so chickenhearted you can't even kill a chicken." Florence asked to be allowed to prove herself next time her mother needed a chicken. Next time her mother needed *three* chickens. Florence successfully passed the test but killed no more chickens in her entire lifetime.

Another time, a basketball player was injured in the college gym during a game. Florence thought, "If I were a doctor, I would have to aid this injured player." The thought so overwhelmed her that she fainted and had to be carried out of the gym. This experience greatly discouraged her. But Professor Kurtz told her, "If you had studied medicine, you would know just what to do and would not need to faint."

Florence entered Missionary Medical College at Battle Creek, Michigan, following college graduation and roomed with a Church of the Brethren woman, Miss (Dr.) Nickey, who became her longtime friend. Later this school merged with the University of Illinois College of Medicine, one of the best in the country. Florence graduated in 1914, one of 6 women in the class, along with 104 men. She felt that "the men were all real gentlemen and did not seem to resent having women in the class." She interned at Women's Hospital in Philadelphia, where she appreciated the hospitality of the Joseph Bechtel family.

Florence Cooprider (Friesen) (1887-   ), medical missionary to India.

In 1916, Florence went to India under the Mennonite mission board and became the only doctor in Dhamtari.

> For the next five years she was busy—treating leprosy, helping women with difficult deliveries, treating hookworm, helping children survive malaria during the first year of life, adjusting to the lizards that crawled over every wall eating bugs, avoiding scorpions on the bedroom floor at night, pushing cars through swollen streams during rainy season, and treating sick missionaries.[16]

In 1922, on her first furlough, Florence married P. A. Friesen, whose first wife, Lena, had died in India. The couple returned to Sankra, where he had been working. Here Florence set up the first of many roadside clinics.

> More people began coming—sometimes 200 people a day—and soon Florence was going to six villages for clinics. She had a car outfitted with a medicine cabinet on the outside so that less packing and unpacking had to be done at each clinic. About two-thirds of the patients were lepers.[17]

How did people in India respond? Elsie D. Kaufman reported in the December 1, 1925, issue of the *Monthly Letter* of the Mennonite Woman's Missionary Society: " 'Ah,' said a Hindu woman, 'your God must be a very good god, to send a doctor to women. None of our gods ever sends us a doctor.' "

While Florence treated patients, her evangelist husband preached and taught. Florence reared two children of her own and four stepchildren. In 1941 the Friesens retired from work in India. From 1945 until 1953 they lived in Greensburg, Kansas, where Florence practiced medicine and her husband served as pastor of a church. Because Greensburg was thirty miles from the nearest hospital, Florence delivered babies in her basement and kept mothers and babies there until they were ready to go home.

> Throughout her medical career Florence had the support of her parents and her husband. It was P. A. who insisted that she start medical practice in Greensburg, and he helped take care of those babies when they cried at night.[18]

At the time of this writing she lives in Schowalter Villa in Hesston, Kansas.

M.D.: Esther Smucker Hodel (1902-____)[19]

Esther Hodel also felt called to be a medical missionary to the women of India but was diverted to service in the homeland because of a health problem. Born near Tiskilwa, Illinois, she was valedictorian at Tiskilwa High School in 1920, received an AB degree from Goshen College in 1925, and an MD from Women's Medical College at Philadelphia in 1931.

Dr. Hodel considers a particular childhood dream one of the outstanding experiences of her life. In the dream she was sleeping under the middle one of three oak trees actually located at the Willow Springs Church near Tiskilwa. She dreamed (a dream within a dream!) that Jesus came to her and walked and talked with her. "His voice sounded like music, heavenly music, and we talked about those very ferns and flowers and the murmuring brook. That early dream has really had an influence upon my life and my thinking and my feeling of nearness to God and to his Christ."[20]

As a junior in medical school Esther suddenly became ill with chills and high fever, was hospitalized, and had to remain flat on her back for five weeks. The X-rays showed a solid left lung with fluid surrounding it. The doctors diagnosed it as tubercular pneumonia and really did not expect her to live longer than six months. She tells the story in these words:

That night I did not sleep; I argued with God all night, but He never gave in; after all, wasn't I preparing to be a doctor among the women of India? So how could He let me be this ill? But by morning I finally was the one to give up, and I said, "Well, God, if it is your will that my work for you here on earth is finished and that I shall come home to You soon, I'll be very happy to come and be with You in glory." With that turning of myself and the future days and years into God's hands, He gave me peace. By daylight I could laugh with the sparrows who were chirping out on the roof of the hospital. . . . I went home, and still had temperature, but that summer was called to partake in a special study of heart and kidney with some of my teachers on Lake Champlain in upper New York State. That fall I was O.K. and returned to med school. They never would say my lung was healed until after my first pregnancy. . . . It left a big scar in my lung which still frightens X-ray people who do not know my history.

In 1934, Esther opened medical practice at Morton, Illinois, at the invitation of Dr. Bacon, her mentor through medical school and internship. The same year, she married John P. Hodel, Mennonite agricultural specialist from Germany. They had three children. Dr. Hodel practiced medicine in Morton for forty years and retired to Carlsbad, New Mexico, in 1974.

The Mennonite women whose stories have been told in this chapter are but a few of those who have exercised the gift of healing. Some of them had specialized education to prepare for their work. Others utilized a natural aptitude or practiced a Spirit-given gift. Their skillful, loving care has blessed many. The appendix which follows is but a partial listing.

EXHIBIT 9
A Partial Listing of Health-Care Workers

Buckingham Douglass, Maude. Graduated from LaJunta Mennonite School of Nursing in 1929. Theron Schlabach calls her "perhaps the Mennonite Church's most versatile and effective rural missioner of her time."[21]

In 1922 Maude Buckingham and her husband, Edward traveled to Colorado because he was ill with tuberculosis. They were so poor that they had to hitchhike, but the sanitarium in LaJunta took him in. The couple professed a faith in Christ, but he had not been baptized. He soon died. But before he did, he renewed his faith and received baptism; and after his death Maude Buckingham worked for a time at the sanitarium and joined the Mennonite fellowship. Wanting to return to Arkansas and serve there, she attended school at Hesston College and LaJunta, and became a nurse in 1929.

By 1930 she had returned to Arkansas, where she soon married John Douglass, who had a four-year-old daughter by a former marriage. Maude became a registered midwife and began work at Mountain Home, Culp, and other places in Arkansas. Paul Erb says:

The nearest doctor was at Batesville, forty miles away, which was utterly beyond reach for a poverty-stricken community. So to meet the needs, she was also a doctor, even a veterinarian. When her daughter Darlene was one month and one day old, she was out again on the mountain trails, calling on the sick who needed her. Her skills became a legend in the community.[22]

Maude also introduced scientific, advanced farming methods into the area. Her work "attracted Mennonite preachers and lay workers to her area, who helped establish Sunday schools, Bible schools, a mission farm, some small businesses, a twelve-grade Mennonite school, and some five Mennonite congregations, most notably Bethel Springs at Culp."[23]

Among the nurses who aided Maude Douglass were Ruth Cressman (Mrs. Clifford) Strubhar, a midwife as well as a nurse, Mary (Mrs. John) Detweiler, and Rhoda (Mrs. David S.) Wenger.

Cressman, Una (1905-_____). Registered nurse. Spent nineteen years in Argentina as a missionary. Worked in the clinic at Pehuajo and in the boys' orphanage at Bragado. With Selena Gamber Shank, set up a clinic for Indians in the Chaco in 1948. Was later joined by her sister Mabel (1914-_____), also a registered nurse. Mabel served for two years in England following World War II.

Deputy (Mrs. Jacob) Brubaker, Mary (1913-_____). Graduated from Rockingham Memorial Hospital School of Nursing, Harrisonburg, Virginia, in 1940. Received MS in nursing education from University of Pennsylvania in 1956. Taught at Rockingham Memorial for ten years. Aided in postwar reconstruction in Austria.

Devitt (Mrs. Henry) Harder, Bernice (1883-1945), Carstairs, Alberta. Born in Breslau, Ontario. Attended Toronto Bible College. Acquired her nurse's training at Youngstown, Ohio. Married Henry J. Harder from Missouri at her parents' home near Didsbury, Alberta, in 1922. The WMSC account of her work in the West Zion congregation in Carstairs says:

Always a leader and organizer, she brought new life to the outlook in our church.... Her presence was needed and felt on the local Hospital Board. At that time holding such positions was rather frowned upon by the church. But quietly and effectively she served and drew our Sewing Circle into sharing the work.[24]

(Many nurses, like Mrs. Harder, have in the past given up active nursing following marriage and thrown their creative energy into homemaking and work in local congregations.)

Gamber (Mrs. J. W.) Shank, Selena (1893-____). Director of LaJunta Mennonite School of Nursing, 1933-37. Served in Argentina from 1923 to 1950. Began a clinic for Indians in the Chaco. At this writing, lives at Schowalter Villa, Hesston, Kansas.

Gehman (Mrs. Harvey) Ruth, Emma (1881-1951). Operated a nursing home in Quakertown, Pennsylvania, prior to her marriage. At one time she had ten maternity cases in her home. The Quakertown Community Hospital is an outgrowth of her work. After her marriage she operated with her husband a home for the elderly at Bally, Pennsylvania.[25]

Godschalk, Sallie (1864-1949). Practical nurse from the Doylestown, Pennsylvania, congregation. Also a leader in the sewing circle. Beginning about 1920, annually gathered dried fruits, vegetables, and nuts for shipment to missionaries in India for their Christmas celebration. Enjoyed singing and led songs in church and Sunday school.[26]

Graber, Lena (1910-____). Took nurse's training at Bloomington, Illinois, 1932-35. Did postgraduate work in obstetrics in Philadelphia in 1937. Received BA in natural science from Goshen College in 1942. Served under Mennonite mission board in India and Nepal for 26 years. Pioneered nursing education in Nepal.

Miller, Nora (1898-1954). The first full-time instructor at LaJunta Mennonite School of Nursing. Director of education there from 1925 to 1950. At her death her co-worker Edna Amstutz wrote:

> In the School and Hospital where she served so selflessly these many years, her works stand as monuments on every hand. Then there are the many intangibles—skilled and tender service to her patients, the inspiration of high ideals and standards to her students, warmth and understanding to her friends, a tower of strength, wisdom, and encouragement to her co-workers—who but God alone can measure the harvest of this rich sowing?[27]

Mosemann, Orpah B. (1910-____). Associate professor of nursing emerita at Goshen College, now living in Harrisonburg, Virginia. Received diploma in nursing at Lancaster General Hospital in 1938, BS in nursing at Western Reserve University in 1950. Taught nursing at Goshen College from 1950 to 1971. First director of the school of nursing there.

Moyer, Bessie C. (1901-____). Graduated from nurse's training at Montgomery Hospital in Norristown, Pennsylvania, in 1933. CPS nurse at Camp Sidling Hill, 1941-42. Nursed at Eastern Mennonite Home, Souderton, Pennsylvania, 1943-56, and at Grand View Hospital, 1956-69. Entered Hatfield Mennonite Home in 1974.[28]

Oyer, Lydia (1884-____), Ashley, Michigan. A leader in the early years of Mennonite nursing education. Maude Swartzendruber says of her: "For a time Sister Oyer served as nurse, X-ray technician, and laboratory technician, as well as instructor of nurses."[29] Author of *Lydia Heatwole: Pioneer in Mennonite Nursing.*

Rohrer, Emma (1877-1972), Wadsworth, Ohio. One of three graduates in the first class at LaJunta, 1918. "She served her alma mater for approximately 15 years. She then returned to her home near Wadsworth, Ohio, where she served as a private duty nurse for many years."[30]

Schmiedendorf (Mrs. Simeon) Hurst, Edna (1913-   ), Preston, Ontario. Received nurse's training in Pennsylvania. Graduated from Eastern Mennonite College in 1939. Stationed with her husband at Nyabasi, Tanganyika, where they worked with the Kuria tribe. A linguist as well as a nurse. With her husband, helped put the Kuria language into writing. Translated the Gospel of John from Swahili into Kuria. Mother of five children. At this writing, lives at Fairview Nursing Home in Cambridge-Preston, Ontario.[31]

Sharp Lehman, Stella (1893-1953). Graduated in the first class at LaJunta, 1918. Minister's wife; mother of seven; widowed early; faithful to the Lord; entertained missionaries whenever possible.[32]

Shenk (Mrs. J. Norman) Kaufman, Lillie (1889-1971). Medical missionary to Tanganyika, 1935-39, and India, 1945-48. Born near Elida, Ohio, daughter of Abram J. and Malinda (Good) Shenk. Influenced as a girl by her missionary uncle, J. A. Ressler. In 1926 wrote a series of four articles for the *Youth's Christian Companion* entitled "Opportunities for Medical Missionaries." Received MD degree from Women's Medical College of Pennsylvania in 1930. Studied at the London School of Tropical Medicine and Hygiene in 1935. Married J. Norman Kaufman, minister, in 1941. Served as a physician and surgeon in East Peoria, Illinois, while her husband was pastor of the Pleasant Hill congregation.[33]

Suter, Margaret (1832-1922), Virginia. Skillful in nursing the sick; often assisted country doctors with serious accident cases before a hospital was located nearby. Would often walk several miles in the evening to a home where someone was seriously ill to nurse and comfort the person through the night.[34]

CHAPTER 11

WMSC and Its Forerunners

Thus far this study has focused on women in their roles as wives, mothers, "aunts," and in their ministries in the local congregation, in teaching and healing, and in missions both at home and abroad. Now the study turns to women in their own organization. Emerson's observation that history is biography, proves true in this case. Without Clara Eby Steiner would a churchwide organization have existed in the second decade of the twentieth century?

A reporter writing about Amelia Ingold (Mrs. Jacob B.) Heiser (expert quilt-maker of Fisher, Illinois) transposed some letters and came up with the initials WSMC—"Women Sewing for the Mennonite Church." Mennonite women have indeed done much sewing and quilting over the years for the outreach programs of the church, but the goal of the founders of the Mennonite women's organizations was not limited to sewing.

This chapter will attempt to list chronologically and describe briefly circles or societies (both names were used) organized in the first decade of the twentieth century. Exhibit 10 (pp. 209, 210) lists others. Some general characteristics of these societies will be noted. This chapter will tell the story of the "takeover," as the women called it, of the Mennonite Woman's Missionary Society

by the mission board in 1928. It will present a brief biography of
Clara Eby Steiner, for she more than any other woman had a
dream of a unified work among Mennonite women, and worked
tirelessly from 1911 to 1926 to make that dream a reality with the
help of her co-workers: Naomi Blosser, Mary Yoder Burkhard,
Mary Ann Nahrgang Cressman (see chapter 6), Mary Ann
Smucker Gerig, Stella Shoemaker Kreider, Amelia Bergey
Nahrgang, Crissie Yoder Shank (see chapter 9), Martha Whitmer
Steiner (see chapter 7), and Ruth A. Yoder. And finally, the
chapter will summarize the work done between 1930 and 1950.

Early Years

Many accounts of early women's groups mention hauling
sewing machines in horse-drawn buggies to the place of meeting.
The West Liberty Sewing Circle at Inman, Kansas, in 1909, had a
rule that required all members "to bring their own horse feed and
dinner." At Line Lexington in the Franconia area, men attended
the first meetings in order to conduct the devotions. Would it
have been too dangerous to allow women themselves to do this?
Once the Clinton Frame women in northern Indiana could not
find a container large enough to hold the vegetable soup they
were making and ended up using a well-scrubbed bathtub. Orpha
Mishler Brenneman (1887-   ) of Albany, Oregon, was nom-
inated to be the first president of the sewing circle there because
she was the only woman who drove a car.

The women often faced opposition. Sometime before 1905,
Mary Yoder and Mary Speicher of the Oak Grove congregation in
Ohio had to make a public confession in church for the "sin" of
trying to start a sewing circle. At Clinton Amish-Mennonite
Church in northern Indiana, women replied to a critic that they
had consulted the bishop. The critic replied, "The bishop is not
the church!" He was right, of course.

Many early groups crossed denominational lines. On the
Eastern Shore of Maryland they met with Church of the Brethren
women; in Hawkesville, Ontario, with Presbyterians. Women in
the Clinton Church mentioned above were greatly influenced by

Lutheran sisters, and women at Prairie Street Church in Elkhart by United Brethren sisters. Perhaps it is time to reclaim this ecumenical heritage.

Early Financial Contributions

In 1894 "sisters of the A.M. Church, Holden, Mo." contributed $1.20 to the work of the Chicago Home Mission.[1] In 1897 women from Leaman Place, Pennsylvania, gave $2.00 for the same purpose. By 1898 women were contributing to the Mennonite Orphans' Home near Orrville, Ohio. "Sisters in Ontario" gave cash; "sisters in Indiana," clothing and two comforters; women in Mahoning County, Ohio, "a quantity of dress goods, three handkerchiefs, one-half bushel dried apples, one gallon maple syrup, shoes and boys' clothing." And the women of Mechanicsburg, Pennsylvania; Ontario; Wayne County, Ohio; and South English, Iowa, contributed various monetary donations. In 1898 also, the Sisters' Aid Society of McPherson, Kansas, sent $15.00 "to support one or more orphans." Across the church, women empathized deeply regarding the plight of orphans. This concern continues to this day, as Mennonite women seek ways to aid refugee children.

Early Sewing Circles

The distinction of being the first organized women's group in the Mennonite Church probably goes to the Paradise congregation in Lancaster County, Pennsylvania. As early as 1895, Annie E. (Mrs. Amos A.) Ressler (1867-1945) directed the work of ten women who made garments in their homes. The clothing was then sent to a small group of women in Scottdale, Pennsylvania, who distributed the items to hospitals and the poor. Later that year Mary A. (Mrs. Ezra H.) Mellinger (1865-1927) invited a number of the women in the Paradise congregation to her home to sew for poor families and the hospitals of their own Lancaster area. This led to the organization on September 2, 1897, of the Paradise Sewing Circle. Mary Mellinger was its first president and Mrs. Harry F. Metzler the first secretary.

By September 1911 a sufficient number of sewing circles existed in this conference to form the Associated Sewing Circles of the Lancaster Conference District. Mary Mellinger was active in sewing circle work, as well as in the Sunday school, for many years.[2] Her obituary says, "Sister Mellinger gave her very life to this work."[3] An interesting story about her death has been handed down. A few hours before passing away she suddenly exclaimed, "Oh, it is so beautiful!"

The earliest minutes of a Mennonite sewing circle submitted to the WMSC collection are from the Science Ridge Church at Sterling, Illinois:

> November 14, 1900
> The sisters met at the J. L. Reisner home to organize a sisters' sewing circle. 17 sisters were present. Francis Rutt presided.
>
> Two comforts were tied and some carpet rags sewed. The president read Col. 3 and led in prayer. Officers elected were
> Mrs. Hettie Burkhart, Pres.
> Mrs. Anna Rutt, assistant
> Anna L. Andrews, Sec.
>
> The meeting closed by singing "Blest Be the Tie." Collection was 25 cents.[4]

J. C. Wenger gives the following account of the first sewing circle organized in the Indiana-Michigan Conference at Prairie Street Church in Elkhart in 1900:

> Mary Brubaker, a member of the United Brethren Church, spoke to Mrs. McClintic and a few other women about starting a sewing circle in the Prairie Street congregation, and they decided to make the attempt. To their great surprise sixty women attended. They did not have enough chairs; so some of the women had to stand. The meeting was held in the Albert Brubaker home, on the corner of Prairie Street and Park. After deciding to organize, the women elected their first officers: Mary Brubaker (hostess to the meeting), president; Mrs. William Kauffman, secretary-treasurer. They met one afternoon each month. The materials needed were donated by different persons who felt led to do so. In the second year Mrs. Rutt was elected president, and a cutting committee was appointed: Anna Brubaker, Mrs. McClintic, and Mary Brubaker. Mrs. Daniel Weldy was inspector. [What did the inspector inspect?] Among

the women who were members in the early years were Mrs. Herman Yoder, Grandma Kulp, Mrs. Kohl, Phoebe (Funk) Kolb, Martha Funk, Mrs. Dr. Mumaw, Mrs. John Lehman, Mrs. John Martin, Mrs. Jacob Mast, Grandma Coffman, Jennie Betzner, Mrs. Rutt, and many others. Most of the sewing done in the early years was for the Chicago Mission. The meetings were held in different homes and sewing machines brought in for the day.[5]

The Bethel Sewing Circle near Garden City, Missouri, was organized in 1901 with Anna Plank (Mrs. Norman) Shepp as its first president. Another early organizing meeting of which we have a record comes from Alpha, Minnesota:

The first meeting was held at Ida Snyder's on April 10, 1902, with two present and offering 20 cents. Among some of the things sent to the Home Mission at Chicago during the years that followed were buckwheat flour and honey, a product raised here at that time. Also things were

Amelia Heiser (1897-   ), Illinois, quilt-maker.

shipped to the Orphans' Home and Old People's Home in Ohio and to
the Kansas City Mission. One of the barrels sent to Chicago contained a
large number of homemade garments, five comforters, a large bundle of
calico and muslin, a cured pork shoulder and homemade sausage to fill
the barrel given by Sam Shearer. Freight charges were 54 cents from
Alpha to Chicago.[6]

Lydia (Mrs. Abram) Huber organized the Lititz Sewing
Circle in Lancaster County, Pennsylvania, in 1905 and served as
its only officer from 1905 to 1913. In 1914, Lydia Mosemann
(Mrs. Benjamin) Leaman (c. 1871-1949) became superintendent,
a position she held until 1949, when she was succeeded by Susan
(Mrs. Henry) Shenk. In 1918, Maud Kaylor (Mrs. Elmer) Eby became secretary-treasurer of the organization and served until
1960—a term of 42 years.[7] Is this a record for length of term in office?

The Oak Grove Sewing Circle at Smithville, Ohio, also
began in 1905, with Lydia Smiley (Mrs. C. Z.) Yoder (1846-1922)
as the first leader. Anna V. Yoder—a member of the congregation
and a worker in the Canton, Ohio, mission—was responsible for
the birth of the organization. She pleaded with the ministers of
the church to allow the establishment of a women's sewing circle
to sew for the poor of the Canton mission area. The ministers,
feeling there should not be a women's organization in the church,
were reluctant to give their permission but finally consented.[8]
Was Anna Yoder more persuasive than the two Mary's had been
earlier? (See p. 186) Was Lydia Yoder's selection as leader a diplomatic act which allowed her husband, the prominent C. Z. Yoder,
to prevent subversive activity by keeping a watchful eye on what
went on?

The South Union Sewing Circle of West Liberty, Ohio, had
its first meeting in January 1906 at the home of Mrs. A. Y.
Hartzler, with Nancy Ann Yoder Hartzler (1861-1949) and Ar-
menon Yoder (Mrs. D. S.) Yoder (1857-1938) as leaders. They sent
their sewing to Tennessee. At the second meeting they made garments for the children's home at West Liberty.

The *Gospel Witness* on August 9, 1906, reported from Ephrata, Pennsylvania:

The sisters met at the home of Mary Hess to organize a sewing circle for the benefit of Home and Foreign Missions, Aug. 7. The following officers were elected: President, Mary Hess; vice president, Anna Wolf; secretary, Lizzie Witmer; treasurer, Emma Oberlin. The name of the organization will be Mennonite Aid Society. Motto, "It is more blessed to give than to receive."[9]

Thanks to the late Erma Miller Erb, we have the words of Nora (Mrs. Samuel) Yoder (1877-1962) about the first meeting of the Sisters Mission Association of the Clinton Amish-Mennonite Church near Goshen, Indiana, on January 3, 1907:

In 1898 we were invited to a Lutheran ladies aid. We were very much impressed with what we saw and heard. They had Scripture reading and prayer and were a busy, social bunch.

At that time we had the Chicago Mission and the Fort Wayne Mission, and we thought, "Why don't we do something for our mission stations?" About that time we also had a study of missionaries instead of young people's meetings. We studied several books, among them David Livingstone's life and mission work and Isabel Thoburn. This gave us more of a mission spirit than we ever had before.

In January 1907 we called a meeting and organized our first Sisters Mission Association. We selected a president and a secretary-treasurer. [These officers were Nora herself as president, Amanda Kauffman, vice-president, and Lizzie Johns, secretary-treasurer. They appointed Nancy Pletcher and Mary Schrock as a standing committee to purchase "goods etc., for the Association."] Our first offering that day was $2.24. We had our secretary and her husband with the help of the bishop write up the constitution.

We were busy farmers' wives, but we took time out to meet once a month. The sewing met in homes. The sister in whose home we met furnished the sewing machine, or one or two of us would load up our sewing machines in our buggies.[10]

In 1908 at least five additional circles organized. The Weavers Sewing Circle of the Weavers Mennonite Church, Harrisonburg, Virginia, had its first meeting on March 21, 1908, when seventeen women gathered at the home of Susanna Hartman (Mrs. Samuel) Brunk (1843-1913). Among them was Laura Suter (Mrs. Daniel P.) Wenger (1873-1959), who became the first secretary and served until 1930. Her minutes have been preserved. Susanna Brunk had visited a sewing circle at Elkhart, Indiana, and was impressed by what they were doing. After several years she decided to express her convictions about the need for this kind of organization in her congregation.[11]

> Finally at church one Sunday she drew several sisters aside and stated her convictions. To her surprise she found others of the same opinion as she. They decided they should see the church leaders, as they didn't want to do anything which the church wouldn't approve. They talked with Bishop L. J. Heatwole. He thought it was a good idea and took the matter before the Church Council. Here they met with some opposition, but not enough to keep them from starting. Some of the men thought the women couldn't manage such a project and that it would be a regular place of gossip. These men rather made fun of the whole idea.

So the circle came into existence in March 1908, and in its early years work was done for the Chicago Gospel Mission; the Fort Wayne, Indiana, mission; the West Liberty, Ohio, orphans' home; West Virginia missionaries; local mountain missions; ministers' wives; and families whose homes were burned. To raise money for their work they served dinners at auction sales and sold magazine subscriptions, "but were requested by church officials not to do that." Later the Sunday school gave offerings to the sewing circle.

The first women's group to be organized in the Ontario Mennonite Conference was the Waterloo Charity Circle, formed in March 1908 at the home of Mariah (Mrs. Cleason) Shantz (1872-1964), with at least 35 members enrolled. After the opening of the Mennonite mission in Toronto in 1907, the Ontario churches had become aware of the needs of the poor in that city, especially after some of the Toronto children spent several weeks in Mennonite homes in the Waterloo area. Lena Weber—a member of the Waterloo Mennonite Church, who had worked in the Toronto mission—helped to acquaint her home congregation with with the needs in the city. As a result, a number of interested women of the church met in the home of Menno and Sarah Weber for their first sewing.

In time they decided to follow a more systematic plan in their work by organizing, which they did in March 1908 by electing as their president Ida (Mrs. Jacob S.) Snider (1868-1966), as vice-president Sarah (Mrs. Menno S.) Weber, as secretary-treasurer Lena Weber, and as associate treasurer Malinda Snider (Mrs. Norman) Stauffer (1876-1962). They agreed that each member was to pay a monthly fee of ten cents, that the time of meeting was to be the first Wednesday afternoon of each month, that the meetings be held in the homes of the members, and that their meetings should be opened by Scripture reading and prayer. Their first meeting after organization was held in April 1908 in the Weber home. Certain articles were donated at this meeting, but in addition the group "turned out 10 pr. boys pants, 2 pr. drawers, 4 undershirts, 2 underwaists, 3 fl. boys shirts." All of this was sent to the Toronto mission.

In July 1908 sisters of the Berlin Mennonite Church (now First Mennonite Church, Kitchener, Ontario) met to organize a sewing circle. They adopted the name of Sisters' Aid. The officers elected were Barbara Bowman (Mrs. David) Shuh (1857- ?), president; Sarah Weber, vice-president; Mary A. Cressman, secretary-treasurer, and Mary Snider (1863-1930), assistant.[12] A year later they reported that they had a membership of 54. With a fee of ten cents per member per month, they collected a total of $53.70 during their first year. The secretary wrote:

> Four quilts were made, besides the many garments that were purchased and made. The work is now carried on in a systematic way. We had a very busy year and we find that by our united efforts much more is accomplished. This fills a long felt want in our church, as from time to time there came calls for help, which are now supplied by the Sisters' Aid.
>
> At the expiration of the year we again reorganized; all the members present expressed themselves as being well satisfied with the work done, and desired to have it continue.

The first minutes book of the Mount Joy (Pennsylvania) Sewing Circle informs us that "a sewing circle was organized in Florin, Pa., by members of the Old Mennonite Church with the

purpose of doing work for missions. Met at the home of sister Catharine B. Nissley on September 9, 1908 at 1 o'clock." The first
president was Catharine B. (Mrs. Christian L.) Nissley, followed
by Mrs. Amos Bender.

Lydia H. Smith reported from the Waldo Mennonite
Church, Flanagan, Illinois, in December 1915:

> It may be of interest to some to hear about the sewing circle which was
> started seven years ago. They used to meet at the homes the middle of the
> month, but this last summer we have met in the church basement where
> we have seven sewing machines and a table. We meet the first Wednes-
> day of each month.

The first recorded meeting of the West Liberty Sewing
Circle, Inman, Kansas, was held on January 15, 1909, at the home
of Maggie Yoder, with nine women present. The officers were
president, Etta Cooprider; vice-president, Maggie Yoder;
secretary, Nora Miller; assistant secretary, Grace Cooprider; and
treasurer, Susie Brunk. Contrary to the general practice, the West
Liberty Sewing Circle met once a week.

The Freeport (Illinois) Mennonite Church organized its sewing circle on November 2, 1909, at the home of Mrs. Simon
Graybill, with thirteen women present at the first meeting. It was
named the Lancaster Sewing Circle because it was a community
organization in Lancaster Township and occasionally had members who were not Mennonites. The circle met on the first Thurs-
day afternoon of each month. Mrs. J. V. Fornter was the first
manager of the circle, serving until about 1935. In the first year
four of the sewings were for private families, but the rest were for
orphanages and the Chicago mission. During the year 145 garments were made, and the offerings amounted to $46.67.

A brief note from Bowmansville, Pennsylvania, on January
20, 1910, reported, "As the winter is cold much suffering is caused
among the poor. The sisters of this congregation have organized
and appointed a day each week to provide clothing for the
needy." In the *Gospel Herald* of March 10, 1910, appeared this
news item:

The sisters of the Weaver congregation, Cambria Co., Pa., met at Bro. D. H. Yoder's home Feb. 24, 1910, and organized a sewing circle to be known as the "Weaver Church Sewing Society." The work of their first day's meeting was to make ten skirts and seven dresses for the Canton Mission. All expenses were paid with a small balance to their credit. The society was organized as follows: Pres., Sister Ella Luther; Sec., Sister Mary C. Hershberger; Treas., Sister Mary Weaver. The society has decided to meet the first Wednesday of each month.

In December 1911 the sewing circle of the Howard-Miami Mennonite Church, Amboy, Indiana, was organized at the home of Lucinda Penrod (Mrs. Silas) Gerber. As early as 1906 or 1907, Lizzie Miller (Mrs. Noah) King had been instrumental in bringing together women of the church to sew in order to raise money for the Chicago mission.

By 1911 in eastern Pennsylvania the already mentioned pioneer organization emerged, the Associated Sewing Circles of the Lancaster Mennonite Conference. During the next decade other regional organizations were formed, as well as a churchwide organization. These came about largely through the efforts of a remarkable woman, Clara Eby Steiner.

Clara Eby Steiner (1873-1929)

In 1911, Clara Eby Steiner became a widow after seventeen years as an active partner with her husband, M. S. (Menno Simon) Steiner, in the work of the church. Many a church committee had met in their home, sometimes for several days. At the time of his death M. S. Steiner chaired the Mennonite Board of Missions and Charities at Elkhart, Indiana. Suddenly bereft not only of her husband, but also of her church work, Clara felt desolate. The church had accepted her working behind the scenes through her husband but would not accept her doing the same work on her own. Because of the viewpoint of the time she was not even considered as a successor to her husband as board chairman, even though she had the dedication, knowledge, and capability.

On October 3, 1915, she wrote to Daniel Kauffman, editor of the *Gospel Herald:*

You touched a sensitive chord in my experience when you refer to my having at one time been closely associated with the active church life. I became interested in church activities when I began to associate with M. S. while I was yet real young. Later as his wife and confidante I became intensely so. I spent days in secretary work. All the mail coming and going passed through my hands. This, when our babies were small and needed much attention. We often felt that we were not doing justice to the work and had hopes and plans of doing better later on. To be called upon to give it all up before I had reached 40 and just as the children were becoming less helpless . . . and while at the same time calls were constantly going out for more laborers, was crucifying to say the least. I felt that if only I would not have had to give up my husband and the work I had learned to love at the same time I would not have been so utterly forsaken. . . .

One who is an actor can hardly realize how it all appears to one who has stepped aside and looks on. I suppose if I were not a woman I would have thrown some of my convictions across some of the scenes.[13]

In 1926, Clara wrote a history of the Mennonite Woman's Missionary Society, which she had helped to establish. Using the editorial "we," she spoke of her "call":

Clara Eby Steiner, founder of the Mennonite Woman's
Missionary Society, with granddaughter Alice (Loewen),
daughter Charity Hostetler, father Tobias Eby, 1920.

We received a definite call of the Lord to this work in 1911. Because it was so hard to believe that the Lord could use us in work of this kind we applied various tests; the tests, although we considered some of them hard, invariably led onward until it developed into a general organization.[14]

Clara spent the remainder of her life on this work.

She did not think of congregational women's groups as being only sewing circles but as groups that would promote the total program of the church. She wrote to a Virginia sister in January 1917 that the Mennonite Woman's Missionary Society was not to be "a general organization of sewing circles but a general organization of Home and Foreign Missionary Endeavor, including Sewing Circles, Mothers Meetings, Ladies Aids, Missionary Societies, Young Peoples and Childrens Circles or Societies, and Individual Sunday School Classes."[15] She did not, however, see this organization as in any way competing with or rivaling the mission board. In the same letter she wrote, "We work in cooperation and harmony with the Mennonite Board of Missions and Charities. . . . Men will be treated courteously if they care to attend." It is important to take note of this statement, for a later impression, even as late as 1965, seemed to be that the women's organization was intending to send out its own missionaries.[16] Her correspondence indicates that Clara worked diplomatically, tactfully, with persons, congregations, and conference districts.

On October 30, 1917, she wrote a long letter to Emma King (Risser), the district representative for Kansas and Nebraska, a woman active in promoting the Mennonite Woman's Missionary Society in her area.

It is really remarkable how the sisters have responded and say they have felt the need of more united and systematic work; and I am very hopeful that we may all learn and grow in the work together. Perhaps we all feel our inability to do the work justice as you do, but you know the Lord only requires of us what we are able to do. . . . I am sure I would have plenty of work without this; for I must work out of doors so much since my husband is gone, and I must provide for my family. I have done man's work for weeks at a time. I cut some corn this fall but not so much as other years; but I must husk corn yet. My children are all in school and I am left alone to do the work. I keep the boys out as much as I dare but they cannot do everything. I should be out today but it is stormy.[17]

Many people appreciated Clara Eby Steiner's efforts. Stella S. Kreider wrote to her on March 5, 1918:

I must say, Mrs. Steiner, you are to be congratulated; for the progress of the Women's work speaks for your efforts.[18]

But Clara also encountered opposition. In a letter written to Daniel Kauffman on March 4, 1918, she told of an experience with a mission board member:

He told me to go home and raise my children, that was *all* the Lord required of me. . . . I went home and pondered and had some dark hours because of it. I thought of the times that brother had spent in my home sometimes for days in committee work, that he came when it suited him and remained so long as it suited him and this during the years when my children were babies and helpless and he never stopped to inquire whether my babies were sick or needed me but came at his convenience and now when they were so they could help themselves he tried to show me my duty to them as well as the Lord's will to me.[19]

Sharon Klingelsmith comments: "The attitude of this brother and of the Board toward executive work for women came from the concept of the scriptural order: God, man, woman. Woman was always to remain in subjection to man and therefore could not take a leadership position." Yet this attitude was not held by all, for on October 5, 1917, G. L. Bender of the mission board wrote to her, ". . . you make an excellent executive."[20] Bender believed that some day the women might even have their own building.

In 1915 the women asked the mission board whether they could become an auxiliary to that board but were refused. Melvin Gingerich explains why:

. . . there were conservative forces in the church that opposed the churchwide organization. There was the widespread fear that the women's movement would become a competitor with the district and general mission boards and would work independently of them. . . . Lydia Gross reported from Doylestown, Pennsylvania, in November 1917 that the district mission board and the ministers favored sewing circles and raising money for mission purposes but that they preferred that all monies be channeled through their district board. "They do not approve of women having a separate board," said Mrs. Gross.... A letter from Laura Suter from Harrisonburg, Virginia, in November declared, "I have taken pains to consult some of the most influential Bishops in the East and so far have received no encouragement for the national organization.[21]

Mary Burkhard, elected president of the women's organization at the second meeting, in 1916, expressed a beautiful sentiment to Daniel Kauffman: "Let us pray that we may discover the happy place for ourselves to work, and that men and women together in the Mennonite Church may do great things."

Klingelsmith reports on the women's views of the attitudes of male leaders of the time toward their organization, rating G. L. Bender and J. S. Hartzler of Indiana and L. J. Burkholder of Ontario as "enthusiastic advocates"; D. D. Miller, D. H. Bender, and J. K. Bixler of Indiana, and S. A. King of Kansas-Nebraska as "definitely opponents"; and others as somewhere between these two poles. It must be pointed out that at this time men also faced opposition; the mission board itself was suspect to some. One is reminded of the Scripture: "A wide door for effective work has opened to me, and there are many adversaries" (1 Corinthians 16:9).

Clara Eby Steiner was unwavering in her courage and persistence. At a fiftieth-anniversary program held at Goshen, Indiana, on June 24, 1965—"an evening of grateful reminiscences"—Clara Eby Steiner's daughter Esther (Mrs. J. C.) Meyer read a tribute to her mother. It contained these words:

In rush seasons Mother's work was staggering. She did much of the farm work and directed her sons in their performance. She sewed for her daughters and for herself and taught them to sew and cook. She taught a Sunday school class, often entertained guests, and did housekeeping chores in the time that was left. She kept up a heavy schedule as long as she could, even after she became ill.[22]

Work of the Society
The women did a great deal of work for the outreach programs of the church. By March 1921 they had 12 regional

branches, 131 societies, and 3,721 members. During that fiscal year they made 17,201 garments and gave $20,853.64 in cash. They sent overseas 32 tons of new and used clothing for relief in Russia and Turkey. In 1921-22 the society supported missionaries Ruth Blosser Miller and Nellie Warye in India besides financing Dr. Cooprider's medical dispensary (see chapter 10). In addition they had at least ten other projects in South America and at home.

Clara Eby Steiner started a newsletter in March 1919. Issue Number 11, appearing on June 21, 1921, carried the title *Monthly Letter*. Crissie Yoder Shank became the editor in 1923. These newsletters portray an active, intelligent group of women at work for Christ and the church. In the February 15, 1921, issue Mrs. Steiner relays an appeal for more workers from "an experienced missionary": "The type of women needed are thorough Christians, loyal Mennonites, consecrated, of sound physique, with abundant courage, optimism and determination, patience and energy, good judgment and common sense, college education desirable with administrative ability. Other desirable assets: congeniality, ability to view situations from the other person's angle, to be humble among all classes of people, together with a good command of the language."

In the December 1, 1921, issue of the newsletter, Mina B. Esch wrote a tribute to Sister Lena Friesen, who had died a few weeks earlier. In the May 24, 1921, issue Vesta Zook wrote about her relief work in Constantinople, Turkey. Lydia Lehman wrote thanking the society for eight shipments, including clothing, tinned and dried fruit, Christmas boxes, and also for money for a bicycle. Mary A. Cressman in the president's annual message on May 1, 1927, exhorted the sisters to work together in "prayer, influence, and labors."

In 1924 the Mennonite Woman's Missionary Society issued a 32-page *Booklet of Prayer for Missions of the Mennonite Church*, covering every day of the year. Emma Shank, Lydia Lehman, and Alta Erb gathered the materials for the booklet, which was the forerunner of today's *Voice*, the monthly magazine of WMSC, and *Rejoice*, a family devotional magazine.

Affiliation with the Board of Missions and Charities

Turmoil and upheaval came to the Mennonite Church in the 1920s. Goshen College was closed in 1923 because many of its most highly educated teachers were considered too liberal. Churches split. Dedicated persons were prevented from teaching a Sunday school class, or even excommunicated for wearing the wrong shape of headgear. Men and women alike experienced anguish.

The women's society did not escape the tribulation. In the conservative/liberal struggle of the time, "the woman leaders, for the most part, would have to be placed on the liberal side in that struggle."[23] When the Iowa Conference decided in 1921 to have the circles report to and send their money through the district mission board rather than the society, Ella Fisher explained it as a reaction against women having executive authority.[24] Vernon Reiff, treasurer of the mission board, wrote to Ruth A. Yoder, treasurer of the women's organization, in November 1925, suggesting that the name be changed from Woman's Missionary Society to Woman's Sewing Circles. This proposal should have had a familiar ring to Mennonite women, for the *Martyrs Mirror* reports that when Lijsken Dircks was martyred in 1551 by being put into a bag and thrown into the Scheldt River, Catholic officials told her that women should attend to their sewing and leave searching the Scriptures to men.[25]

"The Takeover"

Because of ill health and a heavy work load Clara Eby Steiner wrote to Emma Stutzman (Mrs. S. C.) Yoder in 1925 asking whether she would take over the orders for the India sewing. Rather than an answer from Mrs. Yoder, Clara received a reply from her husband, S. C. Yoder, who was executive secretary of the Mennonite Board of Missions and Charities. He replied that his wife was unable to do this but that the board would be willing to act on this matter at its next meeting. He went on, "Calls have come from different parts of the country asking for a central committee or official secretary appointed by the Board, that could receive all orders or requests for work and distribute them."

On March 4, 1926, a by now rather famous letter appeared in the *Gospel Herald:*

Dear Brother:

At the last Meeting of our Executive Committee *we appointed* [italics mine] a Committee of three sisters of which Mrs. J. B. Moyer, Elkhart, Ind., is Secretary. These sisters are to have charge of the distribution of the Sewing Circle work for the different mission stations and anyone of these stations desiring to have the Sewings work for them, may send their orders to Mrs. Moyer and she with her committee will distribute the order among the different Sewing Circles of the United States. Also if there are any Sewing Circles desiring to have work, they may send their orders to her and she will see that they will get something to do. I remain,

> Very Sincerely,
> S. C. Yoder
> Secy. M. B. of M. & C.

This letter sounded the death knell for the Mennonite

Emma Stutzman (Yoder) (1883-1972), Iowa, later the wife of S. C. Yoder.

Woman's Missionary Society. The president of the women's organization, Mary Ann Cressman of Ontario, read the letter in the *Herald* and wondered what was going on. She wrote to Secretary Yoder:

> I was always under the impression that we were working under and with the General Mission Board, and always told our people so.... the Executive of the Women's Missionary organization to my knowledge has not been informed of any dissatisfaction on the part of the Mission Board and has not been approached upon this matter. May we then be entitled to and kindly ask for an explanation and what the Board's attitude is towards the Woman's Missionary organization.

Mrs. Cressman never received an answer to that letter. The women were understandably upset. Their organization, in existence for over a decade, was being ignored and bypassed. Mary Ann Gerig found her feelings beyond expression but yet felt that the only thing to do was to "take it cheerfully, gracefully."

Crissie Yoder Shank felt that at least Ohio could probably cooperate with the board and still retain an outlook greater than the board's.[25] For two years two Mennonite women's organizations existed—one under the mission board to take care of sewing for missions, another to promote missions. The arrangement did not work in a church too small for two women's organizations, as Clara Eby Steiner and Mary Ann Cressman pointed out. Because of their genuine concern for the church, these women felt that the Christian thing to do was to acquiesce graciously. This they did, but it hurt, as a cross always does.

After meeting with the board committee—D. D. Miller, S. C. Yoder, and S. E. Allgyer—the women drew up a statement printed in their November-December 1927 *Monthly Letter:*

> Since there is at present very evident misunderstanding as to the status of the Mennonite Woman's Missionary Society, and since another committee has been appointed by the General Mission Board to have charge of the sewing work of the circles subject to the approval of the Branches working with the Mennonite Woman's Missionary Society, we, the Executive Committee of this organization, in joint session with the com-

mittee appointed by the General Board and *at the suggestion of their committee* [italics mine] give the further planning and work of this society over to the General Mission Board or such other persons as they see fit to sponsor it.

We reserve the funds on hand with such as may come in, until March 31, 1928.

(Signed)
>   Mrs. M. A. Nahrgang, Pres. (proxy).
>   Mrs. A. J. Steiner, Secretary.
>   Ruth A. Yoder, Treasurer.
>   Mrs. J. S. Gerig, Member.

Martha Whitmer Steiner had succeeded her sister-in-law Clara Eby Steiner as secretary. In the same issue of the *Monthly Letter* she wrote the following:

> Personally, we feel the sisters' missionary endeavor is the Lord's work. His work is too important to allow differences, personal feelings and prejudices to enter. It is only as we can soar above the petty things of life and work unitedly together that the Christ life can be lived and His name be glorified.
>
> >   Yours in Christian love,
> >   Mrs. A. J. Steiner.

In the "Final Report of the Mennonite Woman's Missionary Society," Ruth A. Yoder, who had been treasurer for thirteen years and had disbursed thousands of dollars to Mennonite missions, issued the following statement:[26]

> The funds on hand are being given over to V. E. Reiff, Treasurer of the General Board, to be disbursed as stated above.
>
> The further work of the women and girls is to be carried on by the committee appointed by the General Board. This committee will no doubt organize itself in the near future.
>
> Thanking you for the confidence you have shown me as treasurer, and for the faithful support you have given, I am,
>
> >   Sincerely yours,
> >   Ruth A. Yoder,
> July 15, 1929.   Bellefontaine, Ohio.

The *Gospel Herald* carried a statement issued by the mission board on June 26, 1929:

> The church has not looked with favor on such a movement, not that it was not interested in women's work but because it was feared that the organization of such a society would have a divisive influence. We can see a reason why there should be a women's sewing circle organization, for this is distinctly woman's work.
>
> With a separate missionary society it is different.[27]

What happened to these leaders who pioneered organized women's work in the Mennonite Church? Mary Yoder (Mrs. Jacob) Burkhard, the first president, although rejected by the mission board at Elkhart when she wished to return to India, probably because of her "strong opinions," joined the General Conference Mennonites and served in India under their board from 1924 to 1931. Ruth A. Yoder (1887-1960), treasurer, had been the first primary Sunday school superintendent at South Union Church, West Liberty, Ohio, as early as 1915.[28] In 1922 she had presented an address to the Ohio Mennonite Sunday School Conference—"Worship and Its Place in the Sunday School."[29] Hartford Theological Seminary granted her a Master of Arts in religious education in 1923. Yet in the early 1930s her home congregation told her she could no longer teach a Sunday school class. Why? "She was educated, and she had her own ideas." Also she failed to conform to the "headgear code."[30] She joined the Presbyterians and taught religion in the public schools of Gary, Indiana, and Bluffton, Ohio, from 1924 to 1928 and 1931 to 1936. Martha Steiner died in 1928, Clara Eby Steiner and Crissie Yoder Shank in 1929. Did they die at least partially of broken hearts? Mary Ann Nahrgang Cressman continued as president until 1930, when Lina Zook Ressler (see chapter 8) succeeded her. Mrs. Cressman also served as treasurer of the Ontario Sewing Circles organization from 1927 to 1940.

Possibly the men on the mission board, S. C. Yoder particularly, had no idea of what they had done to these women, for forty years later on the occasion of a fiftieth-anniversary celebration of the women's organization (May 25, 1965), he sent a beautiful letter to the Women's Missionary and Service Auxiliary:

> It is a source of gratitude and satisfaction to be accorded the opportunity of expressing my appreciation of your organization which was founded in the face of opposition from well-meaning people, among whom were some of the leaders of the Mennonite Church. We all owe a debt of gratitude to Ruth Yoder, Mary Burkhard, and Mrs. M. S. Steiner, all of whom have now gone to their "long home." It was their courage, faith, and Christian persistence that finally overcame the obstacles that were in their way and led to the establishment of your Society.
>
> Your efforts have, during the years, borne a rich fruitage and multitudes, known and unknown, seen and unseen, have been blest by your labors of love as you ministered to needs at home and abroad.
>
> As a member of the committee that helped to guide your plans for an organization through the Mission Board, I extend my sincere appreciation to you and to those who labored with you in the past, for your and their faithfulness throughout the years. I wish you every blessing in your labors of love in the years to come. Who knows or who can tell what the needs of mankind will be ere the day closes and time comes to an end. It is my prayer that whatever the conditions or exigencies may be, that your faith, your courage, and your strength may be sufficient for the needs of the time and occasion.
>
> Sincerely yours in the bonds of Christian Service,
>
> S. C. Yoder, Past-Secretary and President of the Mennonite Board of Missions and Charities[31]

Years of Quiet Faithfulness

During the seven years of Lina Zook Ressler's presidency, 1930-37, the Sewing Circles, for that is what they were now called, drafted a constitution in 1931, undertook support of nurses at the LaJunta Mennonite School of Nursing in 1934, strengthened work with junior girls in 1935, and set up a sheet and blanket fund in 1937. These Depression and prewar years were characterized by quiet, steady faithfulness.

Cora Shoemaker (Mrs. Alpha L.) Buzzard (1878-1959) served as president of the organization from 1937 to 1944. Daughter of J. S. and Elizabeth Shoemaker, she was born in Freeport, Illinois, and lived in Washington, Illinois, from 1907 to

1929, then in Goshen, Indiana. Her sister Stella Shoemaker (Mrs. A. E.) Kreider had been the first secretary of girls' work (1923). In 1938 the Sewing Circles set up a cutting room at Kalona, Iowa.

In 1944, Ruth Blosser (Mrs. Ernest) Miller (1893-1977) became president, a post she held until 1950. She served in India with her husband from 1921 to 1937 and from 1956 to 1963. In 1947 at a meeting in Atglen, Pennsylvania, the women changed their name to Women's Missionary and Sewing Circle Organization (WMSO), seeking to affirm that their work was not limited to sewing. Clara Hershberger recalls that during these years they wrote asking the *Gospel Herald* for the privilege of publicizing their work. The answer was that they could have from ten to twelve lines! But the situation must have improved, for later the *Herald* gave them more space.

During these years the women undertook many special projects. "Mules for Mildred," a project of GMSA (Girls' Missionary and Service Auxiliary), provided funds to buy mules for Mildred Eichelberger (1920-   ), who did church planting and evangelistic work in northern Brazil from 1955 to 1969. The women provided funds to help construct Mexican mission apartments in Chicago, a mother's room at Bethel Church in Chicago, and a hostel for missionary children at Hokkaido International School in Sapporo, Japan.

In 1954 another name change occurred; the organization became Women's Missionary and Service Auxiliary (WMSA). Minnie Swartzendruber (Mrs. J. D.) Graber (1902-   ), president from 1950 to 1959, explains:

> . . .this new strain of interest involved the total life of women. They met in fellowship groups, missionary meetings, sunshine circles, in prayer groups, homemakers groups, home builders—and many other types of groups. The General Committee took steps to gather all these groups into one organization. At this time they tried to reach out and include all the overseas sewing circles and other women's groups as well.[32]

In August 1971, at Kitchener, Ontario, the name became Women's Missionary and Service Commission (WMSC), with relational ties to the newly formed Mennonite Board of Congregational Ministries. The women were no longer considered "auxiliary" but copartners in the structure, although WMSC delegates still do not vote in General Assembly.

WMSC now employs an executive secretary—at this writing, Barbara Bender (Mrs. Don) Reber (1925-   )—and has an office with the Mennonite Board of Congregational Ministries at Elkhart, Indiana. At both local and district levels, executive committees include a president, vice-president, treasurer, recording secretary, secretaries of (1) home interests, (2) peace and social concerns, and (3) girls' activities (GMSA). WMSC publishes a monthly, the *Voice*, edited at this writing by Vel Gingerich (Mrs. John) Shearer of Wilkes-Barre, Pennsylvania.

WMSC lists as goals—to:

    a. unite the women and girls of the church, and to coordinate their activities;
    b. help women and girls find and articulate faith;
    c. encourage regular and disciplined Bible study;
    d. promote strengthening the quality of family life;
    e. develop an awareness and appreciation of our Anabaptist heritage;
    f. help women and girls discover, develop, and utilize their individual gifts;
    g. help develop leadership potential among women and girls;
    h. encourage cultivation of person-to-person relationships;
    i. motivate creativity in planning programs and activities;
    j. respond as Christ's representatives to community and worldwide needs.[33]

WMSC states, "We need to see ourselves in the larger family of God (the church, the local community, the world community) asking questions, responding to questions, understanding forces that are shaping church life now and exploring responsibly the issues which will determine continuing faithfulness among the people of God."[34]

FACING PAGE: The women in the photograph at the right (left to right) are (top row) Mary Nunemaker (Mrs. Leroy) Good, Cora Ebersole (Mrs. Joe) Bucher, Sarah Blosser, Amanda Ebersole, Hettie Wilker Hollinger, Eliza Ebersole; (middle row) Jennie Ebersole, Bertha E. Landis (Mrs. C. Norman) Long, Katie Nunemaker (Mrs. Milton) Hess, Alice Landis (Mrs. John) Umble, Essie Landis (Mrs. Charles) Hess, Naomi Reisner (Mrs. Harry) Ditzel, Mamie Landis (Mrs. A. C.) Good; (front row) Ada Book (Mrs. Enos) Nunemaker and Loma Detweiler (Mrs. Almon) Fortner.

EXHIBIT 10
Organized Women's Groups, 1900-1912

Beginning in 1900, the contributions from women's groups are reported frequently in the *Herald of Truth*. Below is a list of new groups mentioned:

1900		Sisters, Columbiana, Ohio
	April	Sisters Sewing Society of Logan and Champaign Counties, Ohio
	December	Oak Grove Sewing Circle, West Liberty, Ohio
1901		Zion Sewing Circle, Ohio
	February	Sewing Circle, Masonville, Pennsylvania
	April	Millersville Sewing Circle, Pennsylvania
	August	Rohrerstown Sewing Circle, Pennsylvania
	October	Sycamore and Bethel Congregations Sewing Circle, Garden City, Missouri
1902		Virginia Sisters
	December	Ladies' Aid Society, Elkhart, Indiana

Women of Science Ridge Mennonite Church, Sterling, Illinois, about 1905.

January   Sisters Sewing Meeting, Sterling, Illinois
February   Manheim Sisters, Pennsylvania
April   Sisters, Smithville, Ohio
May   Sisters, New Stark, Ohio
August   Sisters, Belleville, Pennsylvania

1903   Kinzer Sewing Circle
April   Sisters, Cullom, Illinois

1904   Sisters' Sewing Circle, Freeport, Illinois
March   Dorcas Sewing Circle, Alpha, Minnesota
April   Ladies Aid Society, Goshen, Indiana
August   Sunnyside Sewing Circle, Elkhart, Indiana

1906   Mission Sewing Circle, Elida, Ohio
May   South Union and Walnut Grove, Ohio
July   Sisters Sewing Circle, Ephrata, Pennsylvania
August   Working Girls' Missionary Society, Goshen, Indiana

1907   Willing Workers Sewing Circle, Lancaster, Pennsyl-
             vania
October   East Petersburg Sewing Circle, Pennsylvania

1909   Doylestown Sewing Circle, Pennsylvania
April   Florin Sewing Circle, Pennsylvania

1910   Sewing Circle, Sugar Creek, Ohio
February   Sewing Circle, Nappanee, Indiana
March   Weaver Church Sewing Society, Cambria County,
             Pennsylvania
August   Sewing Circle, Allensville and Belleville, Pennsylvania
September   Sewing Circle, LaJunta, Colorado

1911   Sewing Circle, Flanagan, Illinois
January   Sewing Circle, Elida, Ohio
July   Sewing Circle, Landis Valley and Salunga, Pennsyl-
             vania
August   Mellingers Sewing Circle, Pennsylvania

1912   Dorcas Sewing Circle, Tiskilwa, Illinois
May   Martins Creek Sewing Circle, Ohio
October   Martinsburg and Pleasant Grove Sewing Circle, Penn-
             sylvania

(From Melvin Gingerich, *Mennonite Quarterly Review*, Apr. 1963, p. 114).

EXHIBIT 11

First Public Meetings of the Woman's Missionary Society

Date	Place of Meeting	Officers Chosen	Comments
August 20, 1915	Near Wauseon, Ohio	None	Attended by several hundred "interested sisters from a number of States and Canada." Mrs. W. B. Weaver, Elkhart, led the women in singing "Blessed Assurance." Mrs. A. S. Landis, Goshen, Indiana, acted as chairman, and Mrs. J. E. Hartzler, Goshen, as secretary. Mrs. S. E. Allgyer, West Liberty, Ohio, presented the devotionals. This was followed by a talk on home work by Clara Eby Steiner and a talk on foreign work by Mary Burkhard. After this fourteen women from Colorado, Ohio, Indiana, Virginia, Ontario spoke on their experiences in sewing circles and mission work. No action was taken toward setting up a permanent organization. (Gingerich, p. 215)
August 31, 1916	West Liberty, Ohio	Mary Burkhard, president Clara Eby Steiner, secretary Ruth A. Yoder, treasurer	Several hundred present. The program was on the topic of the benefits and the possibilities of the sewing circles. Four missionaries spoke. They were Miss Della Beckel, Fort Wayne, Indiana; Mrs. B. B. Stoltzfus, Lima, Ohio; Miss Mabel Rheil,

Date	Place of Meeting	Officers Chosen	Comments
			Youngstown, Ohio; and Miss Mayme King, West Liberty, Ohio. Clara Steiner spoke on "Possibilities of More Good." (Gingerich, p. 216)
June 15, 1917	Walnut Creek, Ohio	Above three reelected	Featured speaker was Mae (Mrs. T. K.) Hershey (see chapter 8), who was about to go to Argentina.
August 30, 1917	Yellow Creek near Goshen, Indiana	Mary (Mrs. J. S.) Gerig Anna (Mrs. J. B.) Moyer (added to executive committee) Elected to two-year terms as district representatives: Mrs. Lydia Gross, Doylestown, Pa., Franconia Conference Miss Martha Eby, Lititz, Pa., Lancaster Conference and Amish-Mennonites Mrs. R. M. Luther, Johnstown, Pa., Central and Western Pennsylvania Mrs. Benjamin Stauffer, Maugansville, Md., Washington County, Md., and Franklin County, Pa. Miss Laura Suter, Harrisonburg, Va., Virginia Conference	

Miss Martha Brenneman, Lima, Ohio, Ohio Conference

[Mandy] (Mrs. Mahlon) Shrock, Kokomo, Ind., Indiana area

Mrs. Lydia Smith, Flanagan, Ill., Illinois Conference

Mrs. W. H. Miller, Wellman, Iowa, Iowa and Nebraska

Miss Maggie Driver, Versailles, Mo., Missouri

Miss Emma King, Hesston, Kan., Kansas and Oklahoma

Mrs. J. M. Mishler, Hubbard, Ore., Pacific Coast Conference and Amish-Mennonites

Mrs. M. C. Cressman, Kitchener, Ont., Ontario Conference and Amish-Mennonites

Mrs. N. V. Stauffer, Aldersyde, Alta., Alberta and Saskatchewan Conference (Gingerich, p. 217)

June 5, 1919   East Union
Kalona, Iowa

The three former officers reelected

M. A. Gerig, vice-president
Edith Wenger, young women's secretary
Emma (Mrs. S. C.) Yoder, additional member of executive committee)

Date	Place of Meeting	Officers Chosen	Comments
August 29-30, 1923	Waterloo, Ontario	Mary Burkhard, president Mary Nahrgang (Mrs. M. C.) Cressman, vice-president Clara E. Steiner, secretary Ruth A. Yoder, treasurer Mary Ann Smucker (Mrs. J. S.) Gerig, fifth member of executive committee Crissie Y. Shank, secretary of literature Stella Kreider, secretary of young women's and children's work	A constitution was tentatively adopted at this meeting. Emma H. Shank read a paper, "Bible Readers of South America." Lydia Lehman read "My Task in India."

214

EXHIBIT 12

Officers of WMSC and Its Predecessors

Prepared by Priscilla Stuckey Kauffman

President

Mary Yoder Burkhard (1916-23)
Mary Nahrgang Cressman (1923-30)
Lina Zook Ressler (1930-38)
Cora Shoemaker Buzzard (1939-44)
Ruth Blosser Miller (1945-50)
Minnie Swartzendruber Graber
  (1951-59)
Bertha Miller (1960-62)
Mary Imhoff (1963-65)
Fyrne Yoder (1966-67)
Verna Burkholder Troyer (1968)
Doris Liechty Lehman (1969-73)
Jocele Meyer (1974-79)
Grace Derstine Brunner (1980-   )

Vice-President

Mary Ann Gerig (1919-23)
Mary Nahrgang Cressman (1923-37)
Martha Good (1938)
Alta Metzler (1939-46)
Emma Zimmerman Horst (1947-53)
Orpha Troyer (1954-58)
Hazel Lapp (1959-64)
Verna Burkholder Troyer (1965-67)
Gladys Ropp (1968-70)
Jocele Meyer (1971-73)
Angie B. Williams (1974-80)
Kathryn Bontrager
  Swartzendruber (1980-   )

Secretary

Clara Eby Steiner (1916-26)
Martha Whitmer Steiner (1926-29)
Cora Shoemaker Buzzard (1930-36)
Ethel Estella Cooprider Erb (1937-47)
Alma Yordy (1948-52)
Dorothea Eigsti (1953-58)
Dorothy Swartzendruber (1959-64)
Doris Kramer (1965-69)

Fern Massanari (1970-75)
Janet Kreider (1976-80)
Glenda Mast (1980-   )

Assistant Secretary

Pearl Detweiler Smucker (1930-34)
Viola Wenger (1937)

Executive Secretary

Florence Shantz (1956-58)
Doris Snyder (1959)
Dorothy Snapp McCammon
  (1960-66)
Beulah Good Kauffman (1967-78)
Barbara Bender Reber (1979-   )

Treasurer

Ruth A. Yoder (1916-29)
Anna Stalter (1930-31)
Zaidee A. Reiff (1932-46)
Amanda Frey (1947-54)
Ruth Graybill (1955-75)
Fern Massanari (1976-   )

Secretary of Information
Anna Moyer (1919-23)

Secretary of Literature
Crissie Yoder Shank (1923-29)
Alma Yoder Roth (1930-31)
Lydia L. Lehman (1932-45)
Fanny Hershey Lapp (1946-50)
Lydia F. Shank (1951-54)
Ruth King Duerksen (1955)
Helen Wade Alderfer (1956-57)
Alice Kauffman Gingerich
  (1958-60)
Lois Gunden Clemens (1961-64)
Beulah Good Kauffman (1965-66)
Sylvia Jantz (1967-73)

Alice W. Lapp (1974-80)
Hope Lind (1980-   )

Sewing Secretary

Anna Moyer (1930-35)
Martha Burkholder Good (1936)
Cora Shoemaker Buzzard (1937)
Anna Moyer (1938-41)
Martha Buckwalter Guengerich
    (1942-48)
Elva Lehman Yoder (1949-54)

Secretary of Home Interests

Elva Lehman Yoder (1955-56)
Clara Hooley Hershberger (1957-59)
Marianna Reiff Stutzman (1960-65)
Winifred Erb Paul (1966-71)
Lucy Gotwals (1972-73)
Margaret Swartzentruber (1974-79)
Dorothy Snider (1980-   )

Secretary of Girls' Activities

Edith Wenger (1919- ?)
Vinora Saltzman (? -1923)
Stella Shoemaker Kreider (1923-26)
Viola Wenger (1936, 1938-40)
Mabel Groh (1940-45)
Alma Yordy (1946-47)

Cora Gingrich Groh (1948-53)
Florence Shantz (1954-55)
Frieda Amstutz (1956-61)
Rachel Fisher (1962-64)
Lois Liechty (1965-67)
Dorothy Shank (1968-73)
Grace Slatter (1974-80)
Donella Peachey Clemens (1981-   )

VOICE Editors

Lois Gunden Clemens (1960-78)
Vel Gingerich Shearer (1979-   )

Secretary of Peace and Social Concerns

Marie Althouse Stoltzfus (1965)
Naomi Kauffman Lederach (1966-71)
Evelyn Burkholder Kreider (1972-75)
Loretta Leatherman (1976-79)
Norma Goering (1980-   )

Appointee to MCC Peace Section

Fern Umble (1970-72)
Dorothy Yoder Nyce (1973-77)
Janet Umble Reedy (1978-80)

Coordinator of Spanish WMSC Groups

Mary Bustos (1978-   )

CHAPTER 12

Since World War II

World War II, a cataclysmic experience, affected Mennonites and everyone else. Following the Japanese bombing of Pearl Harbor on December 7, 1941, the U.S. Congress declared war against Japan and the Axis powers in Europe. Canada, as part of the British Commonwealth, had entered the conflict earlier. Mennonites maintained their traditional witness against participation in warfare, and between May 1941 and March 1947 nearly 12,000 conscientious objectors to war served in CPS (Civilian Public Service). Of these, 4,665 were Mennonite.[1] Melvin Gingerich tells the story well in *Service for Peace*.

These men planted trees, put out forest fires, and did experimental farm work, public health education, and a variety of other activities. Mennonite women also participated in CPS. Gingerich lists 132, sixty-seven of whom, just over half, were wives of CPS men. A Mennonite woman in CPS served as nurse, dietitian, matron, or as a combination of any two of these.[2]

Post-World War II Activities

A strong conviction existed that a negative witness against war is not enough. Conscientious objectors during World War II were eager to participate actively in reconciliation and reconstruction. Prayers of thanksgiving ascended when in 1947 they were allowed into Germany, where colossal loss of life and property had taken place.

During the next years MCC (Mennonite Central Committee) did relief and reconstruction work in England, Puerto Rico, India, China, Formosa (now Taiwan), Philippines, Java, Sumatra, Japan, France, The Netherlands, Germany, Switzerland, and Palestine. John D. Unruh in his tabulation of personnel who served in MCC from the late 30s until 1952 lists the names of single women, but identifies married women by their husbands' names only.[3]

This book cannot cover thoroughly the participation of women in the service programs that have proliferated in the last 35 years: VS (Voluntary Service), TAP (Teachers Abroad Program), MDS (Mennonite Disaster Service), and many mission programs. Nor is it possible to give this recent period adequate biographical coverage. Whom should one choose? From MCC, Lydia Liechty (Mrs. M. C.) Lehman (see chapters 8 and 11), Elfrieda Klassen (Mrs. Peter) Dyck, Edna Ruth Miller (Mrs. J. N.) Byler?[4] From VS, Edna Ramseyer (Mrs. E. G.) Kaufman? One can only hope that later researchers will continue the task of gathering information about Mennonite women.

Since World War II a whole new generation is pioneering new areas. Mary Oyer (1924-   ) served as executive secretary of the Joint Hymnal Committee (1967-69) and wrote the introduction to the widely used *Mennonite Hymnal*. Mary Harnish (1917-   ) went in 1950 as a physical therapist to the leprosarium at Shirati Hospital in Tanganyika, where she developed strong, lightweight artificial limbs from a native wood. She operates an orthopedic workshop, constructs and fits prostheses.[5] Melva Kauffman, as part of a Columbia University team, helped develop reading materials for the schools of Afghanistan. Mabel Brunk (1927-   ) pioneered nursing education in Korea. Florence Nafziger (1918-   ) has worked in nursing education in India since 1945. Doris Janzen (Mrs. Paul) Longacre (1940-79) produced two books which are making the "simple life" functional for thousands: the *More-with-Less Cookbook* (Scottdale, Pa.: Herald Press, 1976) and *Living More with Less* (Herald Press, 1980). Phyllis Pellman Good (1948-   ) and her husband, Merle, have vigorously promoted the arts among Mennonites through their work at The People's Place in Intercourse, Pennsylvania, and their publication of *Festival Quarterly*. Dorothy Yoder Nyce (1937-   ) helped form an MCC Peace Section Task Force on Women in Church and Society in 1973 and edited *Which Way Women?* (Akron, Pa.: Mennonite Central Committee, 1980). Emma Sommers (Mrs. Joe) Richards (1927-   ) and Marilyn Kauffman (Mrs. Maurice) Miller (1937-   ), ordained in 1973 and 1976 respectively, serve congregations as pastors, as do others.

Only two women, Lois Gunden Clemens and Ruth Brunk Stoltzfus, have been selected from this recent period for a more extended presentation in this chapter. Both were born in 1915 and grew to young womanhood in the "repressive 20s." Adding their experiences together, they cover all the previous categories of this book except medicine—wife, mother, aunt, educator, servant in the local congregation, servant overseas. Both have creatively transcended barriers and overcome restrictions placed on their freedom. Respected by both men and women, both the older and younger generations, they have spoken from many a Mennonite pulpit and have written for both the Mennonite and secular press.

Lois Gunden Clemens (1915-   )

Lois was born near Flanagan, Illinois, the second oldest of the nine children of Christian J. and Agnes (Albrecht) Gunden (Mrs. Gunden is mentioned in chapter 6). The family lived on a 160-acre farm in the flat, fertile corn belt. Lois recalls:

> Since our grandmother was a regular part of our household, we had the benefits of close intergenerational relationships. We learned to accept the responsibility for doing our share of the routine work as well as the special tasks assigned to us. . . . The long summer days gave us the opportunity for creative play and funtimes, too. . . . When the day's work was

finished, our father and mother often found time to play games with us. During nine months of the year we went to school at the one-room country school located a mile and a quarter from home. Our family participated regularly in all the activities of the Waldo Mennonite Church, where I became a member at an early age.

Our father was sorry he had not had more than minimal schooling, and was therefore eager to give his children the advantages of a college education. In order to make this possible, he moved the family to Goshen, Indiana, in 1930. Since we lived only a few blocks from Goshen College, we were all able to room and board at home while attending college.[6]

After receiving a BA from Goshen College in 1936 with a major in English and French, Lois taught in the one-room school near her childhood home. In 1939 she received the MA degree in French from George Peabody College in Nashville, Tennessee, and began teaching at Goshen College, doing so until her marriage to Ernest R. Clemens of Lansdale, Pennsylvania, in 1958. Also in 1958 she received the PhD degree in French and Spanish from Indiana University.

In 1941, Goshen College granted Lois a leave of absence to direct a refugee children's home administered by MCC in southern France. Following the German occupation of all of France, she was taken into Germany as a civilian war prisoner and held in Baden-Baden—together with the American diplomatic group interned there—for thirteen months, being released in March 1944. She then traveled across the United States and Ontario visiting church communities and CPS units in the interests of MCC.

During her teaching years at Goshen, Lois spent summer months either in pursuing further graduate studies or in doing VS work. She spent two summers with MCC and Mennonite mission board programs in Puerto Rico just as the Puerto Rican Mennonite Church was emerging. For two years she directed a women's summer VS unit at Ypsilanti State Hospital in Michigan. One summer she spent week-long periods with MCC units in California, Mexico, Mississippi, and Louisiana as a representative from the MCC office. Her facility with both French and Spanish often aided her in her service.

Since 1958, Lois Gunden Clemens has served terms on several churchwide boards, including the Mennonite Board of Education, the Goshen College Board of Overseers, the Mennonite Church General Board, and the WMSC General Committee. She edited the WMSC *Voice* from 1960 through 1978. She has also been an area representative to the American Bible Society and a member of its advisory council. She has served on the Nurture Commission of the Franconia Mennonite Conference and has been active in the Plains Mennonite Church.

In 1970, Lois presented the Conrad Grebel Lectures on the role of women in the church. (Herald Press, Scottdale, Pennsylvania, published these lectures in 1971 as *Woman Liberated*.) Lois says of this experience:

> Discussions indicated that when persons found it difficult to accept new biblical insights, this usually resulted from the selectivity with which they

Spencer Cunningham photo

Lois Gunden Clemens (1915-   ), teacher, author, church leader.   Ruth Brunk Stoltzfus (1915-   ), active churchwoman.

customarily approached the scriptures. Their method involved using certain familiar passages to support their viewpoint rather than searching the scriptures to ascertain the total biblical message on the subject. It was obvious that help was needed in learning how to interpret the Bible from a more comprehensive approach.[7]

In 1980, Lois visited Mennonite church communities in Japan as a member of a Fellowship Tour organized by the Mennonite Board of Missions.

Lois says of her life:

As I look back over the breadth of experiences and opportunities which have added depth and joy to my living, I am filled with gratitude to God for the love and mercy by which He has directed me in His ways and the goodness with which He has crowned my days. I praise Him for the goodly heritage that has been mine, both in the family into which I was born and in the church within which I have been nurtured. My family and my church have both been important influences in teaching me the meaning and significance of belonging to the family of God. I pray that God may always use me to pass on to others the legacy of faith that has been given to me.[8]

Ruth Brunk Stoltzfus (1915-   )

Ruth Wenger Brunk, eighth of the nine children of George R. and Katie (Wenger) Brunk, grew up in Denbigh, Virginia. (For her paternal grandmother's story, see chapter 4.) She attended Eastern Mennonite School at Harrisonburg, Virginia, for two years. In 1937 she received a Normal Collegiate Certificate, which enabled her to teach in elementary school for the next five years. In 1941 she married Grant M. Stoltzfus, a historian. They became the parents of five children.

In 1950 at Scottdale, Pennsylvania, Ruth began a popular radio broadcast for women called "Heart to Heart." In an informal, friendly way she spoke about Christian family life. By 1958, when the program became a part of Mennonite Broadcasts under Ella May Miller, it was carried on 32 stations across the United States, Canada, and Puerto Rico. (It continues as "Your Time" under the capable direction of Margaret Foth.) Next Ruth began a ministry of supplying four-column "Family Life" messages to newspapers. She continues a counseling and family-life ministry.

She says of her youth:

> When at 16 I was elected president of the youths' Literary Society, my father [well-known Bishop George R. Brunk] helped with my inaugural address and later with speeches and debates up through two years of college. I took to public speaking like a duck to water and received enough comments to keep me encouraged.... Papa gave me the 620-page *Portraits and Principles of the World's Great Men and Women* (1899). Among its "over fifty leading thinkers" six women were described as "proprietor and manager of a publishing house," "having rare business ability," "able writer," "popular lecturer," "principal of a seminary," and "a personal force in her home and public life."[9]

As a girl, Ruth realized that she could become such a woman. She often helped her father with his business transactions and record-keeping. She found that she enjoyed both business and public speaking. She also became a Christian and was determined to live "in service to the Lord and the church." From age fifteen she participated in church activities as a song leader, Sunday school teacher, and Bible school teacher. The conviction grew within her that her service to the church was to be a speaking ministry. Yet she had no role models to follow.

She recalls vividly a time when her father invited Sarah Lapp, missionary on furlough from India (see chapter 7), to speak from the pulpit in her home church.

> When we got home he [her father] was pleased that she [Mrs. Lapp] had stood a little to the side of the pulpit desk. But for a woman to stand there at all was unusual for the late 1920s, and it left an impression on me.[10]

Ruth says of her father, "While Papa did not believe in the ordination of women, he had much to do with grooming me for a speaking ministry."

Ruth cites other influences on her call. She read Hannah Whitall Smith's *The Christian's Secret of a Happy Life*, a highly approved book, and knew that its Quaker author was a minister. She read a column by Kenneth J. Foreman that "struck fire" with her perception of her own gifts.

> He pointed out that unbalanced people used (or misused) a few Scriptures to restrict the use of women's gifts in the church. He cited active women

in Bible times such as Miriam, Deborah, Huldah, Anna, the four daughters of Philip and others, also Paul's instructions to women who prophesy.... Whenever most preachers spoke on woman's role they pushed the few verses on SILENCE for women but said nothing about the many verses on PROPHESYING for women. So I began studying all those Bible verses about women on which the preachers were all too SILENT.[11]

Ruth tells many stories of God's leading in her life, including this one:

Once while driving from a speaking engagement I had the strong impression that I should stop to see a Christian businessman who had shown interest in putting my broadcast on a new station. I argued, "Lord, I wrote to him about it twice, but he never replied, and I am embarrassed to go."

The answer was, "I said you are to go."

I went. The wife met me at the door and said her husband was out in the field getting corn for their markets. As I walked toward my car puzzled, the man drove in. I said, "Brother B, I am embarrassed to appear to ask you to sponsor my broadcast, but the Lord made me come."

He said, "Sister Ruth, the Lord was talking to me in the cornfield just now about your broadcast, and I told Him I would sponsor it."[12]

Ruth Brunk Stoltzfus's work has generated opposition and verbal criticism, but it has also generated much appreciation. She has spoken in over 200 Mennonite churches. Following a talk by Ruth in an Ohio church in recent years, the pastor asked members of the congregation who wished to do so to join him in laying hands on her and praying for her. She reflects, "Those touches, prayers, and what seemed to be a commissioning, have meant more to me than I can say."

Life in the twentieth century has not always been easy for Lois Gunden Clemens, Ruth Brunk Stoltzfus, and their contemporaries, both male and female. But God has been ever present to guide and direct, and he has been faithful.

CHAPTER 13

Three Hundred Years

What a wide sweep in time and space! From Germantown, Pennsylvania, 1683, to many communities across the United States and Canada, 1983. Three hundred years of history in the New World for Mennonite women and their men.

First came the years of pioneering, when physical survival itself was an achievement. In 1799 and following, the 400-mile trail of the Conestoga took Mennonites loyal to the crown and/or in search of new land to Ontario. In the nineteenth century came the westward expansion. Mennonites established communities in Oregon, Idaho, Nebraska, Alberta, and other exotic-sounding places far away from Lancaster and Mifflin Counties and the Franconia area in Pennsylvania, Rockingham County in Virginia, or Elkhart County, Indiana.

Did this westward expansion of Mennonites differ in any way from that of their neighbors? Always the Mennonites were eager to see a church established as quickly as possible. The church has been central in the lives of most Mennonite women. Like Barbara Bachman Heiser Eyer, Mary Keck Shrock, and Barbara Schultz Oesch, they have rejoiced when a congregation was established in a new community.

The church is the hub of life in a Mennonite community, the center around which the rest of life revolves. The church has supplied meaning and an area of freedom in the lives of Mennonite women. Often those few hours of worship and study on Sunday morning have been the only time in the week that women and men alike felt released from the burden of working to conquer an obdurate frontier, and were able to meditate concerning the meaning of life. It has not been unusual for a family to move from one community to another, like Christian and Anna Yoder of Iowa, in order that their children might enjoy the benefits of a particular kind of church—in earlier years, a Sunday school; in more recent times, an active youth group.

Role of the HERALD

A meaningful medium binding scattered Mennonites together has been the printed page. In 1864, John F. Funk began the *Herald of Truth* (now the *Gospel Herald*), the official church paper. John M. Gingerich and Suzanne Gross, who did extensive research on the volumes covering 1864-94, comment:

> Women during the late 1800s played a definite role in defining the *Herald of Truth*. From the start they were enthusiastic about having a "Mennonite" paper. Subscription lists included many women.... It is surprising how much of the material in the *HOT* was contributed by women—more than half of some issues.[1]

Gross notes further that in the reinforcing of Mennonite values, women authors played a substantial role. Article after article—especially those by Clara Brubaker (see chapter 9) and Mary Pontius—reminded the reader not to conform to the world's evil ways (ways of vanity and materialism), but rather to cultivate a joy in living that comes from humble hard work where each takes a share of the responsibility for his or her brothers and sisters.[2]

Women were correspondents from many communities: Minnie Schload, Ephrata, Pennsylvania; Lizzie M. Wenger, Farmersville, Pennsylvania; Amelia Conrad, Wood River, Nebraska; Barbara Christner, Wayland, Iowa; E. Rose Sutter, Bardo, Alberta; Ruth Friedt, Baltic, Ohio; Eunice Mast, Casselton, North Dakota; Edith Leinbach, Yellow Creek, Goshen, Indiana; Marie Nafziger, Hopedale, Illinois; Mary A. Miller, Greenwood, Delaware; Lena Dirks, Winton, California; Grace Miller, Springs, Pennsylvania.

"The Quickening"

In the late 1800s a warm religious piety resulting from the Great Awakening influenced American Mennonites. Pietism influenced, but never completely swallowed up Mennonites, for an emphasis on nonresistance (peacemaking), nonconformity (being different from the world by following Christ), mutual aid, simplicity, service, and working "as unto the Lord" continued.

In the 1880s also there occurred what Theron Schlabach has called "The Quickening." People became interested in missions and Sunday schools. Phoebe Mumaw Kolb, Lina Zook Ressler, Mary Denlinger—all three played a part in this movement. No one ever assumed that Christian witness was required of one sex only. The Chicago mission in the 1890s and early twentieth century became a training ground for overseas missionaries.

During the first decades of the twentieth century, Rose Lambert and Vesta Zook went to Turkey. Alice Thut Page, Mary Yoder Burkhard, Sarah Hahn Lapp, Lydia Liechty Lehman, and many others went to India with their husbands. Some went alone, as did Anna Stalter in 1905 and Florence Cooprider as a medical doctor in 1916.

In 1890 a churchwide organization, the Mennonite General Conference, was founded. Although women attended those conferences from the beginning, they were not officially represented on boards and commissions in the United States and Canada until 1950, when Maude Swartzendruber, Ethel Zook, and Esther Widmer served on the Mennonite Board of Education as representatives of the LaJunta Mennonite School of Nursing. However, Mary Yoder Burkhard served on the executive committee of the India Mennonite Church in 1906,[3] and Felisa Cavadore shared the office of secretary with D. Parke Lantz in the Argentina Conference in 1923.[4] Are missionaries pioneers for the rest of the church?

Although most Mennonite women in the nineteenth century received only a country school education, here and there a few graduated from academies and colleges. Emma D. Lefevre (Byers) was one of two in the first graduating class at the Elkhart Institute in the spring of 1898. Fannie Coffman taught Bible there in 1901. In 1902, Anna Beck set up a kindergarten. High school and college education became more acceptable and is now considered a necessity by many. When Bertha Leaman wrote a doctoral dissertation in history at the University of Chicago in 1935, little place existed for her in the Mennonite Church, and she became a professor at a state university. Graduate degrees are no longer a novelty, and one can find lawyers and professors among today's younger Mennonite women.

"The Great Repression"

In the 1920s a wave of repression swept over the church. Why? Mennonite women, neither flappers nor suffragettes, became the focus of restrictive dress codes, as did men. In 1921 the Mennonite Publishing House published "Dress: A Brief Treatise Prepared by a Committee Appointed by Mennonite General Conference."[5] Not one woman served on the committee of five which drew up the statement. Wearing the "wrong" style of headgear became grounds for excommunication from church membership. A woman in northern Indiana was excluded from the communion table because she had removed the ribbon ties from her bonnet. Bishops removed from office any ministers who refused to excommunicate women for infractions of dress regulations. This phenomenon of authoritarianism occurred in other denominations as well. A Catholic scholar calls the 1920s "The Great Repression," for Catholic church authorities attempted at that time to cloister nuns and restrict their activities after centuries of freedom in the New World.[6]

Various hypotheses exist concerning the turbulent 20s. Perhaps the turmoil in the church merely reflected the chaos in secular society. Although a costly war had been fought, the world was *not* "safe for democracy." Was the church? Perhaps it was a time of transition, when a group of younger leaders attempted to wrest the positions of power and authority from older, more established leaders, who in turn overreacted by exerting power, honestly believing that they were preserving the "purity" of the church.[7] With power comes the temptation to use it arrogantly. The church has not always been entirely free of such. Did some older leaders act in the manner of proud Diotrephes, who loved to push himself forward as the leader of the Christians and tried to put others out of the church? (See 3 John, verses 9 and 10.) Fortunately, during the 1920s, leaders like Demetrius (3 John, verse 12) also existed—loving and dedicated to truth. In every age, no matter what the circumstances, the Holy Spirit finds ways to work toward Kingdom ends.

Mennonite Woman's Missionary Society

In 1911, Clara Eby Steiner felt an inner call to set up a Woman's Missionary Society. By 1921 this organization had 12 regional branches and 3,700 members, and it had disbursed almost $16,000 to missions the previous year. Crissie Yoder Shank, as editor of the society's publication, promoted the ecumenical study of worldwide mission. She advocated participation in the World Day of Prayer as early as 1924. When the mission board took over the women's organization in 1929, the women acquiesced graciously, but inwardly they wept.

Quiet Faithfulness

During the 1930s, 40s, and 50s, talk of the role of women— missing in earlier years—indicated a narrowing view and the imposition of limitations. yet the women continued to work— quietly, steadily, faithfully. They canned and sewed for missions. They started summer Bible schools. Alta Erb in 1939 made an eloquent, stirring appeal to women to go, give, and pray: "Women have all the opportunities they could hope for and need to fulfill the Great Commission."[8] In 1948, shortly before receiving her doctorate from Ohio State University, Mary Royer addressed the Mennonite World Conference meeting in Newton, Kansas, on

"The Mennonite Contribution to Evangelical Christian Education."

In 1950 the General Conference Executive Committee appointed a committee of three men (Nelson Kauffman, John H. Mosemann, and Truman Brunk) to study "the place of women on church boards." They summed up their five-page report with the following six conclusions:

(1) That we recognize that in redemption men and women have equal status.
(2) That in the divine economy the headship of men is established.
(3) That both on the basis of Scriptural teaching and church practice, the administration of the church's life and service is the responsibility of the brethren.
(4) That we recognize the scriptural basis for a variety of services to the church by our sisters, and we appreciate the wide range of activities in which they serve the church today in line with this basis.
(5) That we encourage the church in *the use of sisters* [italics added] in this wide range of services, but that we be alert to maintain the Biblical principle of the leadership of man.
(6) That inasmuch as our Church Boards have a representative membership, and inasmuch as there are areas of work which are largely or entirely done by sisters, we see no inconsistency in having sisters serving as members of Boards providing they are not given chief executive or administrative responsibilities on the Boards.[9]

Would the conclusions have been different if the study committee had included at least one woman—Lois Gunden Clemens or Ruth Brunk Stoltzfus, for example?

At the time that report was being prepared, Mennonite men and women were in fact working together all around the world through MCC and mission boards. Korea. Egypt. Jordan. Indonesia. Seventy-two countries. Mennonite women worked alongside their brothers on frontiers of need as they once had on the geographical frontier.

In the Arts

On that physical frontier the community did not approve of setting up an easel and doing oil painting on a weekday morning. It endorsed physical work necessary for survival, but not the fine arts, necessary for the soul. Fraktur artist Anna Weber (1814-88) of Ontario, *Scherenschnitt* (paper-cutting) artist Elizabeth Johns Stahley (1845-1930) of Lagrange, Indiana, and designer Anna Steckle Shantz (1872-1940) of Fairview, Michigan, were exceptional in countering that current. Michael S. Bird's *Ontario Fraktur* reproduces some of Anna Weber's sixty to seventy extant drawings. "Tree of 22 Birds," done in 1870, is especially imaginative and beautiful.[10] Edna Shantz, of Goshen, Indiana, now owns some of the work of her mother, Anna Steckle Shantz.

The artistic impulses of most Mennonite women, however, expressed themselves primarily through two acceptable channels, flower gardens and quilts. Music teacher Maryann Amstutz Sommer was remembered for her garden, as was Barbara Bachman Heiser Eyer. In a tribute to her mother on her ninetieth birthday (see p.78), Evelyn King Mumaw recalled watching her "relax with flowers—begonia, coleus, Christmas cactus, and gloxynias inside the house; four o'clocks, mums, peonies, iris and geraniums outside the house."[11] Attendance at any current Mennonite relief sale provides evidence of the continuing satisfaction Mennonite women receive from creating beautiful quilts. In August 1981, 124 large quilts were sold at the Ohio sale, averaging $341 each, for a total of $42,355, all given for the relief of suffering around the world. Mennonite women have traditionally also found aesthetic satisfaction in the orderly way they hung clothes on a clothesline or set a beautiful table with a gleaming white, perfectly ironed cloth, sparkling glassware, and multicolored foods, including "red-beet eggs."

Now that life is less harsh, the attitude toward the fine arts is much more hospitable than it once was, fortunately. Today Esther Kniss (Mrs. Myron) Augsburger (1938-   ) is a sculptor;[12] Sylvia Gross Bubalo (1928-   ), a painter; Ruth Carper Eitzen (1924-   ), a sculptor, painter, and illustrator; Mary Lou Brubaker (1940-   ), a printmaker, painter, and potter; Susanne H. Bishop (1921-   ), a ceramicist with her own pottery business; and Irma Yost, painter and potter.[13] Some conditions do improve with the passage of time.

Two Viewpoints Concerning Women

During the three centuries in the New World, two streams of thought have been present for U.S. and Canadian Mennonite women, often simultaneously in a single congregation or in a single head.

Stream One: *Women are human beings, copartners with men, in need of redemption. As Christians, women have the obligation to follow the Lord Jesus, to testify to the power of the risen Lord, to take the gospel to the ends of the earth, "teaching them to observe all things, whatsoever I have commanded you."*

Stream Two: *Women have a limited role. They should be primarily in the home. Both at home and in the church they should be subordinate to men. Paul teaches that they should be silent in the church.*

Paradoxically, a man may say, "My wife and I are coheirs of the grace of God. She is my equal and partner in Christ and, of course, should enjoy complete freedom to utilize her gifts. But *other women* should remain 'in their place.' " Or he may say, "Of course women are obligated to carry out their calling in Christ. They should use their gifts—preach, serve on committees, whatever the Spirit calls them to do. But *my wife* should be at home to serve me a hot dinner every evening and make sure that I have clean socks."

An old issue of the *Gospel Herald* vividly illustrates this "two streams simultaneously" characteristic. The April 18, 1912, issue carried articles exemplifying both streams. J. C. Kolb of Spring City, Pennsylvania, wrote agreeing with J. H. Mosemann that women should not speak in church, and deploring

> the prevailing tendency ... to ignore the distinction which the Holy Ghost through the Apostle Paul places between men and women in the work of the Lord (I Tim. 2:11-14).... Priscilla helped to teach the eloquent Apollos, but did she teach in the church service—when the "whole church was come together"? Certainly not.[14]

This is Stream Two.

Right beside Kolb's article is one by D. S. Troyer of Protection, Kansas. He begins as follows:

Firmly believing that woman must meet exactly the same conditions for salvation as man, and thereby stands on a level by the side of man in his Christian life, we believe that in order for her to retain and enjoy salvation she must of necessity obey the commandments with man for the promulgation of the Gospel.

Her sphere is that of help-meet. There is one head only for each institution. The Church, of which the bishop is the head as highest officer, may have ministers under him, and may include woman.[15]

This is Stream One.

A third article by J. A. Ressler delineates "respective spheres" for men and women. Both Troyer and Ressler disagree with Kolb's interpretation of the passage from 2 Timothy. This diversity of opinion continues among Mennonites to this day.

Which interpretation predominates? For me Stream One—"workers together in the Kingdom"—has been operative. Others have had different experiences. From the many biographical examples in this book, one can conclude that the church has more often than not been an arena of freedom for Mennonite women. In cases in which women could not or did not exercise their gifts, whether the fault of the church or themselves, they were not heard of at all by others, and are therefore not included here. Women and men alike have often been unfaithful by choosing "the easy way" of not using their gifts in the Lord's service. When the church has limited the freedom of women to use God-given gifts, many have transcended the limitations in creative ways. Still others have been faithful in obscure, unnoticed places. That service has been precious to God, even though it is not mentioned on these pages.

Looking Ahead

What of the future? One clue comes from the responses of Mennonite women during wars. During the American Revolution, Catherine Hesster Schmucker took food to her husband, Christian—sentenced to death and in prison for his faith in Reading, Pennsylvania. Eva Yoder and Esther Bachman sent a letter to the Pennsylvania Assembly on behalf of all the wronged families.

The assembly listened to them and granted their petition. During the Civil War, Susanna Heatwole Brunk sided neither with the Yankees nor the rebels, but supported her husband, Henry, in his conscientious objection to the war and shouldered the responsibility for their young family.

Following World War I, Mennonite women sent thousands of garments to aid their brothers and sisters suffering from famine and deprivation in Russia. Following World War II they went with their husbands and brothers into the mental hospitals, where brutal and inhumane conditions prevailed, and helped begin the modern mental health movement.[16] They went to Europe to help with reconstruction and reconciliation. They have been in both Korea and Vietnam. They and their children have sent thousands of "Christmas bundles." At home, during peace or war, Mennonite women have been builders of community. They have taught Sunday school, practiced hospitality, served funeral dinners for bereaved relatives, and increased the amount of beauty in the world.

Peace. Simple life. Not being conformed to the world, but being transformed by Christ. Teaching the children. Salvation. Following after Christ. Old terms these are, yet deeply meaningful as the Mennonite community approaches a new century and a new millennium. Most Mennonite women deeply desire to live harmonious, purposeful, socially responsible lives in the spirit of Christ.

Can Mennonite women and their men meet the challenges of living in a world where individuals continue to need salvation, a world of technology, atomic energy, space exploration, and dwindling global resources? With Jesus Christ the risen Lord within and going on before, the answer resounds, "Yes!"

Notes

CHAPTER ONE

1. John C. Wenger, *The Mennonite Church in America* (Scottdale, Pa.: Herald Press, 1966), p. 57.

2. John C. Wenger, *History of the Mennonites of the Franconia Conference* (Telford, Pa.: Franconia Mennonite Historical Society, 1937), p. 12.

3. Lois Barrett in *Study Guide: Women in the Bible and Early Anabaptism*, ed. Herta Funk (Newton, Kan.: Faith and Life Press, 1975), p. 33.

4. Quotation supplied by Leland Harder, Elkhart, Indiana.

5. Thieleman J. van Braght, *Martyrs Mirror* (Scottdale, Pa.: Mennonite Publishing House, 1950), pp. 977-79.

6 *Ibid.*, pp. 979-83.

7. Wolfgang Schäufele, "The Missionary Vision and Activity of the Anabaptist Laity," *Mennonite Quarterly Review*, Apr. 1962, p. 107.

8. *Martyrs Mirror*, p. 1122.

9. Schäufele, p. 108.

10. George Williams, *The Radical Reformation* (Philadelphia: The Westminster Press, 1962), pp. 506-07.

11. Menno Simons, *The Complete Writings* (Scottdale, Pa.: Herald Press, 1956), p. 836.

12. *Ibid.*, p. 887ff.

13. *Ibid.*, pp. 836-37.

14. *Ibid.*, pp. 1028-29.

15. *Ibid.*, p. 1061.

16. Harold S. Bender, "Women, Status of" in *Mennonite Encyclopedia*, IV, 972-74.

17. *Martyrs Mirror*, p. 185. According to Wenger, modern research has established the date of her execution as May (not March) 27, 1549.

18. The *Ausbund* is the oldest hymnbook of the Swiss Anabaptists, dating from 1564. It is still in use by the Amish of North America.

CHAPTER TWO

1. John L. Ruth, '*Twas Seeding Time* (Scottdale, Pa.: Herald Press, 1976), p. 171.

2. Frank Epp, *Mennonites in Canada, 1786-1920* (Toronto: Macmillan of Canada, 1974), p. 81.

3. Evelyn K. Mumaw, Harrisonburg, Virginia, in WMSC Collection.

4. Richard Kerwin MacMaster, with Samuel L. Horst and Robert F. Ulle, *Conscience in Crisis* (Scottdale, Pa.: Herald Press, 1979), p. 182.

5. *Ibid.*, p. 441.

6. Ruth, p. 145.

7. *Ibid.*, p. 138.

8. Ruth Stutzman and Esther Kauffman, Kalispell, Montana, in WMSC Collection.

9. Mabel Snyder, Ontario, to Alice Koch, April 15, 1980, in WMSC Collection.

10. Paul Erb, *South Central Frontiers* (Scottdale, Pa.: Herald Press, 1974), p. 162.

11. Interview with Ruth Yoder Miller—granddaughter of Margaret Heatwole—April 1981, conducted by Elaine Sommers Rich, Bluffton, Ohio.

12. Nellie I. Kinsie, Cambridge, Ontario, in WMSC Collection.

13. Eva Yeackley Reeb, Milford, Nebraska, in WMSC Collection.

14. Mary Eiman Swartzendruber, *Mountains and Prairies and a Girl Named Mary*

(Harrisonburg, Va.: privately published, 1978).
    15. MacMaster, pp. 441-42.

CHAPTER THREE
    1. Menno Simons, *The Complete Writings* (Scottdale, Pa.: Herald Press, 1956), p. 1038.
    2. Roland Bainton, *What Christianity Says About Sex, Love and Marriage* (New York: Association Press, 1957), p. 91.
    3. January 1, 1900.
    4. Mathilda K. Voth, *Clear Shining After Rain* (North Newton, Kan.: Mennonite Press, 1980), p. 49.
    5. Minnie Swartzentruber Graber, interview with Arlene Mark, Elkhart, Indiana, September 2, 1980.
    6. John C. Wenger, *History of the Mennonites of the Franconia Conference* (Telford, Pa.: Franconia Mennonite Historical Society, 1937), p. 28.
    7. Letter from Lorraine Roth, Kitchener, Ontario, to Elaine Sommers Rich, October 30, 1980.
    8. *Christian Zook Yoder: A Memorial and Tribute* (Goshen, Ind.: Goshen College, May 1959), p. 14.
    9. J. S. Shoemaker, *The Ideal Christian Home* (Scottdale, Pa.: Mennonite Publishing House, 1925), p. 76.
    10. Ira D. Landis in *Mennonite Encyclopedia*, II, 712.
    11. *Mennonite Encyclopedia*, II, 138; Lorraine Roth, Kitchener, Ontario.
    12. Hilda Troyer, Gridley, Illinois, in WMSC Collection.
    13. Harry F. Weber, *Centennial History of the Mennonites of Illinois 1829-1929* (Goshen, Ind.: Mennonite Historical Society, 1931), p. 281.
    14. Gerald L. Mumaw, Elkhart, Indiana, in WMSC Collection.
    15. Mary Royer and Christina Royer Neff, Goshen, Indiana, and Lebanon, Pennsylvania, in WMSC Collection.
    16. *Gospel Herald* obituary, May 8, 1919, p. 111; J. A. Ressler in preface to *Memories: A Collection of Poems* by Susan Good Hostetler (Scottdale, Pa.: privately published, ca. 1920).
    17. Kathryn Yoder Miller, Salem, Oregon, in WMSC Collection.
    18. Materials about Mrs. Bender are from an April 8, 1981, interview by Priscilla Stuckey Kauffman and from a six-page handwritten autobiography, a photocopy of which is the WMSC Collection.
    19. Hubert R. Pellman, *Eastern Mennonite College 1917-1967* (Harrisonburg, Va.: Eastern Mennonite College, 1967), p. 53.

CHAPTER FOUR
    1. Linda Grant DePauw and Conover Hunt, *Remember the Ladies: Women in America 1750-1815* (New York: Viking Press, 1976), p. 36.
    2. Lorraine Roth, Kitchener, Ontario, nine-page paper in WMSC Collection.
    3. In the New World, Amish and Mennonites were one group until 1854, when a division occurred.
    4. Katherine Meyer Yoder, Wayne County, Ohio, ten-page paper in WMSC Collection.
    5. This account was written by Katherine Royer (Goshen, Indiana), great-granddaughter of Catharine Holly Stoltzfus.
    6. Ethel Estella Cooprider Erb, *Through Tribulation to Crown of Life: The Story of a Godly Grandmother* (Hesston, Kan.: The Book and Bible Room, ca. 1944); personal let-

ter from Ruth Brunk Stoltzfus to Elaine Sommers Rich, in WMSC Collection.

7. Amos Gingerich, *The Faith and Life of the Family of Frederick Swartzendruber,* (Parnell, Iowa: privately published, ca. 1958); LaVerne Hostetler, Goshen, Indiana, in WMSC Collection.

8. Edna Heiser Cender, Fisher, Illinois, in WMSC Collection.

9. Elsie Hooley Mann, Faribault, Minnesota, in WMSC Collection.

10. C. Henry Smith, *Mennonite Country Boy* (Newton, Kan.: Faith and Life Press, 1962), p. 175.

11. Adella Brunk Kanagy, Fairfax, Virginia, in WMSC *Voice,* Aug. 1977, p. 7.

12. Evelyn King Mumaw, Harrisonburg, Virginia, "Into the Tenth Decade" (eight-page paper in her personal possession), p. 8.

CHAPTER FIVE

1. Mary Royer, "Aunt Lydia," *Gospel Herald,* June 10, 1947, p. 230.

2. Martha Yoder, Middlebury, Indiana, in WMSC Collection.

3. Hazel Lapp, Sterling, Illinois, in WMSC Collection.

4. Edna Mast, Cochranville, Pennsylvania, in WMSC Collection.

5. Kathryn Aschliman, Goshen, Indiana, in WMSC Collection.

6. Helen Wade Alderfer, Scottdale, Pennsylvania, MCC Peace Section Task Force on Women and Society Report, March-April 1981, pp. 4-5.

7. Alice Lapp, Goshen, Indiana, in WMSC Collection.

8. Irene Horst, *Reflections of 704* (Narvon, Pa.: privately published, 1977); Lawrence Horst in WMSC Collection.

9. Betty Buckwalter, Wellman, Iowa, in WMSC Collection.

CHAPTER SIX

1. John C. Wenger, *The Doctrines of the Mennonites* (Scottdale, Pa.: Mennonite Publishing House, 1950), p. 82.

2. Hope K. Lind, Eugene, Oregon, in WMSC Collection.

3. Personal letter to Elaine Sommers Rich, January 21, 1981.

4. A copy of this letter is in the N. A. Lind files, Archives of the Mennonite Church, Goshen, Indiana.

5. Paul Erb, *South Central Frontiers* (Scottdale, Pa.: Herald Press, 1974), p. 51.

6. *Gospel Herald* obituary, January 27, 1948, p. 93; letter from Simon Gingerich to Paul Erb, March 31, 1981, in WMSC Collection; letter from Erb to Elaine Sommers Rich, July 10, 1981, in WMSC Collection.

7. Grace Showalter in WMSC Collection.

8. *Gospel Herald,* Dec. 4, 1951, p. 1182.

9. John S. Coffman Collection, Archives of the Mennonite Church, Goshen, Indiana (copy in WMSC Collection).

10. Y.P.C.A. Historical Committee, *Mennonite Church History of Howard and Miami Counties, Indiana* (Scottdale, Pa.: Mennonite Publishing House, 1916), p. 90.

11. Emma Richards, Villa Park, Illinois, in WMSC Collection.

12. Gladys B. Hostetler, Goshen, Indiana, in WMSC Collection.

13. Carolyn Augsburger, Ruth Bauman, Harold E. Bauman, and Russell R. Oyer in WMSC Collection.

14. Theron F. Schlabach, *Gospel Versus Gospel* (Scottdale, Pa.: Herald Press, 1980), p. 103. He tells the interesting story of the controversy surrounding the Youngstown mission (1908-23) on pages 99-108.

15. Carolyn Augsburger, Youngstown, Ohio, in WMSC Collection.

16. Nona M. Kauffman, Goshen, Indiana, in WMSC Collection.

17. *Gospel Herald,* Nov. 11, 1909, p. 527.

18. *Gospel Herald*, July 15, 1909, p. 254.

19. Grant M. Stoltzfus, *Mennonites of the Ohio and Eastern Conference* (Scottdale, Pa.: Herald Press, 1969), p. 256.

20. Grace Showalter, Harrisonburg, Virginia.

21. Dorcas Kauffman, *Bethel Church Newsletter*, West Liberty, Ohio, June 1981.

22. Mary Graber Conrad Wade Good, Elkhart, Indiana, in WMSC Collection.

23. John L. Ruth, *Franconia Conference News*, Sept. 1980, p. 6.

24. Personal letter to Elaine Sommers Rich, May 1980, in WMSC Collection.

25. Personal letter to Elaine Sommers Rich, October 1980, in WMSC Collection.

26. Ruth L. Rittgers, Imlay City, Michigan, in WMSC Collection.

27. Nancy L. Kauffman, "Dora Shantz Gehman" (unpublished paper, 1980), in WMSC Collection.

28. Elizabeth Hershberger Bauman, Goshen, Indiana, in WMSC Collection.

29. Article on "Summer Bible School" in *Mennonite Encyclopedia*, IV, 654.

30. Mabel Hackman, Des Allemands, Louisiana, in WMSC Collection.

31. P. Erb, p. 410.

32. Nona M. Kauffman, Goshen, Indiana, in WMSC Collection.

33. Hope K. Lind, Eugene, Oregon, in WMSC Collection.

34. Elva May Schrock Roth, Morton, Illinois, in WMSC Collection.

35. Lorna L. Bergey, New Hamburg, Ontario, in WMSC Collection.

36. Alice Nahrgang Koch, New Hamburg, Ontario, in WMSC Collection.

37. John Umble, *Goshen College Bulletin* XLV, No. 6 (Golden Anniversary Alumni Directory [Apr. 1951]), 17 and 29.

38. Florence Voegtlin, Tofield, Alberta, in WMSC Collection; Fern B. Shantz, "Everybody Likes Nora," *Purpose*, Feb. 26, 1978.

39. Frances Coan Zehr, Northbrook, Illinois, in WMSC Collection.

40. Lorraine Roth, Kitchener, Ontario, in WMSC Collection.

CHAPTER SEVEN

1. James O. Lehman, *Creative Congregationalism* (Smithville, Ohio: Oak Grove Mennonite Church, 1978), p. 71.

2. Olga Kennel Berky, Bluffton, Ohio, materials from Mrs. Petter, in WMSC Collection.

3. Noah Byers, "The Times in Which I Lived," *Mennonite Life*, VII, No. 2, 78.

4. Letter from Floyd Byers, Goshen, Indiana, to Elaine Sommers Rich, in WMSC Collection; interviews with M. F. Sprunger and Elfrieda Howe, Bluffton, Ohio.

5. Catherine M. Kurtz, Pocomoke, Maryland, in WMSC Collection; Rebecca Kauffman, "If It Doesn't Seem Fair," *Christian Living*, Oct. 1956, p. 24.

6. Elma Bixler and Frieda Amstutz, Orrville, Ohio, in WMSC Collection.

7. Hope K. Lind, Eugene, Oregon, in WMSC Collection.

8. Katherine Royer, Goshen, Indiana, in WMSC Collection

9. John Steiner, Goshen, Indiana; Katie Steiner and Sam Steiner, Waterloo, Ontario, in WMSC Collection.

10. Mary Smucker, Goshen, Indiana, in WMSC Collection.

11. Hubert R. Pellman, *Eastern Mennonite College 1917-1967* (Harrisonburg, Va.: Eastern Mennonite College, 1967), p. 22.

12. Interview with Priscilla Stuckey Kauffman, Goshen, Indiana, August 1981.

13. Mary Miller, *A Pillar of Cloud: The Story of Hesston College 1909-1959* (North Newton, Kan.: Mennonite Press, 1959), p. 109.

14. For more detailed information, see Phyllis Pellman Good, *Paul and Alta* (Scottdale, Pa.: Herald Press, 1978).

15. Pellman, pp. 78 and 207.

16. *Ibid.*, p. 95.

17. *Ibid.*, pp. 78 and 207.

18. Letter from Arthur E. Barbeau, West Liberty, West Virginia, to Elaine Sommers Rich, in WMSC Collection.

19. *The Mirror*, XI, No. 6 (Dec. 1979).

20. Salome Bauman has written a tribute to her mother Lydia Ann Groff Bauman (1862-1949), which is in the WMSC Collection.

21. June B. Weber, Newport News, Virginia, in WMSC Collection.

22. Thelma Getz Showalter, Broadway, Virginia, in WMSC Collection.

23. John Sylvanus Umble, *Mennonite Pioneers* (Elkhart, Ind.: Mennonite Board of Missions and Charities, 1940), p. 92.

24. Pauline Lehman, St. Anne, Illinois, in WMSC Collection.

CHAPTER EIGHT

1. Letter from Lina Zook to A. B. Kolb, in Archives of the Mennonite Church, Goshen, Indiana, reported by James O. Lehman, *Creative Congregationalism* (Smithville, Ohio: Oak Grove Mennonite Church, 1978), p. 147ff.

2. John Allen Lapp, *The Mennonite Church in India 1897-1962* (Scottdale, Pa.: Herald Press, 1972), p. 67.

3. *Mennonite Historical Bulletin*, XI., No. 3 (July 1979), 2.

4. Priscilla Stuckey Kauffman, letter to Elaine Sommers Rich, April 9, 1981, in WMSC Collection.

5. Personal letter to Elaine Sommers Rich, August 12, 1981, in WMSC Collection.

6. Theron F. Schlabach, *Gospel Versus Gospel* (Scottdale, Pa.: Herald Press, 1980), p. 29.

7. Lapp, p. 27.

8. *Herald of Truth*, Apr. 1, 1902, p. 103.

9. *Herald of Truth* Jan. 1, 1900, pp. 6-7.

10. Schlabach, p. 334.

11. Ruth Ressler, Waverly, Ohio, in WMSC Collection.

12. *Herald of Truth*, Nov. 15, 1892, p. 338.

13. John M. Gingerich, Goshen, Indiana, in WMSC Collection.

14. Emma Oyer, *What God Hath Wrought* (Elkhart, Ind.: Mennonite Board of Missions and Charities, 1949), p. 11.

15. Schlabach, p. 334.

16. Ruth Ressler in WMSC Collection.

17. Lehman, p. 147ff.

18. John Umble, *Goshen College 1894-1954* (Goshen, Ind.: Goshen College, 1955), p. 268.

19. Ruth Ressler.

20. J. A. Ressler letter to A. K. Kurtz, August 18, 1904, American Mennonite Mission Superintendent's Correspondence, Archives of the Mennonite Church, Goshen, Indiana, quoted by Barbara Bixler Lamb, "The Role of Women in the Mennonite Missionary Movement 1890-1910" (unpublished paper, 1978), p. 27.

21. Words of Cheer, Apr. 22, 1934.

22. *Gospel Herald*, June 10, 1909, p. 170.

23. *Gospel Herald*, Apr. 15, 1909, p. 37.

24. Telephone interview with Robert Kreider, North Newton, Kansas, February 25, 1981.

25. *Mennonite Historical Bulletin*, XXXIX, No. 4 (Oct. 1978), p. 3.

26. WMSC Collection.

27. Letter from David A. Shank, Abidjan, Ivory Coast to Elaine Sommers Rich,

October 1, 1980, in WMSC Collection.

28. Letter from Mary Royer, Goshen, Indiana, to Elaine Sommers Rich, December 3, 1980.

29. Melvin Gingerich, "The Mennonite Woman's Missionary Society," *Mennonite Quarterly Review*, Apr. 1963, p. 220.

30. For information about Lydia Shenk Shank see Helen Good Brenneman, *Ring a Dozen Doorbells* (Scottdale, Pa.: Herald Press, 1973), pp. 160-75.

31. The story of Phebe's call to Africa is told in the chapter entitled "Phebe's Promise," in David W. Shenk, *Mennonite Safari* (Scottdale, Pa.: Herald Press, 1974), pp. 19-21; Carol Duerksen in the Hesston College *Alumni News*, Feb. 1974. The account in this chapter combines these two sources.

32. Lapp, pp. 128-29.

33. Beatrice Hershey Hallman, Goshen, Indiana, in WMSC Collection.

34. Herbert Zook, New Castle, Pennsylvania, in WMSC Collection.

35. *Gospel Herald* obituary, Nov. 10, 1981, p. 846.

36. "Esther Ebersole Lapp," undated pamphlet published by Mennonite Woman's Missionary Society, Indiana-Michigan branch, ca. 1919 (in possession of Hazel Lapp, Sterling, Illinois).

37. Lapp, p. 70.

38. Carolyn C. Wenger, Lancaster, Pennsylvania, in WMSC Collection.

39. Lorraine Roth, Kitchener, Ontario, in WMSC Collection.

40. Beatrice Hershey Hallman, Goshen, Indiana, in WMSC Collection.

41. Mahlon M. Hess in *Missionary Messenger*, Jan. 1970.

42. *Ibid.*, p. 9.

43. *Gospel Herald* obituary, Jan. 11, 1934, p. 879.

44. Lorraine Roth, Kitchener, Ontario, in WMSC Collection.

CHAPTER NINE

1. Confusion exists concerning the Ebersole birth date. Harry F. Weber in *Centennial History of the Mennonites of Illinois 1829-1929* (Goshen, Ind.: Mennonite Historical Society, 1931) and Mamie Ebersole in the WMSC Collection list it as 1870. An obituary from her hometown newspaper—contributed by Lila G. Ebersole of Sterling, Illinois—and the *Gospel Herald* obituary (Mar. 23, 1933) list it as 1860, as does John Sylvanus Umble in *Mennonite Pioneers* (Elkhart, Ind.: Mennonite Board of Missions and Charities, 1940).

2. Emma Oyer, *What God Hath Wrought* (Elkhart, Ind.: Mennonite Board of Missions and Charities, 1949), p. 5.

3. Umble, *Mennonite Pioneers*, p. 49.

4. Weber, p. 602.

5. Oyer, pp. 5, 7.

6. A. C. Good, *A Life Sketch* (Sterling, Ill.: Crown Printing, 1980), p. 17.

7. *Gospel Herald*, Mar. 23, 1933, p. 1087.

8. Weber, p. 285.

9. Alta Mae Erb, *Studies in Mennonite City Missions* (Scottdale, Pa.: Mennonite Publishing House, 1937), p. 31. This is the source on which I have relied most for names of women in home missions during this period. It was designed as a study guide for use in churches.

10. Edna Bowman, Preston, Ontario, in WMSC Collection.

11. The white net cap which women church members wore during worship services.

12. A. M. Erb, pp. 183-85.

13. Oyer, p. 43.

14. Priscilla Stuckey Kauffman, "Clara (Brubaker) Shank, 1869-1958, Daughter of the

Quickening: Rural Missionary in Missouri" (unpublished paper, 1981), of which there is a photocopy in WMSC Collection. Unless otherwise indicated, material about Clara Shank is from this source.

15. Paul Erb, *South Central Frontiers* (Scottdale, Pa.: Herald Press, 1974), p. 105.
16. *Ibid.*, p. 131.
17. Theron F. Schlabach, *Gospel Versus Gospel* (Scottdale, Pa.: Herald Press, 1980), p. 159.
18. A. M. Erb, p. 192; L. L. Swartzendruber, *The Child: A History of the Mennonite Orphans' Home, West Liberty, Ohio* (Scottdale, Pa.: Mennonite Publishing House, 1931); Jocele Thut Meyer, Brooklyn, Ohio, in WMSC Collection.
19. Mary Maple Berkshire, Elkhart, Indiana, in WMSC Collection.
20. *Bluffton News*, Sept. 26, 1907.
21. A. M. Erb, p. 192.
22. Minnie Beidler (age 93, Bluffton, Ohio), interview with Ted Cunningham, 1981.
23. John A. Hostetler, *God Uses Ink* (Scottdale, Pa.: Herald Press, 1958), p. 4-A.
24. *Youth's Christian Companion*, Mar. 25, 1945, p. 479.
25. Hostetler, p. 94.
26. Alice K. Gingerich, *Life and Times of Daniel Kauffman* (Scottdale, Pa.: Herald Press, 1954).
27. *Ibid.*, p. 105.
28. *Gospel Herald* obituary, Dec. 11, 1919, p. 702.
29. *Hi-Lights of the Mennonite Publishing House*, Oct. 24, 1969.
30. *Ibid.*, Apr. 19, 1968.
31. Paul Erb in telephone conversation with Elaine Sommers Rich, July 10, 1981.
32. A book of her complete poems, *Prairie Praises*, was published posthumously by her children in 1978 (Lahla Miller Selzer and Sanford E. Miller, Protection, Kansas).
33. Information concerning Esther Eby Glass is from Edna K. Mast, Cochranville, Pennsylvania, in the WMSC Collection, and Virginia Glass Schlabach, "A Memorial for Esther Eby Glass," *Christian Living*, Apr. 1973, pp. 6-9.
34. Lorraine Roth, Kitchener, Ontario, in WMSC Collection.
35. Umble, chapter 9.
36. Rhoda Lehman, Sarasota, Florida, and Irene Stauffer, Paradise, Pennsylvania, in WMSC Collection.
37. Barbara Campbell Showalter and Mary E. Suter, Harrisonburg, Virginia, in WMSC Collection.
38. Ira D. Landis, in *Missionary Messenger*, Apr. 1958, p. 4.
39. John E. Lapp, Souderton, Pennsylvania, in WMSC Collection.
40. A. M. Erb, p. 57. Some confusion exists concerning the two Lizzie Mussers. Irene Horst, Narvon, Pennsylvania, says this one worked at Lancaster, not Reading (letter to Elaine Sommers Rich in WMSC Collection).
41. Irene Horst, in *Pennsylvania Mennonite Heritage*, July 1981, p. 9.
42. *Gospel Herald* obituary, Nov. 6, 1962, p. 990; Hope K. Lind, Eugene, Oregon, in WMSC Collection.

CHAPTER TEN

1. John E. Lapp, Souderton, Pennsylvania, and Wilbur and Velma Hostetler, Goshen, Indiana, in WMSC Collection.
2. Shirley Yoder in *Oregon Mennonite Centennial News*, No. 2 (June 1976).
3. Lucille Krabill (West Liberty, Ohio), *Mother Told Me*, privately published booklet in WMSC Collection, p. 9.
4. Bessie Hailey, Stuarts Draft, Virginia, in WMSC Collection.
5. Edna Mast, Cochranville, Pennsylvania, in WMSC Collection.

6. Maude Swartzendruber, *The Lamp in the West* (Newton, Kan.: LaJunta Mennonite School of Nursing Alumnae Association, 1975), p. 22.

7. Lydia Oyer, *Lydia Heatwole: Pioneer in Mennonite Nursing* (privately published, 1958), p. 35; John Sylvanus Umble, *Mennonite Pioneers* (Elkhart, Ind.: Mennonite Board of Missions and Charities, 1940), chapter 10.

8. Oyer, p. 17.

9. *Ibid.*, p. 35.

10. Quoted in Oyer, p. 16.

11. Oyer, p. 36.

12. Mary Liechty Smucker, Goshen, Indiana, in WMSC Collection.

13. Swartzendruber, preface.

14. *Ibid.*, appendix, pp. 359-61.

15. Mary Lou Cummings, ed., *Full Circle: Stories of Mennonite Women* (Newton, Kan.: Faith and Life Press, 1978), pp. 82-86.

16. *Ibid.*

17. *Ibid.*, p. 85.

18. *Ibid.*, p. 86.

19. Elva May Roth, Morton, Illinois, in WMSC Collection.

20. From a speech given in 1978, in WMSC Collection.

21. Theron F. Schlabach, *Gospel Versus Gospel* (Scottdale, Pa.: Herald Press, 1980), p. 122. (Another source of material about the work of Maude Douglass is an unpublished thesis by Linden M. Wenger for Union Theological Seminary, Richmond, Virginia, entitled "A Study of Rural Missions in the Mennonite Church," 1955.)

22. Paul Erb, *South Central Frontiers* (Scottdale, Pa.: Herald Press, 1974), p. 416.

23. Schlabach, p. 122.

24. Lilly Steckly, Carstairs, Alberta, in WMSC Collection.

25. John E. Lapp, Souderton, Pennsylvania, in WMSC Collection.

26. *Ibid.*

27. Edna Amstutz, "A Tribute to a Beloved One," *Alumnae News* (LaJunta, Colo.), XVII, No. 1 (Jan. 1954), 10.

28. John E. Lapp, Souderton, Pennsylvania, in WMSC Collection.

29. Swartzendruber, p. 24.

30. *Ibid.*, p. 22.

31. WMSC Collection (no author given).

32. Ethel L. Slabaugh, Whitmore Lake, Minnesota, in WMSC Collection.

33. *Gospel Herald* obituary.

34. Mary E. Suter, Harrisonburg, Virginia, in WMSC Collection.

CHAPTER ELEVEN

1. Rather than document each item in this chapter, I refer readers to two sources which have been relied on extensively in the writing of this account: Melvin Gingerich, "The Mennonite Woman's Missionary Society," *Mennonite Quarterly Review*, Apr. and July, 1963, pp. 113-223; and Sharon Klingelsmith, "Women in the Mennonite Church, 1900-1930," *Mennonite Quarterly Review*, July 1980, pp. 163-207. Used with permission of Mennonite Quarterly Review.

2. Gingerich, p. 115.

3. *Gospel Herald* obituary, June 30, 1927, p. 304.

4. Hazel Lapp, Sterling, Illinois, in WMSC Collection.

5. John C. Wenger, *The Mennonites in Indiana and Michigan* (Scottdale, Pa.: Herald Press, 1961), p. 31.

6. Mary Hartzler, Jackson, Minnesota, in WMSC Collection.

7. Maud Eby quoted by Gingerich, p. 118.

8. Gingerich, p. 118; James O. Lehman, *Creative Congregationalism* (Smithville, Ohio: Oak Grove Mennonite Church, 1978), p. 195.

9. Gingerich, p. 119.

10. Undated clipping, *Mennonite Weekly Review,* probably spring 1962.

11. The account of this and the next ten organizations is told largely in the words of Melvin Gingerich (pp. 120-122), with minor additions. Permission secured from *MQR.*

12. Mary Snider worked for many years at an orphanage in Waterloo and adopted a son.

13. Draft of this letter is in Archives of the Mennonite Church, Goshen, Indiana (quoted by Klingelsmith, pp. 169-70).

14. Archives, quoted by Gingerich, p. 123.

15. Archives, quoted by Klingelsmith, p. 188; *Mennonite Historical Bulletin,* Jan. 1980, p. 3.

16. Speech by Minnie Graber at fiftieth-anniversary celebration, Goshen, Indiana, in WMSC Collection.

17. *Mennonite Historical Bulletin,* Jan. 1980, p. 4.

18. *Ibid.,* p. 5.

19. Archives, quoted by Klingelsmith, p. 197.

20. *Ibid.,* p. 170.

21. Gingerich, pp. 221-22.

22. Clara Hooley Hershberger, Glendale, Arizona, fiftieth-anniversary program, June 25, 1965, Goshen, Indiana, in WMSC Collection.

23. Klingelsmith, p. 194.

24. *Ibid.,* p. 190.

25. Thieleman J. van Braght, *Martyrs Mirror* (Scottdale, Pa.: Mennonite Publishing House, 1950), p. 515.

26. Archives, quoted by Klingelsmith, p. 202.

27. *Gospel Herald,* June 6, 1929, p. 194.

28. John Sylvanus Umble, *Ohio Mennonite Sunday Schools* (Goshen, Ind.: Mennonite Historical Society, 1941), p. 118.

29. *Ibid.,* p. 476.

30. Loren King (age 75, West Liberty, Ohio, superintendent of the Sunday school in the early 1930's), interview with Joseph Horner, September 1981.

31. Clara Hooley Hershberger, Glendale, Arizona, in WMSC Collection.

32. *Ibid.*

33. *WMSC Handbook,* Jan. 1975, p. 9.

34. *Ibid.,* p. 8.

CHAPTER TWELVE

1. Melvin Gingerich, *Service for Peace* (Akron, Pa.: Mennonite Central Committee, 1949), p. 1.

2. At this writing John Bender of Elkhart, Indiana, is undertaking a study of the contribution of women in CPS.

3. John D. Unruh, *In the Name of Christ* (Scottdale, Pa.: Herald Press, 1952).

4. At this writing Marion Keeney·Preheim, Newton, Kansas, is undertaking a study of women leaders in MCC, *Something Meaningful for God.*

5. Susan Godshall, Rheems, Pennsylvania, in *Missionary Messenger,* June 18, 1979.

6. Lois Gunden Clemens, Lansdale, Pennsylvania, in WMSC Collection.

7. *Ibid.*

8. *Ibid.*

9. Ruth Brunk Stoltzfus, Harrisonburg, Virginia, in WMSC Collection.

10. *Ibid.*

11. *Ibid.*
12. *Ibid.*

CHAPTER THIRTEEN

1. John M. Gingerich and Suzanne Gross, progress report on WMSC Bibliography Project, May 30, 1980, in WMSC Collection.

2. Suzanne Gross, interim report for WMSC, May 28, 1980, in WMSC Collection.

3. Barbara Bixler Lamb, "The Role of Women in the Mennonite Missionary Movement 1890-1910" (unpublished paper), 1978.

4. Theron F. Schlabach, *Gospel Versus Gospel* (Scottdale, Pa.: Herald Press, 1980), p. 213.

5. Melvin Gingerich, *Mennonite Attire Through Four Centuries* (Breinigsville, Pa.: Pennsylvania German Society, 1970), p. 182.

6. Mary Ewens, in Rosemary Ruether and Eleanor McLaughlin, *Women of Spirit: Female Leadership in the Jewish and Christian Traditions* (New York: Simon and Schuster, 1979), p. 257.

7. For this insight I am indebted to Dr. James Juhnke, North Newton, Kansas.

8. Alta Mae Erb, "The Great Commission and Woman's Sphere," *Gospel Herald*, June 1, 1939, p. 205.

9. Report of committee appointed by General Conference Executive Committee to study the place of women on church boards, Chicago, Ill., Apr. 20-21, 1950, pp. 4-5.

10. Michael S. Bird, *Ontario Fraktur* (Toronto: M. F. Feheley Publishers Limited, 1977). "Tree of 22 Birds" is now owned by Dr. and Mrs. Lawrence Commings of Kitchener, Ontario.

11. Evelyn King Mumaw (Harrisonburg, Virginia), "Into the Tenth Decade" (unpublished paper in possession of the author).

12. Mrs. Augsburger was granted an honorary Doctorate of Fine Arts by Grove City College on May 17, 1981.

13. *Mennonite Artists Contemporary* (Goshen, Indiana, 1975, 1980). These two volumes list many additional artists.

14. *Gospel Herald*, Apr. 18, 1912, p. 35.

15. *Ibid.*

16. See my fictionalized account of conditions in the mental hospitals of that time— *Tomorrow, Tomorrow, Tomorrow* (Scottdale, Pa.: Herald Press, 1966).

Bibliography

Books

Bainton, Roland. *What Christianity Says About Sex, Love and Marriage.* New York: Association Press, 1957.

Beaver, R. Pierce. *American Protestant Women in World Mission: A History of the First Feminist Movement in North America.* Grand Rapids, Mich.: Eerdmans, 1980.

Bird, Michael S. *Ontario Fraktur.* Toronto: M. F. Feheley Publishers Limited, 1977.

Boulding, Elise. *The Underside of History: A View of Women Through Time.* Boulder, Colo.: Westview Press, 1976.

Brenneman, Helen Good. *Ring a Dozen Doorbells,* Scottdale, Pa.: Herald Press, 1973.

Burkhard, Mary. *Life and Letters of Jacob Burkhard.* Goshen, Ind.: Privately published, 1936.

Burkholder, L. J. *A Brief History of the Mennonites in Ontario.* Mennonite Conference of Ontario, 1935.

Clemens, Lois Gunden. *Women Liberated.* Scottdale, Pa.: Herald Press, 1971.

Cummings, Mary Lou, ed. *Full Circle: Stories of Mennonite Women.* Newton, Kan.: Faith and Life Press, 1978.

DePauw, Linda Grant, and Conover Hunt. *Remember the Ladies: Women in America 1750-1815.* New York: Viking Press, 1976.

Erb, Alta Mae. *Studies in Mennonite City Missions.* Scottdale, Pa.: Mennonite Publishing House, 1937.

Erb, Ethel Estella Cooprider. *Through Tribulation to Crown of Life: The Story of a Godly Grandmother.* Hesston, Kan.: The Book and Bible Room, ca. 1944.

Erb, Paul. *South Central Frontiers.* Scottdale, Pa.: Herald Press, 1974.

Funk, Herta, ed., *Study Guide. Part I: Women in the Bible and Early Anabaptism; Part II: Lesson Helps for All We're Meant to Be.* Newton, Kan.: Faith and Life Press, 1975.

Gingerich, Alice K. *Life and Times of Daniel Kauffman.* Scottdale, Pa.: Herald Press, 1954.

Gingerich, Amos. *The Faith and Life of the Family of Frederick Swartzendruber.* Parnell, Iowa: privately published, ca. 1958.

Gingerich, Melvin. *Mennonite Attire Through Four Centuries.* Breinigsville, Pa.: The Pennsylvania German Society, 1970.

——————. *Service for Peace.* Akron, Pa.: Mennonite Central Committee, 1949.

Goering, Gladys V. *Women in Search of Mission: A History of the General Conference Mennonite Women's Organization*. Newton, Kan.: Faith and Life Press, 1980.

Good, Phyllis Pellman. *Paul and Alta: Living Wisdom*. Scottdale, Pa.: Herald Press, 1978.

Horst, Irene. *Reflections of 704*. Narvon, Pa.: privately published, 1977.

Hostetler, John A. *God Uses Ink*. Scottdale, Pa.: Herald Press, 1958.

Hostetler, Susan Good. *Memories: A Collection of Poems*. Scottdale, Pa.: privately published, ca. 1920.

Juhnke, James C. *A People of Mission*. Newton, Kan.: Faith and Life Press, 1979.

Kauffman, J. Howard, and Leland Harder. *Anabaptists Four Centuries Later*. Scottdale, Pa.: Herald Press, 1975.

Lambert, Rose. *Hadjin and the Armenian Massacres*. New York: Fleming H. Revell, 1911.

Lapp, John Allen. *The Mennonite Church in India 1897-1962*. Scottdale, Pa.: Herald Press, 1972.

Lehman, James O. *Creative Congregationalism*. Smithville, Ohio: Oak Grove Mennonite Church, 1978.

Longacre, Doris Janzen. *Living More with Less*. Scottdale, Pa.: Herald Press, 1980.

——————— *More-with-Less Cookbook*. Scottdale, Pa.: Herald Press, 1976.

MacMaster, Richard Kerwin, with Samuel L. Horst and Robert F. Ulle. *Conscience in Crisis*. Scottdale, Pa.: Herald Press, 1979.

Miller, Mary. *A Pillar of Cloud: The Story of Hesston College 1909-1959*. North Newton, Kan.: Mennonite Press, 1959.

Miller, Ursula. *Prairie Praises*. North Newton, Kan.: Mennonite Press, 1978.

Nyce, Dorothy Yoder, ed. *Which Way Women?* Project of MCC Peace Section Task Force on Women. Akron, Pa.: Mennonite Central Committee, 1980.

Oyer, Emma. *What God Hath Wrought: In a Half Century at the Mennonite Home Mission*. Elkhart, Ind.: Mennonite Board of Missions and Charities, 1949.

Oyer, Lydia. *Lydia Heatwole: Pioneer in Mennonite Nursing*. Privately published, 1958.

Pellman, Hubert R. *Eastern Mennonite College 1917-1967*. Harrisonburg, Va.: Eastern Mennonite College, 1967.

Rich, Elaine Sommers. *Tomorrow, Tomorrow, Tomorrow*. Scottdale, Pa.: Herald Press, 1966.

Ruether, Rosemary, and Eleanor McLaughlin. *Women of Spirit: Female Leadership in the Jewish and Christian Traditions*. New York:

Simon and Schuster, 1979.

Ruth, John L. *'Twas Seeding Time*. Scottdale, Pa.: Herald Press, 1976.

Schlabach, Theron F. *Gospel Versus Gospel: Mission and the Mennonite Church, 1863-1944*. Scottdale, Pa.: Herald Press, 1980.

Sergio, Lisa. *Jesus and Woman*. McLean, Va.: EPM Publications, 1975.

Shank, Crissie Y. *Letters from Mary*. Scottdale, Pa.: Mennonite Publishing House, 1924.

Shenk, David W. *Mennonite Safari*. Scottdale, Pa.: Herald Press, 1974.

Shoemaker, J. S. *The Ideal Christian Home*. Scottdale, Pa.: Mennonite Publishing House, 1925.

Simons, Menno. *The Complete Writings*. Scottdale, Pa.: Herald Press, 1956.

Smith, C. Henry. *Mennonite Country Boy*. Newton, Kan.: Faith and Life Press, 1962.

Stoltzfus, Grant M. *Mennonites of the Ohio and Eastern Conference*. Scottdale, Pa.: Herald Press, 1969.

Swartzendruber, Mary Eiman. *Mountains and Prairies and a Girl Named Mary*. Harrisonburg, Va.: privately published, in 1978.

Swartzendruber, Maude. *The Lamp in the West*. Newton, Kan.: La-Junta Mennonite School of Nursing Alumnae Association, 1975.

Umble, John Sylvanus, ed. *Goshen College Bulletin*. Vol. XLV, No. 6 (Golden Anniversary Alumni Directory [Apr. 1951]).

——————. *Goshen College 1894-1954*. Goshen, Ind.: Goshen College, 1955.

——————. *Mennonite Pioneers*. Elkhart, Ind.: Mennonite Board of Missions and Charities, 1940.

——————. *Ohio Mennonite Sunday Schools*. Goshen, Ind.: Mennonite Historical Society, 1941.

Unruh, John D. *In the Name of Christ*. Scottdale, Pa.: Herald Press, 1952.

van Braght, Thieleman J. *Martyrs Mirror*. Scottdale, Pa.: Mennonite Publishing House, 1950.

Voth, Mathilda K. *Clear Shining After Rain*. North Newton, Kan.: Mennonite Press, 1980.

Weber, Harry F. *Centennial History of the Mennonites of Illinois 1829-1929*. Goshen, Mennonite Historical Society, 1931.

Wenger, John C. *The Doctrines of the Mennonites*. Scottdale, Pa.: Mennonite Publishing House, 1950.

——————. *History of the Mennonites of the Franconia Conference*. Telford, Pa.: Franconia Mennonite Historical Society, 1937.

——————. *The Mennonite Church in America*. Scottdale, Pa.: Herald Press, 1966.

——————. *The Mennonites in Indiana and Michigan*. Scottdale, Pa.:

Herald Press, 1961.

Wiebe, Katie Funk, ed. *Women Among the Brethren*. Hillsboro, Kan.: Board of Christian Literature of the General Conference of Mennonite Brethren Churches, 1979.

Williams, George. *The Radical Reformation*. Philadelphia: The Westminster Press, 1962.

WMSC Handbook. Elkhart, Ind., 1975.

Y.P.C.A. Historical Committee. *Mennonite Church History of Howard and Miami Counties, Indiana*. Scottdale, Pa.: Mennonite Publishing House, 1916.

Mennonite Quarterly Review

Gingerich, Melvin. "The Mennonite Woman's Missionary Society." Apr. and July 1963.

Klingelsmith, Sharon. "Women in the Mennonite Church, 1980-1930." July 1980.

Schäufele, Wolfgang. "The Missionary Vision and Activity of the Anabaptist Laity." Apr. 1962.

Unpublished Research Papers

Friesen, Richard. "Attitudes Toward the Status of Women in the History of the Mennonites." 1972.

Kauffman, Priscilla Stuckey. "Clara (Brubaker) Shank, 1869-1958, Daughter of the Quickening: Rural Missionary in Missouri." 1981.

Lamb, Barbara Bixler. "The Role of Women in the Mennonite Missionary Movement 1890-1910." 1978.

Sawadsky, Hedy, "The Role of Anabaptist Women According to the *Martyrs Mirror* from 1527 to 1559." 1960.

Zercher, Janette. "Women's Role in Church Committees Among Three Mennonite Conferences."

Index

Elaine Sommers Rich has been a contributor to the church press for many years. Since 1973 she has been a fortnightly columnist for *Mennonite Weekly Review*. She was on the editorial staff of *Japan Christian Quarterly* (Tokyo) from 1974 to 1978. She edited a devotional book for women, *Breaking Bread Together* (Herald Press, 1958), and wrote *Hannah Elizabeth* (Harper & Row, 1964), *Tomorrow, Tomorrow, Tomorrow* (Herald Press, 1966), and a book of poetry, *Am I This Countryside?* (Pinchpenny Press, 1981).

Elaine and her husband, Ronald L. Rich, are parents of four grown children. She received a BA from Goshen College in 1947 and an MA from Michigan State University in 1950. In addition to rearing her family, Mrs. Rich has taught part-time in Christian colleges and has maintained a lively interest in the work of the church at home and abroad. She has served on various boards and committees at local, district, and national levels.

Born in Plevna, Indiana, she has lived in North Newton, Kansas; Mitaka, Tokyo, Japan; and now in Bluffton, Ohio, where she is adviser to international students at Bluffton College.